INDIRA GANDHI

A Personal and Political Biography

by ANAND MOHAN

MEREDITH PRESS   New York

Library of Congress Catalog Card Number: 67-16513

MANUFACTURED IN THE UNITED STATES OF AMERICA FOR MEREDITH PRESS

VAN REES PRESS   •   NEW YORK

Preface

THE source material for this book was gathered in India during the months of May, June, and July 1966. The bulk of it was collected in a series of interviews with persons listed below. Owing to the very little documentation available on Mrs. Gandhi's life, the technique of extensive interviewing of her relatives, teachers, friends, co-workers, colleagues in government, members of her official and household staffs, and some of her critics suggested itself as the only possible course.

The memories of persons interviewed ranged from total recall to partial amnesia. In some cases memories seem to have played tricks, even when there was no play of motive, while in others they have appeared to be a matter of convenience. In reconstructing Mrs. Gandhi's life from so wide a variety of versions and such extensive data there obviously arise problems of selectivity, exclusion, weighing, and balancing, for all of which I assume sole responsibility. I have handled these problems with as decent a regard for truth as I could muster. All I can honestly claim is that I have done it free of malice.

Attribution of statements has been made where authorized, and anonymity has been maintained where requested. In spite of all the care I have taken to observe the sacredness of facts, some errors must certainly have crept in, and I tender my sincere apologies to whomever I might have wronged in the process, however unwittingly. Comment is free, and I hope that my own in this book is fair. If the reader considers it unfair I can only beseech him or her to take it as resulting from error of judgment rather than from deliberate intent.

My debts are legion. I am beholden to the Prime Minister for so graciously agreeing to talk to me in spite of her having accepted the awesome burden of office at the most critical juncture of the country's history since 1947. I am indebted to the following persons in New Delhi who have furnished information for one or more chapters of the book: Mr. Morarji Desai, M.P., former Minister of Finance; Mr. Y. B. Chavan, Minister of Home Affairs; Mr. C. Subramaniam, Minister of Food and Agriculture; Mr. Asoka Mehta, Minister of Planning; Dr. Sushila Nayar, Minister of Health; Dr. Syed Mahmud, former Minister of State in the Ministry of External Affairs; Mr. Suresh Desai, Mr. Uma Shankar Dikshit, Mrs. Shyam Kumari Khan, Mr. Pyare Nath Kathju, Mrs. Tarakeshwari Sinha, Mr. M. R. Sherwani, Dewan Chaman Lall, Mr. M. R. Masani, and Mr. V. K. Krishna Menon, all Members of Parliament; Mrs. Violet Alva, Deputy Chairman of the Rajya Sabha; Mrs. Kamaladevi, Chairman, All-India Handicrafts Board; Mrs. Achamma Matthai, Chairman, Central Social Welfare Board; Mrs. Durgabai Deshmukh, former Chairman, Central Social Welfare Board; Mrs. Mohammed Younus, Director, Kashmir Government Emporium; Miss Shanta Gandhi, Assistant Professor, National School of Drama; Mrs. Muriel Wasi; Mrs. Jai Dordi; Miss Vimla Sindhi; Miss Prema Manai; Dr. Raghubhai Nayak; Mr. Krishna Kripalani, Secretary Sahitya Akadami; Mr. B. R. Nanda, Director, Nehru Museum; Mr. Y. N. Verma, Joint Secretary, Ministry of Information and Broadcasting; and Mr. Bhabani Prasad Banerji and Mrs. Mukul Banerji of the central office of the All-India Congress Committee.

I am thankful to the following members of the Prime Minister's official and household staffs for finding the time to talk about her: Mr. N. K. Seshan, Miss Usha Bhagat, Mr. Yashpal Kapur, Mrs. Amy Crishna, Mr. A. James, and Mr. Vinod Behari Barua.

In Lucknow I was privileged to interview Mr. Kailash Nath Kaul, Mrs. Sheila Kaul, and Dr. and Mrs. Ishwar Topa, to all of whom I express my sincere appreciation. In Allahabad I am grateful to Mrs.

Tehmina Gandhi, Mr. Faredun Gandhi, Mrs. Kamala Bahuguna, President of the District Congress Committee, and the gardeners of Anand Bhavan—Data Din and Ram Avatar—for offering valuable information. In Bombay, Mrs. Nayantara Sahgal, Mr. P. A. Narielwala, and Mrs. Coonverbai Vakil all gave their precious time most graciously.

I am immensely indebted to Mr. H. Y. Sharada Prasad, Deputy Information Adviser to the Prime Minister, for providing me with copies of the Prime Minister's official statements and speeches, for making valuable suggestions, and for his unfailing courtesy, sympathy, and encouragement.

I am grateful to Mr. P. N. Haksar, India's Deputy High Commissioner in London, for the lengthy interview he gave me in between his official duties.

In Washington, D.C., I am deeply beholden to India's Ambassador to the United States, His Excellency Mr. B. K. Nehru, for permitting me to interview him and his illustrious mother, the late Mrs. Rameshwari Nehru, and also for his most fruitful introductions and kind intercession on my behalf at a very crucial juncture.

In New York, Mr. Arthur S. Lall, Professor of International Relations at Columbia University and former Ambassador of India to the United Nations, and Mr. Hasan Naim, Administrative Attaché in the Permanent Mission of India to the United Nations, have both introduced me to helpful sources of information in India. I am obliged to Mr. M. Gopala Menon, Resident Director of the Indian Investment Center in New York, who talked at length about the Prime Minister. I must tender my appreciation to India's energetic and ebullient Consul for Information and Cultural Affairs in New York, Mr. Nirmal J. Singh, who patiently cleared the clogged bureaucratic byways leading to New Delhi.

My thanks are due to Mr. N. R. Mehta of *The Leader* of Allahabad, to the News Editor of *The Statesman* of New Delhi, and to the Librarian of the Indian Council of World Affairs, New Delhi, for letting me use their old newspaper files.

I wish to thank the following authors from whose works I have quoted: *The Nehrus, Motilal and Jawaharlal*, by B. R. Nanda, published by George Allen & Unwin Ltd., London; *An Autobiography, Letters from a Father to His Daughter, Glimpses of World History, The Discovery of India*, and *A Bunch of Old Letters*, all by Jawaharlal Nehru, copyright of which now vests in Mrs. Indira Gandhi; *Nehru's Letters to His Sister*, edited with an introduction by Mrs. Krishna Hutheesing, published by Faber & Faber, London, and *With No Regrets*, an autobiography by Krishna Hutheesing, published by Oxford University Press, London; *Prison Days* by Vijaya Lakshmi Pandit, published by The Signet Press, Calcutta; *Prison and Chocolate Cake* by Nayantara Sahgal, published by Alfred A. Knopf, New York; *After Nehru, Who?* by Welles Hangen, published by Rupert Hart-Davis, London; *Rabindranath Tagore* by Krishna Kripalani, published by Grove Press, Inc., New York, copyright © 1962 by Krishna Kripalani; and *A Study of Nehru*, edited by Rafiq Zakaria and published by The Times of India, Bombay. I am grateful to Mr. Harsh Dev Malaviya, editor of *The Socialist Congressman*, New Delhi, for permitting me to use some of the material which has appeared in past issues of his journal.

I know that some of my readers will be annoyed with me for not having provided references to the quotations I have introduced. I am equally sure that others will appreciate my desire not to let footnotes interfere with the free flow of the narrative. I have by no means written a work of historical research or reference, and this should be sufficient to explain the deliberate omission of citations. At any rate, it is a lapse that does not disturb me, since I find myself in the distinguished company of Mr. Harold Nicolson, whose example in *The Age of Reason* I have followed.

My sister-in-law, Miss Shail Lal, took the pains to transcribe the tapes. My friends, Miss Roopan Munshi and Mrs. Saroj Sathija, did some interviewing on my behalf in Bombay after my departure and have dug out some valuable facts.

This book could hardly have been written without the assistance of a very dear friend of my wife's and mine, Mr. R. Ramanujam, *Newsweek's* New Delhi Correspondent. He was a reliable guide, an able adviser, an expert in his profession, and a cheerful companion.

My wife and I are grateful to him also for interviewing some persons on our behalf in Delhi after our departure.

I am immensely indebted to my good friend, Mr. Sevaklal M. Master, librarian at Columbia University, New York, for preparing the excellent index.

My wife and I are thankful to our friends, Mr. Keval Misra in Allahabad, Mr. and Mrs. Devendra Malaviya and Mr. Duli Chand in New Delhi, and my brother-in-law, Bipin B. Lal in London, for extending to us several courtesies.

My wife's parents, Mr. and Mrs. Radhe Behari Lal, made our stay in Bombay most pleasant and met our exacting demands, and we are most grateful to them.

My wife, Kusum, sat in on most of the interviews and participated in their give-and-take. Owing to the shortage of time, she also had to conduct several of the interviews on her own. She has done the entire research for the book, read through the manuscript, passed critical judgment on it, and endured the boredom of typing it. Rather than stop with thanking her, I should in all honesty say she is the co-author of this book. I also owe her more than thanks for putting up with my various moods during these past few months of hectic travel and hard work.

Finally, I am most appreciative of the patience and understanding shown to me throughout by Mr. Robert W. Lutnes, Executive Editor of Meredith Press.

A. M.

New York
November 1966

To my parents

Contents

INDIRA GANDHI

I

Death of a Prime Minister

A PALE and diffident sun hesitantly pierced the blanket of mist that covered the sprawling but somnolent city of New Delhi on the wintry morning of January 11, 1966. As the capital city of India came to life, it learned the numbing news that the nation's Premier had seen the last of life in the far-off, fabled Soviet Central Asian town of Tashkent.

Lal Bahadur Shastri, independent India's second Prime Minister, had been at the helm of affairs for barely nineteen months. After the exit of Jawaharlal Nehru, India's first Premier, Shastri's entry onto the stage in June 1964 seemed like the comic relief provided by the clown in a murky Shakespearean tragedy. Small of stature and slight of build, soft in speech and shy in manner, his very sight was a provocation for laughter. Even his fleeting appearance in newsreels sent a sustained twitter through the audiences of cinema halls.

But all this was to change in a year's time. The undersized man tackled his oversized job with solemn purpose and steely determination. The anonymity of a man who they said would be lost in a crowd of two yielded place to the image of a stalwart towering above the crowd. In the conduct of the short war with Pakistan in August and September of 1965 Shastri revealed unsuspected sources of strength.

Forced to pit the inferior Indian-manufactured Gnats and the old Mysteres and Hunters against the superior might of Pakistan's

3

American-supplied F-86 Sabre jets and F-104 supersonic fighters, and India's obsolete World War II vintage Shermans and the more recent Centurions against Pakistan's invincible Patton tanks, Shastri was literally cast in the role of a David battling Goliath. No one was surprised more than the Indians themselves when Shastri pulled off the miracle and came out on top at the conclusion of hostilities in the last week of September.

Every year the nation celebrated October 2 as Mahatma Gandhi's birthday. Hardly anyone cared to remember that it also happened to be the birthday of Shastri, the then Prime Minister. But not so in 1965; even the father of the nation, Mahatma Gandhi, receded into the background and let the limelight fall on another man who answered the call to greatness. *This* October 2 was Lal Bahadur Shastri's birthday, and his grateful admirers surprised him with a cake shaped to look like a Patton tank. Knife in hand he pierced it with boyish glee and then exclaimed sheepishly: "Now I too have destroyed a Patton tank!"

Three months later he traveled to Tashkent to meet with President Ayub Khan of Pakistan and negotiate a peace under the auspices of Soviet Premier Aleksei Kosygin. Shastri was asked to give up at the conference table the gains that were won on the battlefield. He matched the equanimity which he showed in the adversity of war with the magnanimity of a victor, and signed the Tashkent agreement. He clasped President Ayub's hand, buried the hatchet, and saved the peace. It was when he had covered himself in a blaze of glory and retired to bed, unsuspecting and defenseless, that cowardly Death struck him in the heart.

Shastri woke from his sleep at 1:25 A.M. with a bout of severe coughing and complained of acute pain and congestion in the chest. His personal physician gave him an injection; even before it could take effect, he collapsed and died at 1:32 A.M. A team of seven Soviet physicians and surgeons arrived at the scene within moments and attempted to revive his heart, but in vain. The 587 days of the short-lived Shastri regime had come to an end.

As soon as the news reached Home Minister Gulzarilal Nanda in New Delhi, he telephoned his cabinet associate, Mrs. Indira

Gandhi, then Minister of Information and Broadcasting, and asked her to proceed immediately to Rashtrapati Bhavan, the official residence of India's President, Dr. Sarvepalli Radhakrishnan. At 3:15 A.M. the President administered the oath of office to Nanda to act as Interim Prime Minister. Indira Gandhi and Finance Minister Sachin Chaudhuri, who were present, were reinstalled in their respective offices.

All this procedure was no doubt according to precedent. For a few years before his death, Mr. Nehru had left the post of Deputy Prime Minister vacant, with the intention of letting it fall into desuetude. When Mr. Nehru died, the Ministry of Law was of the opinion that since there was no Deputy Prime Minister it was necessary constitutionally for someone to be sworn in as Prime Minister. That was how on May 27, 1964, some two and a half hours after Nehru died, Gulzarilal Nanda had been hurriedly sworn in to act as Prime Minister.

But only six days later poor Nanda had been edged off from the pinnacle of power when his party, the Indian National Congress, chose Lal Bahadur Shastri as the permanent Prime Minister. Now, nineteen months later, Dame Fortune smiled on Nanda again, and this time he resolved that the office should not elude his permanent grasp.

When Nanda rushed to have himself sworn in as Acting Prime Minister, it was not out of any concern for the observance of constitutional proprieties. In fact, a school of constitutional lawyers is of the opinion that, as in the United States, in India too it is the President who is the chief executive, and that the death of the Indian Prime Minister does not leave a vacuum at the top of the government any more than the demise of the American Secretary of State does. It can of course be argued with equal force that the President of India, like the monarch of England, simply reigns but does not rule, and it is the Prime Minister in both countries who is the repository of effective power. But these constitutional niceties aside, what actually prompted Nanda into his precipitate predawn action was the instinct for political survival.

By noon, more than a million stunned people swarmed into New

Delhi's Palam airport and lined the 12-mile-long route to Shastri's residence at No. 10 Jan Path. At 2:30 P.M. when a silver-gray Aeroflot IL-18 with Soviet insignia on its tail taxied to a halt on the tarmac, a hushed silence descended on the crowd. Its door swung open, six officers of the rank of major general, representing the three services, entered the aircraft with a stretcher and brought out the slender body draped in the Indian tricolor flag. A chorus of incoherent groans rent the air when the multitudinous crowd fixed its gaze on the white cap which was still in place on a head propped up by pillows. An Air Force man, lined up for the guard of honor, collapsed, and Shastri's second son swooned.

The body was borne past the President, the Vice President, members of the Cabinet, Governors and Chief Ministers of States, and the members of the diplomatic corps, all with grief written large on their faces. An interservice guard of honor of a hundred men presented arms, reversed them, and bowed their heads. As the body was placed on the same gun carriage that had borne the body of Jawaharlal Nehru, the tearful crowds broke through police lines to shower rose petals and marigolds, snatch one last *darshan* of the departed leader, and wail *Lal Bahadur amar rahe* ("May Lal Bahadur be immortal"). The Navy band played "Abide with Me," then the gun carriage left in procession, flanked by 120 soldiers, to the tune of the "Funeral March" played by the crack Rajputana Rifles.

A distraught and disconsolate Lalita Shastri lunged forward as her husband's remains were brought into the portals of the house at 4 P.M. She emptied her heart of all its convulsive grief, but the impassive face of Lal Bahadur Shastri responded with a stony silence. She patted his cheeks and fondled his chin, but no warm blood coursed through his icy countenance. Up on the veranda the late Prime Minister's eighty-five-year-old mother and ninety-two-year-old uncle seemed like silent apparitions while heartrending wails emanated from the private rooms of the Shastri residence.

The body was now bathed in the waters of the holy Ganges, and the family priest, Pandit Rajaram of Allahabad, performed the last religious rites. Amid the chanting of hymns the flag-draped body was carried to the portico and placed on a raised flower-bedecked platform. Incense filled an air that was already heavy with the fragrance of roses, marigolds, jasmine, and winter annuals. The five largest nurseries of Delhi were denuded of all their floral wealth, and urgent requests were dispatched to Bombay and Calcutta nurseries to air-freight more. Surrounded by his four sons, two daughters, and his wife—now clad in white and with the familiar red vermilion mark on the forehead removed to signify her widowed status—and flanked by two officers who kept an all-night vigil with their swords unsheathed, Lal Bahadur Shastri lay in state, his mien in an aspect of forgiveness for those thousands who, having mocked him in life, now filed past him in reverence and contrition.

When the news of Shastri's death reached him on the morning of January 11, Kumaraswami Kamaraj, the president of the ruling Congress Party, was in his native Madras. Kamaraj had found himself trapped in Madras once before—when Nehru died. Now, as then, he rushed to Delhi in a Fokker Friendship aircraft to help find a successor to the late Prime Minister Shastri.

A burly, dark-skinned sixty-three-year-old mountain of a man, Kamaraj is probably one of the most distinguished school dropouts of the world. Orphaned early in childhood, he belongs to the lowly caste of Nadars, who tap the white sap of the coconut palm and ferment it either into a mild brew called toddy or a bitter, strong one called arrack. With neither an educational background nor a social pedigree, he joined the only profession that calls for no formal qualifications—politics. Although his name literally means "the Prince of Carnal Love," he has remained to this day a confirmed bachelor, politics continuing to be his zealous mistress. Kamaraj cannot speak Hindi or English, the two official languages of India. A man of few words, he can only speak his native tongue, Tamil. But quite early in his newfound career this earthy peasant demonstrated his native ability for using the only language that is of any consequence in organizational politics—arm-twisting.

There were three things uppermost in the mind of Kamaraj when Nehru died—to ensure an orderly succession, to prevent his party's going to pieces in the process of finding a successor, and to find a successor who would toe the Nehru line. He convened his party's

Working Committee and made a moving appeal for unity and solidarity. The committee then resolved that the new leader should be elected unanimously, and authorized Kamaraj as president to ascertain the consensus of the party on its preference for leadership. With this mandate in his pocket, Kamaraj proceeded to do what comes to him naturally. He collared some two hundred in the rank and file of the party, who were in Delhi to mourn Nehru's death, and indicated or—depending on whom he was talking to—dictated what the consensus should be. That was how Lal Bahadur Shastri, the conciliator and compromise candidate, had been chosen as Nehru's successor.

As Kamaraj once again winged northward to Delhi on Shastri's death, he knew there could be no repeat performance of his "Operation Consensus." He had alienated the leading contenders by thwarting their ambitions. And he had laid himself open to the charge that, rather than ascertain honestly the consensus of the party, he had dishonestly imposed his own preference on it. It was no longer possible for him to dissemble as the disinterested president of a party who rose above the din of its dissensions. For the moment, he did not let these thoughts disturb him and waited dutifully at the airport to do reverence to Shastri's body. Later that day he called on President Radhakrishnan, the Acting Prime Minister Nanda, the Minister of Information and Broadcasting, Mrs. Indira Gandhi, and the Chief Ministers of a few key states. Having reconnoitered the political battlefield, Kamaraj kept his counsel till the cremation of Shastri's body.

All through the night of January 11, hundreds of thousands of people poured into Delhi by train, bus, and bullock-cart from places far and near to pay their last homage to Shastri. As they arrived in the city they lined the route along which the funeral procession was to march. They clambered onto roof tops, lined the balconies, hung onto ventilators, stood on window sills, sat on compound walls, and climbed trees and waited patiently with the wilting flowers in their hands.

By seven-thirty on the morning of January 12, the main gates of Shastri's residence were closed to the unending stream of mourners that came to have one last look at the body. The night vigil at the catafalque came to an end with the echoes of "Lead, Kindly Light" sung by the choir of Christ's Church. Preparations were afoot to receive the large number of foreign dignitaries that arrived in the city to pay their last respects on behalf of their peoples.

Among the earliest callers were Vice President Hubert H. Humphrey and Secretary of State Dean Rusk, who walked up to Mrs. Shastri with folded hands and then stood in silence for two minutes before the body. Soon after came the Soviet Premier Aleksei Kosygin on his second visit. The Dalai Lama placed a white scarf on the body in the Tibetan tradition, followed by President Radhakrishnan and Lord Mountbatten, both of whom placed wreaths. Mrs. Indira Gandhi and her Cabinet colleagues, Congress President Kamaraj, Ambassadors, senior government officials, and servicemen then filled the rest of the portico.

At nine-fifteen the scores of members of the Shastri household stepped forward and one by one washed his feet. Mrs. Lalita Shastri slipped her gold bangles off her wrists and placed them on her dead husband's chest to signify her status of widowhood. At nine-thirty the Navy band played the first poignant notes of the "Funeral March." The column of uniformed men from the three services, led by the Brigade of Guards with their scarlet berets and turbans, marched in studied slow step. According to Hindu custom, women do not visit the cremation ground, and as the gun carriage moved out of the gates of the house, Lalita Shastri's tear-filled eyes cast their last longing, lingering look on the bier.

The carriage inched forward, navigating through a sea of humanity. Traversing Jan Path, the procession came to the intersection with Raj Path and turned right toward the historic India Gate. Its beautifully laid out, spacious lawns were packed to capacity. But its recently erected railings had a tale of irony to tell. They were meant to control the joyous crowds during the celebration of Republic Day a fortnight hence. The procession wended its way through Curzon Road and negotiated the turn into the inner circle of Connaught Place. The press of the people in their multitudes was immense as the cortege entered the heart of the city.

They broke through police cordons and through the chains of human arms formed by members of the National Cadet Corps. A man hobbled erratically on his wooden crutches and flung a garland at the cortege. A blind woman groped in her enveloping darkness to feel what others saw. A young widow wailed that she had lost her loved one as a victim of the recent war and her beloved leader was now a casualty of the peace. When the procession neared a railroad crossing, the restless passengers of an express train brought it to a halt on the overhead bridge and had a glimpse of the body that passed beneath.

When the procession reached the end of the eight-mile-long route it was in full view of the vast concourse of humanity that had gathered for the cremation in what is fast developing into India's national cemetery. Most conspicuous in it are Shantivan, the memorial to Jawaharlal Nehru, and, farther on, Rajghat, the memorial to Mahatma Gandhi. Across the road to the south is the monumental Red Fort, and in the brightness of high noon is clearly visible the dome of the Divan-e-Khas where the Mogul emperors in their plenitude of power once held court with their nobility. On the north flows the river Jumna, perennial witness to the pomp, circumstance, and catastrophe of Indian history.

The carriage halted 150 yards from the brick-and-mortar platform on which the funeral pyre was to be lit. Standing by the pyre to receive Shastri's body were acting Prime Minister Nanda, Defense Minister Y. B. Chavan, Mrs. Indira Gandhi, and others. As the priests, led by Pandit Rajaram, chanted Sanskrit *slokas* and blew conch shells, senior army officers, led by the three service chiefs, lifted the body from the carriage and placed it on the pyre. Religious rites over, the priest handed the torch of burning wood to Shastri's eldest son, the twenty-four-year-old Hari Krishan. Head bowed and holding the torch in his folded hands, he circled the funeral pyre thrice. Thirteen men of the Brigade of Guards fired three shots into the air. Hari Krishan lit the pyre. A pencil-thin column of black smoke snaked its way up. The skies were rent by the spontaneous cry: "*Janata ka pradhan mantri amar rahe*" ("May the people's own prime minister remain immortal!") The buglers sounded the "Last Post," and Shastri's second son, the eighteen-year-old Sunil, fell unconscious.

The priests poured some fifty kilograms of *ghee* (clarified butter) on the pyre's seven maunds of combustible sandalwood. Soon the rising flames licked the crackling wood. Sixty kilograms of incensed ingredients and a liter of water from the holy Ganges were sprinkled on the pyre. In an hour's time Lal Bahadur's corporeal frame was reduced to ashes.

2

The Reluctant Candidate

ALL through the day of the cremation, Kamaraj went through the motions of mourning, making sure tactfully that his physical presence was observed at the obsequies. But his mind was engrossed in the issue of succession. At seven-thirty in the morning Kamaraj called on acting Prime Minister Nanda. Nanda recapitulated to him how he had given up in 1964 the prize that was already in his possession when he stepped down in favor of Shastri and responded to the Congress president's fervent appeal to preserve party unity. But at the time of Nehru's death, argued Nanda, there was at least a national Prime Minister in Lal Bahadur Shastri, whereas there was none in sight now around whom all elements of the party would rally.

Nanda then advanced the argument which he hoped would clinch the issue. The General Election was due in just a year's time. Why does the party have to waste its substance in an intraparty wrangle in a preelection year? Anyone who remembers the slaughter in San Francisco's Cow Palace in July 1964 would have seen great merit in Nanda's argument. Possession is nine tenths of title, and Nanda calculated that if only he hung on to his chair till after his party was returned to power in the ensuing General Election, he would have his title perfected. Kamaraj did the listening as usual without committing himself. His own interest was in the procedure to be adopted for choosing a successor, rather than in the result of the procedure adopted. As the chief of his party, his instinct told him to avert internecine feuding and fall back on unanimity. Whether Nanda was allowed to remain or asked to get out mattered little to Kamaraj. His only concern was that whatever the Congress decided must be decided upon unanimously.

Under the Indian Constitution the President of the Republic invites the leader of the party with a majority in Parliament to become the Prime Minister and to form a government. In India, as in England, political parties have two different wings, the parliamentary and the organizational, each wing choosing its own leader. During the seventeen years that Nehru was Prime Minister, there never was a contest for parliamentary leadership. In all of the three General Elections the Congress party obtained a majority, and its members in Parliament chose Nehru mechanically as their leader. When Nehru died, every effort was made to avoid a contest because the Congress Party had convinced itself that, unless it papered over its differences, it would crack down the middle.

During the last years of Nehru's life it was an interesting pastime for Western observers to speculate on what might happen when Nehru departed from the scene. Since British political parties are based upon ideology, the common belief of most British observers was that the Indian National Congress would break up into Right and Left factions once the cement of Nehru's unifying influence was removed, thus endangering the country's political stability. Since until recently most Americans let the British do the thinking for them on matters Indian, this had become the prevailing American view also. But what is astonishing is that it should have become the official dogma of the leading lights of the Indian National Congress itself. They need only have remembered that the Democratic and Republican parties in the United States are both coalitions of diverse interests, and neither is ideologically cohesive. And yet, neither the Taft-Eisenhower wrangle for power in 1952 nor the Scranton-Goldwater scramble for preeminence in 1964, both of which were portrayed by American commentators as the classic representation of the Conservative-Liberal dichotomy, tore the Republican party at the seams.

All this notwithstanding, the Indian National Congress believed that what others said of it amounted to a law of nature. Little effort was therefore required of Kamaraj in 1964 to convert the already converted. He easily persuaded the two chief contenders, Gulzarilal Nanda and Morarji Desai, to withdraw from the race. And in a great show of unanimity he got Nanda to propose the name of Shastri, and Desai to second it.

But myths die hard, and once again in 1966 feverish attempts were being made to avoid a contest at all costs. A procession of Chief Ministers of several states waited on Kamaraj on the afternoon of January 12, 1966, to reiterate that a contest would be suicidal and that the consensus must be ascertained. Meanwhile the executive committee of the Congress Parliamentary Party met informally to discuss the procedure for electing Shastri's successor. Most of those present felt that the election must be unanimous. But if a contest became unavoidable, they felt that the members must be polled informally and the candidate securing the largest number of votes should then be elected unanimously.

At the time of Shastri's death, the most formidable contender for his vacant office, Morarji Desai, was in Bhubaneswar in the eastern state of Orissa, some one thousand miles away from New Delhi. Replying to newsmen, he said "...a smooth change-over would be a tribute not only to Shastri but also to the country." The optimists read sweet reasonableness into his statement and concluded that he would accept any mechanism devised by the Congress President to obtain unanimity. But Congress President Kamaraj knew better.

Morarji Ranchhodji Desai has always been noted for being inflexible of purpose and unbending in will. Ever since he came under the influence of Mahatma Gandhi, he has pursued with puritanical zeal such idiosyncrasies as the prohibition of alcoholic beverages and the adoption of homeopathic medicines. It is perhaps symbolic of the man's self-imposed asceticism and austerity that he can celebrate even his birthday only once in four years—on the twenty-ninth of February. At seventy, he is spare in build but still stands upright, both in bearing and character. Although he describes himself as a Gandhian and a socialist, his political enemies have labeled him the friend of the exploiting capitalist and of the imperialist West. Extremely personable and charming though he is, Morarji does not forgive easily his political enemies, and although he attributes the happening of most events to the will of an inscrutable Providence, he ascribes some to the animus of perverse humans. Some honest Congressmen admit that in choosing free India's second Prime Minister they were not expressing unanimity in favor of Shastri so much as "unanimosity" against Desai. At any rate, Morarji himself suspected that in June 1964 Kamaraj engaged not in an "Operation Consensus" but in an "Operation Animus."

When Morarji returned to New Delhi from Bhubaneswar he realized it would be bad politics to make indecent haste with a public announcement of his candidacy only hours after Shastri's death. So his colleagues let it be known quietly that their man's white cap of homespun cotton was in the ring. This was no surprise to Kamaraj, who had expected it all along. It only confirmed his well-grounded fears that the party must brace itself for some fierce infighting. For tactical reasons, however, Kamaraj continued to harp on the theme of unanimity. The more he bandied that word about, the more he thought it would dissuade Morarji from running. When newsmen surrounded Kamaraj in his house after the cremation, he drew their attention to the unanimous desire of State Chief Ministers for a unanimous election of the Prime Minister. "Do you think it is possible?" asked one journalist. "I hope so," he answered. Since the Chief Ministers' wish seemed father to Kamaraj's thought, a skeptical correspondent volunteered it would be "quite an achievement." With an oracular shake of his balding head, he grunted, "Yes," and retreated into the house.

All through the forenoon of January 12 New Delhi wore a deserted look. Offices and shops and banks remained closed, and the city's spacious streets, its tree-lined pavements and wide vistas were quite empty of man, animal, and vehicle. But by late afternoon they were darting in different directions to one condolence meeting or the other in this city of distances. The weak winter sun departed early, and the chill set in. With nightfall, people gathered in small clusters under street lamps, wearing woolens or swathed in shawls, purged and purified by the day's events, and prepared to probe the

subject of succession with guilt-free consciences. The faint and muf-
fled tones in which the issue was discussed the previous day gave way
to a more audible and assertive expression. Gossip, hearsay, wishful
thinking and thinkful wishing threw up the names of all the various
candidates, possible and improbable. Uppermost among these were
the names of the Defense Minister, Y. B. Chavan,* and the Minister
of Information and Broadcasting, Indira Gandhi.

Yeshwantrao Balwantrao Chavan, with his stocky frame and easy
manner, exudes confidence that the defense of the country is safe in
his hands. He is a descendant of the Marathas, a hardy south-central
Indian mountain race that marauded the imperial hordes of the
Moguls in the seventeenth century. To this inherited reputation must
be added his recently acquired credentials of having conducted with
cocksureness the war with Pakistan in September 1965. His compatriots feel that Chavan has enabled them once again to walk with
their heads held high after the humiliating reverses inflicted on them
by Communist China in October 1962.

A revolutionary in his student days, and later a small-town crimi-
nal lawyer, Chavan became in 1956 the youngest Chief Minister of
the wealthiest state in India, Bombay. When, in 1960, Bombay was
ultimately divided along linguistic lines into the two states of Maharashtra and Gujarat, Chavan headed the former and became one
of India's most efficient and successful Chief Ministers. Intellectually
curious but not ideologically hidebound, Chavan enjoys the political
advantage of not being associated in the public mind with any one
faction of his party. Genial and affable, he has few political enemies.

Chavan had accompanied Shastri to Tashkent to assist him in the
peace negotiations with Pakistan. He flew back to Delhi with Shastri's body on the afternoon of January 11 and busied himself for the
rest of the day assisting with preparations for the funeral. Next day,
however, in his palatial and well-appointed bungalow at No. 1 Race
Course Road, he found time to meet with Mr. V. P. Naik, the Chief
Minister of Maharashtra. Since Chavan was Maharashtra's favorite
son, Naik no doubt wanted to boost his candidacy. Chavan was not

* In a Cabinet reshuffle of November 1966, he was made Minister of Home
Affairs.

unwilling to run, but if there is one faculty more than any other which is his political asset, it is his Rooseveltian sense of timing and grasp of the situation.

The best situation for Chavan to be in was one where he would be drafted as the candidate most acceptable or least offensive to all the warring factions. If a draft seemed unlikely and a contest inevitable, he must enter it with such overwhelming support as to leave no doubt of his victory. If principle is what matters most to Morarji Desai, all that matters to Yeshwantrao Chavan is success. Chavan realized that he had been a member of the federal government for just over three years and had yet to reach the commanding heights of national politics before he could expect any massive popular support. Being ambitious he was willing to take risks, but being practical he wanted the risks to be within limits. He decided that the best thing was to float a balloon and see how it would stand up to the impending political storm. He therefore let Naik slip out the word that "Barkis is willing."

Late in the evening on January 12 Chavan visited Kamaraj for the ostensible purpose of acquainting him with what had transpired at Tashkent. Kamaraj was no more eager to listen to that story than Chavan was to tell it. When he switched to the real issue, Chavan did indeed play his cards well. Rather than disturb Kamaraj's composure by telling him that he had one more "contestant" on his hands, Chavan reassured him by saying that he was merely an "aspirant." He would run, but not unless he had the Congress chieftain's blessing. Kamaraj listened as usual but said nothing, although he must indeed have been flattered to hear at least one person tell him that he was still the unquestioned kingmaker.

Not unquestioned, really, as Kamaraj was soon to learn. But meanwhile there came a development which even politically prescient Kamaraj did not expect. In 1964 Kamaraj managed to get Shastri elected largely with the astute manipulation of men by three Tammany-style politicians—Atulya Ghosh, S. K. Patil, and Sanjiva Reddy. The alleged unsavory tactics of this triumvirate soon earned them the sobriquet of "the Syndicate." In 1966 the Syndicate was still powerful enough singly to block the election of anyone it did

not approve, although powerless singly to get anyone elected. As
president of the Congress party in the state of West Bengal, Ghosh
has easy access to the moneybags in Calcutta and is in a position to
control party affairs in the two neighboring states of Bihar and
Orissa, and in Assam. Patil, with his easy access to the moneybags
in Bombay, has long been able to lord it over in the affairs of the
state Congress party there. Besides, Patil had been a successful federal Minister of Food—a portfolio regarded as the graveyard of many
a political ambition—and was now an efficient Minister of Railways.
Sanjiva Reddy operates from his political base in the southern state
of Andhra Pradesh, was a past President of the Indian National Congress, and was now the federal Minister of Steel.

The members of the Syndicate were hopelessly divided among
themselves and could not unite behind any of the candidates whose
names were being bruited about. In the circumstances, the Syndicate
at first resorted to the expedient of entering the fray itself. First Patil
and then Reddy offered themselves as possible candidates. Quite
obviously, however, neither thought his chances were bright, and
the objective was apparently to establish bargaining counters to obtain Cabinet positions for themselves. But on the night of January 12,
after Chavan had left, staking out his claim with the Congress president, the Syndicate repaired to Kamaraj's house with the serious offer
that it would support Kamaraj himself for the Prime Ministership.
The Syndicate's idea, of course, was to see that Kamaraj the kingmaker became king so that Ghosh in turn could become the kingmaker. Once again Kamaraj gave the impatient men a patient hearing, but his impassive face revealed no feeling.

By all accounts Kamaraj sleeps soundly, and he pondered if it were
worthwhile lying uneasy with a crowned head. He did not take long
in deciding to reject the proffered crown—not because he is any
self-effacing saint but because he is a sound student of psychology.
Kamaraj had made an able administrator and effective Chief Minister of his native Madras State for a full decade, from 1954 to 1963.
Then he came out with a suggestion which since its adoption in 1963
has come to be known as the Kamaraj Plan. What he suggested was
that senior Congressmen who were holding federal and state offices

With the dawn of January 13 enlightenment came to Kamaraj, and by the simple process of elimination he arrived at the name of Indira Gandhi. As daughter of Jawaharlal Nehru, she had the right genealogical connection. Like her father, she was a charismatic leader capable of attracting vast crowds to the polling booths in an election year. She had been a member of the party's Working Committee for many years, and her record as Congress president in 1959 was quite distinguished. She had no political enemies, and she might well be the candidate behind whom most of the factions would unite. And she appeared to be the only candidate capable of beating Morarji Desai in a straight contest.

Beyond the substantial benefits which would accrue to his party from her candidacy, it occurred to Kamaraj that Mrs. Gandhi as Prime Minister might be useful to her country too. Her youth might give the nation the much-needed dynamism. India's image in the world would also improve, since Mrs. Gandhi certainly had style, poise, grace, and sophistication. Her acquaintance with the leaders of all the major Powers and scores of lesser Powers would enable her to conduct diplomacy in high key. Kamaraj now turned his attention to how best he could ensure Mrs. Gandhi's nomination and eventual election.

None of the contending groups was yet privy to Kamaraj's private decision. Meanwhile the dying embers of acting Prime Minister Gulzarilal Nanda's political ambitions were rekindled by the hope that the party's inability to arrive at unanimity might well leave him in the saddle. But why should he not spur the party-horse a little to trot about with himself in the saddle rather than wait patiently till he was thrown off its back? So the nervous Nanda carried his petition once again, importuning Kamaraj to let him stay a while in the saddle. Luckily for Nanda, a nonaligned section of the Congress Parliamentary Party veered around to the view that it might be conducive to unity in the party and stability in the country to let Nanda function as the Prime Minister until the ensuing election.

Nanda also hoped that his present political stance as a centrist would be more acceptable to Kamaraj and to the party majority. As Nehru's Minister of Planning, Nanda had once been a fire-eating

must resign and take to organizational work so that the party's
which was dimmed in the General Election of 1962 and in t
elections of 1963, might be refurbished.

Jawaharlal Nehru, shrewd politician that he was, saw the
tion as extremely serviceable—one with which he could get
the Ministers he did not like. Kamaraj himself resigned as Chi
ister of Madras, and in appreciation of his sterling suggestion,
made Kamaraj the president of the Indian National Congress
It was bad enough that Shastri took back into office some
Ministers who were sacked under the Kamaraj Plan, thus e
the party to the grave charge that it played a hoax on the
Could the author of the Plan himself now get into one of the
offices of the land by the back door? And that, too, just be
General Election?

Kamaraj had also to give some thought to the balancing ol
regional, religious, and linguistic factors. The President of
public, Dr. Radhakrishnan, was a southerner, Prime Ministe
a northerner, and Vice-President Zakir Hussain a Muslim. If
were to become Prime Minister now, both the head of state
of government would be southerners, and the vast Hindi-
region of the north would go unrepresented.

These were not the only considerations either. It was
to be the Chief Minister of an outlying state, occupied with
interests, and handing out patronage, but quite another to
hub of national affairs and in the vortex of international
Again, it was one thing to manage party matters, reward t
ent and chastise the unruly, but quite another for Kamaraj
a Parliament of which he has never been a member, the
and conventions of which were alien to his experience, a
arena of which a vigilant opposition is eager to embarrass
ernment at every step. Finally, although Kamaraj undoubt
sessed sound common sense and an unerring political in
untutored mind was erratic both in the perception of poli
articulation. Kamaraj ended his nocturnal soliloquy with
judgment that he was not the man for the office, but that
hour for sleep.

socialist. But now, as Shastri's Home Minister, Nanda was eager to put out many a domestic fire. This naturally affected his philosophy —if such it was—and he began to accept increasingly the prescription of that character in Ibsen who argued for "discreet moderation and moderate discretion." At any rate, his conversion seemed to have pleased some prominent businessmen, and they commenced canvassing openly for Nanda.

Unfortunately for him, however, Nanda had a redoubtable enemy in one of his erstwhile Cabinet colleagues, T. T. Krishnamachari. TTK, as he was popularly called, also hails from Kamaraj's Madras State. But in contrast to Kamaraj's rustic simplicity and boorish manner, TTK sports an urbane sophistication and a cultivated air. An astute Brahmin and an adept opportunist, TTK was wont to employ devious ways in his pursuit of power. As Nehru's Finance Minister TTK had reached a position of preeminence when he was forced to resign in 1958 under a cloud of suspicion as a result of a scandal unearthed by none other than Indira's husband, the late Feroze Gandhi. But the adroit TTK staged an astonishing comeback as Shastri's Finance Minister. But TTK could not change his proverbial spots, and it was not long before an impressive group of Members of Parliament leveled serious charges about his official conduct. Shastri's last important act in office before he left for Tashkent was to fire TTK.

TTK suspected that the man actually responsible for his ouster was Nanda, and hapless Nanda had provided sufficient cause for suspicion. When he became Home Minister in 1963, he had pledged to root out corruption. But rather than do this through courts of law, where the rights of the accused are protected, Nanda was alleged to have maintained a private court to entertain complaints of corruption, to have employed private eyes to investigate, and then rendered his private judgment on each case. His methods were generally denounced by other Ministers and officials who said their integrity was being attacked unjustly for purely political reasons by persons permitted by Nanda to remain in the sanctuary of their anonymity. TTK was a political intimate of Kamaraj, and, thirsting for a retaliatory blow against Nanda, he insisted that Kamaraj give short shrift to Nanda's ambitions. Kamaraj hardly needed this prodding since he was anyway convinced that the Prime Minister's shoes were a few sizes too large for Nanda.

Kamaraj's immediate concern was to raise Indira Gandhi's standard. But in doing so he had to be careful not to give the impression that she was *his* candidate. She had to be projected as the candidate of an overwhelming majority of the party, so that he could, in the guise of the protective shepherd, approach the recalcitrant minority and plead with them not to go astray but remain with the flock.

During the forenoon of January 14 Kamaraj went to the national headquarters of his party on Jantar Mantar Road to attend the crucial meeting of the Working Committee—an organ comparable to the national committee of an American political party. The committee was convened to decide the date, time, and procedure for the election of Shastri's successor. Since the Chief Ministers of all the states happened to be in town for Shastri's funeral, Kamaraj invited them too to attend the meeting—a move the deeper significance of which will presently become clear.

Members and invitees walked up the stairs to the second floor of the building, kicked off their footwear, and filed into a modest-sized room with book-lined walls. Morarji Desai and Indira Gandhi sat next to each other, insulated in their woolen shawls from the cold dampness of the room, still unaware that they would be pitted against each other in a fight to the finish a few days hence. The embarrassing interludes of silence were filled with occasional small talk as the members squatted on sheeted mattresses and leaned against white bolsters. The lean and lanky crossed their legs and froze their sitting positions, but the weightier ones frequently shifted their bulk this way or that to find the most comfortable resting position in that all too restless atmosphere. In the center of a row along one length of the room sat Kamaraj, his elbows poised on a wooden lectern covered by a printed tablecloth and the palms of his hand supporting his massive jaws.

Kamaraj tapped the knob of a chromium-plated call bell to bring the meeting to order. The first suggestion from the floor was that an attempt be made to find a consensus, as was done successfully in

1964. The motion was discussed in the most desultory fashion, with Kamaraj, the patent-owner of "Operation Consensus," evincing the least interest in the suggestion. Morarji Desai then intervened in the debate and maintained firmly that a free, fair, and unfettered election must be held, as he put it, "in the interests of democratic tenets." Some of the committee members were surprised to hear the staunch support given to Morarji by Jagjivan Ram, who controlled a solid block of eighty votes of Parliamentarians belonging to the former untouchable class. Another member interposed to say that a regular contest might create bad blood and cause a rift which might be difficult to heal in time for the General Election. Morarji countered with the argument that an election was a decent, democratic device intended to prevent bitterness rather than cause it. He then went on to utter the significant warning that the procedure decided upon by the committee "should not leave any room for a sense of bitterness," implying that anyone's attempt to steamroller his right to contest would be deeply resented by his supporters.

The offshoot of the discussion was the decision to call a meeting of the Congress Parliamentary Party at 11 A.M. on January 19 to elect its leader, who would then automatically become Prime Minister. A belated suggestion was then made that a committee of four, including Kamaraj and Morarji, be appointed to search for unanimity between now and the holding of the election. However, Kamaraj and Morarji were both opposed to the appointment of a formal committee, but both welcomed the idea of striving for unanimity—Morarji still hoping he might be chosen unanimously, and Kamaraj still hoping that someone else might be elected unanimously.

The meeting ended in a surprisingly short three quarters of an hour. One more surprise was in store for the committee members. Their jaws dropped as they saw Morarji and Kamaraj drive away together to the latter's residence. It was their first face-to-face encounter after nineteen months during which each was *persona non grata* to the other. Kamaraj had deprived Morarji of the Prime Ministership in 1964. In 1965 Morarji had opposed, although unsuccessfully, a second term of the Congress presidency for Kamaraj. Could two such sworn enemies agree except to disagree? Their meeting ended after a brief twenty-minute confrontation. Morarji put Kamaraj on notice that he was determined to contest, and added it would be nice if Kamaraj refrained from his reputed pressure tactics and allowed a free election. Kamaraj wished Morarji all the luck in the world—mumbling to himself no doubt that he would need it—but protested innocently that it would be a denial of freedom if he prevented anyone from running against Morarji.

The battle lines were now clearly drawn, and Kamaraj went into action. The same afternoon he conveyed to the powerful Chief Minister of Madhya Pradesh, Dwarka Prasad Mishra—a sixty-five-year-old former member of the opposition Praja Socialist Party and a long-time critic of some Nehru policies—Morarji's determination to contest. Kamaraj then convinced Mishra that only one candidate—Indira Gandhi—had the right mixture of qualities and credentials to give Morarji a drubbing. However, the Parliamentarians were not to know that Mrs. Gandhi had the backing of the Congress president, since it would certainly alienate their sympathies. Mishra was therefore advised to caucus with other Chief Ministers and announce jointly with them that there existed a tremendous ground swell of sympathy for Mrs. Gandhi at the grass-roots level, and they would therefore support her candidacy.

But would this stratagem work? Their experience as Chief Ministers told both Kamaraj and Mishra that at this particular juncture it ought to work exceedingly well. In a few weeks' time, a third of the membership of the Rajya Sabha, or the upper house of the Indian Parliament, would retire by rotation and be up for reelection. But unlike the United States Senators who are now chosen directly by the people as a result of the Seventeenth Amendment, members of the upper house of Parliament in India are chosen indirectly by state legislatures. The state legislatures are controlled by their respective Chief Ministers. If Parliamentarians want to get reelected, they had better do whatever the Chief Ministers tell them. Similarly, the entire membership of the Lok Sabha, or lower house of Parliament, would also contest in the General Election in a year's time. Once again, it is the Chief Ministers who more or less decide who should run for

Parliament from their respective states. If Parliamentarians want to be the Congress Party's nominees once again in the General Election, they had better be in the good books of their Chief Ministers and do their bidding. With the strategy mapped out all to their mutual satisfaction, Mishra took leave of Kamaraj.

Kamaraj sent word through his emissaries to Indira Gandhi not to be surprised if she heard her candidacy being discussed openly the next morning. He advised her to say, in answer to newsmen's possible questions, that she entertained no personal ambition to become the Prime Minister. However, Mrs. Gandhi was to stress that she would be glad to accept the candidacy for wholly impersonal reasons. One such reason could be an irresistible request from senior party members to bail them out of trouble. Suppose someone queried her about unanimity? Well, she was to say she would welcome a unanimous election, but she was not the least bit frightened of a contest.

Kamaraj then summoned the members of the Syndicate to his residence for a late-night session. He first disabused them of any notion they might have of persuading him to accept the Prime Ministership. He went over with them, in very great detail, the merits and demerits of every candidate in the field. He warned the Syndicate not to underestimate the support Morarji could muster. It was not enough for the Syndicate to take the negative approach of opposing Morarji. Time was running out, and the Syndicate ought to think in positive terms of uniting behind someone who could defeat Morarji. Kamaraj indicated—no doubt stressing that he was being very objective about it—that Indira Gandhi possessed a decent chance of defeating Morarji. But the Congress President did not succeed in converting the Syndicate wholly to his point of view.

As planned the previous day, D. P. Mishra invited his counterparts from other states for a meeting at Madhya Pradesh Bhavan, a red-and-white brick bungalow owned by his state in Chanakyapuri, the fashionable diplomatic enclave of New Delhi. Present were the Chief Ministers of seven states—Madras, Andhra Pradesh, Mysore, Maharashtra, Rajasthan, Bihar, and Orissa. Deciding with dispatch upon their course of action, the eight Chief Ministers drove directly to Kamaraj's house and informed him of their intention to support

Indira Gandhi. Word spread fast in New Delhi about this supposed
sudden development—a development which in fact had been incu-
bating in Kamaraj's feverish brain for the past few days.

But the development did produce the desired electric effect. Gulzarilal Nanda was the first contender to telephone Mrs. Gandhi and
congratulate her. He told the press he was bowing out of the contest "in view of the wide measure of agreement over Mrs. Gandhi's
candidature." Yeshwantrao Chavan went over swiftly to Mrs. Gandhi's house to offer her his felicitations and unstinted support. The
Chief Ministers then called on the presiding deity of the Syndicate,
Atulya Ghosh, and requested him to convey their decision to Morarji
and couple it with the appeal that he withdraw from the race and
make the election unanimous. Schooled in the language of power,
Ghosh realized the import of a decision made by eight Chief Ministers, decided that the Syndicate should make common cause with
them, and went to Morarji with a bid to surrender. But schooled as
Morarji was in the language of principle and indifferent as he was to
the charge that he adhered to his weird principles with mulish obstinacy, the outcome of the Ghosh-Morarji meeting was quite pre-
dictable.

Ghosh walked out with empty hands, and Morarji came out wring-
ing his hands to meet the press. "My position will not change until
the election is over," he insisted, and scoffed at the idea of Chief
Ministers—who themselves were not entitled to vote—trying to influence it. He stressed that even so, only eight Chief Ministers had
supported Mrs. Gandhi, implying that eight other uncommitted ones
might well support him. Surveying the unusually large assemblage
of news-hungry reporters anxious to spin their yarns, the stern disciplinarian remarked, "You should leave me for more legitimate
activity," and returned religiously to his daily Gandhian routine of
spinning yarn.

In another part of the city, at his residence on Jantar Mantar Road,
a confident Kamaraj also held court. He told newsmen that almost
all the Chief Ministers had met and told him that Mrs. Indira Gandhi
should be chosen unanimously. There was only the permissible degree of exaggeration in what he claimed. For, since the eight Chief

Ministers' decision was flashed across the nation's teleprinters, the bandwagon started rolling. The Chief Ministers of four more states—Assam, West Bengal, Punjab, and Himachal Pradesh—called long distance to confer with Kamaraj and pledge their support to Mrs. Gandhi. A clever correspondent asked if Kamaraj endorsed the Chief Ministers' decision. But the agile Kamaraj, who had to pretend he endorsed nothing and nobody, simply said he would consider the decision for what it was worth in his still continuing quest for unanimity. A mischievous correspondent interjected: "Does unanimity mean that Mr. Morarji Desai should step down?" Kamaraj growled: "Don't put that question." Another tormentor persisted: "Do you support Mrs. Gandhi yourself?" And the irate Kamaraj admonished: "Don't ask that question." The last but least provocative of the questions shot at him was whether he was at least happy with the Chief Ministers' decision. His white walrus moustache accenting a widening grin, the kingmaker confided, "I am always happy," and on that happy note everyone dispersed.

Attempting in vain to conceal her quiet satisfaction, a coy Mrs. Gandhi met reporters in a third quarter of the city. She had called earlier on Dr. Sarvepalli Radhakrishnan, the white-turbaned, bespectacled, septuagenarian President of the Republic, to acquaint him with what had transpired during the day. As the constitutional head of state, the President has little disposition to invite the odium of any faction by appearing to support any other. Dr. Radhakrishnan's constitutionally enforced nonalignment in domestic politics was further reinforced by his own professional training and personal temperament. Long recognized by the world of intellect as the most eloquent exponent of Indian philosophy, he had now been assigned the role of Plato's philosopher-king, to abjure all popular sentiment, factional intrigue, and mob passion. Fittingly therefore, as Mrs. Gandhi took leave of him, Dr. Radhakrishnan gave her his paternal, not presidential, blessing.

Mrs. Gandhi admitted to the assembled newsmen, however, that she did receive some purely political blessing—from acting Prime Minister Nanda, Defense Minister Chavan, and Railways Minister and Syndicate member Patil. Eager to extract her explicit admission

of Kamaraj's implicit support, a correspondent asked who had conveyed to her the decision of the Chief Ministers. She replied with a
smile that she learned about it from the Press Trust of India—the
national news agency. Did she tell Kamaraj she would accept the
nomination? No, she told him she would do whatever he asked her
to do. "What did he ask you to do?" "He has asked me to stay at
home until he calls me." A foreign correspondent jumped the gun:
"How does it feel to be the first woman Prime Minister of India?"
Thrown off guard momentarily, she said: "I shall not be the first
woman Prime Minister," referring to the fact that Mrs. Sirimavo
Bandaranaike of Ceylon was the first woman ever to become Prime
Minister. But she regained her concentration hastily and added that
she could not anticipate events, and at any rate she was a human
being who happened to be a woman by the sheer accident of birth.
Soon after the pressmen left, hundreds of ordinary citizens gathered
all evening on January 15 on the narrow grounds in front of Mrs.
Gandhi's small but comfortable bungalow on 1 Safdarjung Road to
felicitate her on what they felt was a certain victory.

For three days prior to the polling on January 19, New Delhi became the cockpit of concerted canvassing, large-scale lobbying, and
hectic horse-trading. In addition to all the Chief Ministers who were
already there, the presidents and secretaries and other petty officials
of the various state branches of the Congress Party descended from
the sunny skies on Palam Airport in the manner of an unseasonal
flight of migratory birds. They looked eagle-eyed for their unwilling prey in scores of identical one-storied white buildings—the subsidized housing for Members of Parliament on the tranquil lawn-laid
North and South Avenues, in the tree-shaded compounds of Meena
Baug on Maulana Azad Road, and in the quarters on the noisier
Ferozeshah Road. The scene was a microcosm of India itself, em-
bracing its diversity of races, its variety of tongues, its plurality of
religions, its multiplicity of attire. The visiting delegations of party
workers immediately went to work on Members of Parliament belonging to their respective states, persuading the still uncommitted
to make their pledges, needling the halfhearted to confirm their
pledges, and pressuring the already committed to switch their pledges.

At the start of the canvassing it appeared that Mrs. Gandhi might poll about 300 and Mr. Desai about 250 of the 551 votes to be cast by the members of the Congress Parliamentary Party. A healthy feature of this polarization of forces was that it accorded not with the horizontal divisions of language, caste, and community—along which, according to some foreign observers, India is doomed to disintegrate —but with the vertical division of power, between the "haves" and the "have-nots," and the "ins" and the "outs." In most of the states the Chief Minister, who is the leader of the Congress Party in the legislature, controls one center of power, while the president of the state party organization controls a rival center of power. In some cases there are dissidents within the party's legislative group who are exploited by the organizational faction. It is one continual jockeying for power, position, and advantage till that quinquennial circus called the General Election alters the composition of forces and redraws the vertical line.

In state politics the divisions are often along horizontal lines, but in national politics these very horizontal groupings range themselves along the vertical line. This was very much in evidence in the Gandhi-Desai contest. At the outset, the Chief Minister of the eastern state of Orissa supported Mrs. Gandhi, but a former Leftist Chief Minister of that state favored Mr. Desai. The Chief Minister of the central Indian state of Madhya Pradesh, D. P. Mishra, was instrumental in engineering the near-unanimous support of other Chief Ministers for Mrs. Gandhi, but the dissidents in his own state favored Mr. Desai. In the populous North Indian state of Uttar Pradesh the lady Chief Minister, whose own womanly sympathies lay with Mrs. Gandhi, was herself at the mercy of a faction which supported Mr. Desai, while a second faction rooted for Mrs. Gandhi. The Chief Minister of the adjoining state of Bihar came out for Mrs. Gandhi, but the dissidents wanted Mr. Desai. The Chief Minister of the Himalayan state of Kashmir supported Mrs. Gandhi, but a former Chief Minister was inclined toward Mr. Desai. In the other North Indian state of Punjab the Chief Minister announced himself for Mrs. Gandhi, but the president of the local party organization favored Mr. Desai. In the northwestern state of Rajasthan and the southern state of Mysore the Chief Ministers were ardent supporters of Mrs. Gandhi, but their former Chief Ministers were outspoken advocates of Mr. Desai.

Horizontal divisions did play a minor role, and these were noticeable in three instances. The west Indian state of Gujarat went almost solidly for Mr. Desai because he is from that state and speaks its language, Gujarati. Its adjoining state, Maharashtra, went almost solidly for Mrs. Gandhi, partly because the Maharashtrians still harbor their traditional antipathy for Mr. Desai's linguistic group. Likewise, the four South Indian states, Andhra Pradesh, Mysore, Madras and Kerala, whose languages are of Dravidian origin, and the East Indian state of West Bengal were opposed to Morarji Desai because of his strident insistence upon making Hindi, a North Indian language, the sole official language of India. These states want the indefinite continuance of English as an associate official language, a demand with which Mrs. Gandhi sympathizes. The last serious horizontal division—that based on caste—was represented by Mr. Jagjivan Ram, credited with controlling the votes of some eighty Members of Parliament who were formerly untouchables. Mr. Ram originally seemed to sympathize with Mr. Desai's claims but switched to Mrs. Gandhi after having been assured of a post in Mrs. Gandhi's Cabinet. However, both the Desai and Gandhi camps deny that the untouchables constitute a monolithic bloc, voting on considerations of caste alone.

As in American politics, the two main contenders, Mrs. Gandhi and Mr. Desai, traversed the high road, leaving it to their campaigners to take the low road. The common people of the capital, who had no part in this contest, had an earful from the travelers on the low road. They heard from Mrs. Gandhi's camp that Morarji's moneybags were buying up the votes of Members of Parliament, that Nehru's socialist policies would be reversed by Morarji, who was just a front-man for big business, that under Morarji—who was nicknamed "Moral-ji" for his excessive moralizing—there would be a ruthless invasion of privacy and personal freedom, and that Morarji would sell India down the drain to the Western Powers. They then heard from Mr. Desai's camp that Mrs. Gandhi's henchmen were terrorizing Members of Parliament to vote for her, that she was the captive candidate of extreme socialists who would take the country to rack and ruin, that under the Gandhi regime the state would become a Leviathan extinguishing every trace of individual liberty, and that Mrs. Gandhi would put India under the tutelage of the Kremlin.

Like the American people, the Indian people too were relieved to know that their Republic survived these frightful forebodings. Both candidates in truth have long and proud records of service to the country; both are individuals of integrity and high principle; both are personally incorruptible; both are believers in social justice and the welfare state; and both are firm believers in India's right to pursue an independent foreign policy.

Even when the canvassing was at its briskest, neither candidate resorted to horse-trading. Jagjivan Ram switched his bloc of votes to Mrs. Gandhi only after Morarji Desai had refused to offer him an advance commitment of a Cabinet post. Mrs. Gandhi also refused to pay any price to anybody, and Jagjivan Ram is believed to have obtained the commitment from Kamaraj. Likewise the Syndicate demanded and obtained as its price—but not from Mrs. Gandhi—the dismissal of two members from the old Shastri Cabinet and their substitution by two others acceptable to the Syndicate.

The arguments of the campaigners on the high road were clothed in legal raiment or invested with constitutional sanction. The chief of these arguments related to the role of the Chief Ministers in the nomination of Mrs. Gandhi. Mr. Desai's supporters alleged that the actual voters were members of the Congress Parliamentary Party, that no extraneous influence or pressure must be brought to bear on them, and that democratic practices would be endangered if members were not allowed to cast their ballots without let or hindrance. This was countered by Mrs. Gandhi's colleagues, who reasoned that it was not improper for anyone to seek to influence Members of Parliament so long as the latter cast their votes by secret ballot, and that since the various states constituted several focuses of power in a federal structure, the Chief Ministers as repositories of that power were bound to exercise it.

What was surprising was the participation by members of the opposition parties in an essentially intraparty argument. Seven prominent members of the non-Communist opposition parties excoriated the role of the Chief Ministers as "a negation of democracy." The octogenarian leader of the conservative Swatantra Party, Mr. Chakravarti Rajagopalachari, deplored any contest and desired that Acting Prime Minister Nanda should lead the lame-duck Parliament until the General Election of 1967. The unnerved Nanda suspected that this unexpected conservative endorsement was his kiss of political death. At the other end of the political spectrum, Mrs. Gandhi was embarrassed when she received the unsolicited endorsement of Mr. S. A. Dange, the leader of the pro-Moscow Indian Communists, who also suggested that the names of Morarji's supporters should be published, presumably for the purposes of victimization.

Continuing the legal argument, a member of the Congress Party suggested that the Prime Minister should belong to the lower house of Parliament, as in England. The intent of this seemingly innocuous suggestion was to disqualify Mrs. Gandhi, who happened to be a member of the upper house, and facilitate the election of Mr. Desai, who belonged to the lower house. The knight-errant to rush gallantly to the aid of the lady was none other than Mr. Bhupesh Gupta, the leader of the pro-Peking Indian Communists, who developed, for a change, a sudden love of constitutionalism and discovered that both houses were equal under the law of the land.

But not all opposition members yielded to the temptation of becoming strange bedfellows of Congress members. A spokesman for the Revolutionary Socialist Party declared that in respect of their claim to be socialists, both Mrs. Gandhi and Mr. Desai were dissimulators, and there was nothing to choose between Tweedledum and Tweedledee. The most notorious of India's maverick Parliamentarians professed to see no principle involved at all in the contest unless it be hereditary monarchy versus puritanism!

As the date for polling drew near, the situation crystallized, and it appeared certain that Mrs. Gandhi would obtain a minimum of 350 votes. Various tactics were employed by her supporters to arrive at this goal. Members of Parliament were asked to declare themselves openly in favor of Mrs. Gandhi, which a sizable number did. The ones who were reluctant to come out in the open were directed to give written pledges. During the last three days of the canvassing, Members of Parliament cut off all communication with their personal friends in the enemy camp, since even the most innocuous conversation could be construed as fifth-column activity. If there were personal matters to be talked about, they would much rather scribble a note and pass it on stealthily than be caught conversing in the open and become suspect in the eyes of the high command. When accosted by reporters, the Parliamentarians appeared enigmatic and talked in riddles.

The developments of January 18, the last day before polling, were the most dramatic. Of these, the one event which had the greatest demoralizing effect on the Morarji camp was the switch of the Harijan leader, Jagjivan Ram. He was pestered for days by pressmen to indicate his preference, but he replied only to say he would not reveal his *modus operandi*. When reporters once caught Jagjivan Ram in an extremely jovial mood with Kamaraj, they asked the Congress chief to tell them with whom the untouchable leader was. But the wily Kamaraj only said, "He is with all of us," which was precisely what the calculating Jagjivan was trying to be—all things to all men —until he knew for certain on which side his bread would be buttered.

The other crucial event was the highly publicized meeting between Mrs. Gandhi and her aunt, Mrs. Vijaya Lakshmi Pandit. It was rumored that Mrs. Pandit, now a Member of Parliament from the state of Uttar Pradesh, favored the election of Morarji Desai. The Uttar Pradesh Congress Party was divided into two equally strong factions, one headed by its president, Mr. Chandra Bhan Gupta, and the other by a dissident leader, Kamalapati Tripathi. The state's Chief Minister, Mrs. Sucheta Kripalani, favored Mrs. Gandhi, but was forced to maintain a discreet silence because she was wholly at the mercy of Mr. Gupta, who was an active supporter of Morarji Desai. The belated endorsement of the niece by the aunt helped make up the minds of some wavering Parliamentarians in the Gupta faction to side with Mrs. Gandhi.

It was also on this day that Kamaraj's lieutenants set afloat a rumor that there was a massive defection from the Morarji camp. Simultaneously, they started another rumor that Morarji's withdrawal from the race was imminent. The credibility of this rumor was maintained by the intermittent efforts made throughout the day to weaken Morarji's defenses and compel him to yield. The first of these efforts was by Jagjivan Ram during an hour-long session in the morning that ended vaingloriously. The second was made by a powerful four-man delegation consisting of a Chief Minister, a former Chief Minister, a Minister of the federal Cabinet, and the president of a state Congress party committee, and ended as infructuously as the first.

At six o'clock in the evening came the widely billed and long-awaited event. Accompanied by the Chief Minister of Madras to act as his interpeter, Kamaraj drove to Desai's house on Thyagaraj Marg. A few score reporters, press photographers, and TV cameramen, and a few hundred curious hangers-on lay in wait there. As flash bulbs popped, the cameras could catch only the pleasant exteriors which both Desai and Kamaraj wore for a full five minutes before going into a huddle. The outcome of the meeting was too obvious for words when twenty-five minutes later Kamaraj emerged tight-lipped, his eyes emitting sparks of fury, and his waving arms clearing a pathway through the jungle of crowds to his waiting car. Unanimity died an ignominious death, and both leaders buried it unceremoniously in their respective press conferences minutes later.

During the afternoon, Morarji had sent every Member of Parliament a three-page letter. In it he made an unmistakable reference to Kamaraj, charging that "those who, by virtue of their positions had a special responsibility to be above personal prejudices and animus, seem to have decided that the search for unanimity should mean the elimination of all those whom they do not like." Morarji also pointed out that "the responsibility and the right to choose a leader rest squarely on the Members of Parliament" and asked them not to allow their right "to be eroded by the use of extraneous pressures," meaning the intervention of Chief Ministers. Morarji's friends felt that this impersonal letter, flaunting his highfalutin principle, would hardly endear him to Members of Parliament whose personal support he was seeking. They therefore persuaded him to talk to each member individually on the telephone, which he did till a late hour in the night.

At the other end of town, in her modest home on Safdarjung Road, Mrs. Indira Gandhi said it was for Members of Parliament to judge and decide on the merits of the respective candidates, and added: "My beliefs and convictions are well known to my fellow party members. There is no need for a reaffirmation on my part." Mrs. Gandhi's staff had little doubt about how the majority of Members of Parliament would judge and decide, and sniffing the yet faint but sweet scent of victory in the air, they went ahead with their preparations for a celebration the following day. Over Mrs. Gandhi's objections, they erected in the foreground of the compound a *shamiana*, a colorful tentlike canopy for holding the expected overflow of guests and friends. Arrangements for a press conference were made, some three hundred chairs were brought during the night, and so were extra utensils for making tea and coffee.

Indira Gandhi's day started early on the morning of January 19. At 6.45 A.M. she set out on a visit to Shantivan and Rajghat, where Jawaharlal Nehru and Mahatma Gandhi had been cremated, made a floral offering and stood prayerfully with her folded hands. From there she drove to Teen Murti House, where she had lived with her father for seventeen years when he was Prime Minister of India. With moist eyes, she stood in silence for a while in front of her father's portrait; then she returned home.

By ten thirty, the Congress Party members of both houses of Parliament started trickling in and entered the high-domed Central Hall of Parliament, a huge rotunda carpeted with green baize and forming the core of a magnificent pantheon in red sandstone. From the teak-paneled walls hung life-size portraits of the men who once fashioned India's freedom and now seemed to stand there as mute witnesses to the preservation of that freedom by those seated below in the semicircular rows of chairs upholstered in bottle-green.

Morarji Desai entered the Central Hall at 10:45 A.M., went around greeting members with folded hands, and sat in one of the front rows. Five minutes later Indira Gandhi walked in, draped in a white sari and with a plain tan woolen shawl wrapped around her shoulders. She was presented with a bouquet of flowers by an admirer, and a woman Member of Parliament pinned a rose on her shawl, bringing nostalgic memories of the days when her father, Jawaharlal Nehru, strode like a colossus into this very hall and held the audience captive. Mrs. Gandhi too went round greeting the members, approached Morarji's seat to shake hands with him to the applause of the assemblage, and occupied a chair in the seventh row.

Loud cheers greeted the arrival of Kamaraj minutes before the meeting was to begin. He sat in his presiding chair, flanked by Acting Prime Minister Nanda and the Minister of Food and Agriculture, Chidambaram Subramaniam, who was to act as his interpreter.

After a brief address Kamaraj invited nominations from the floor. A former Chief Minister of Mysore, Mr. K. Hanumanthaiya, proposed Morarji Desai's name, and a leader from Rajasthan, Tikaram Paliwal, seconded it. Acting Prime Minister Gulzarilal Nanda proposed Indira Gandhi's name, and it was seconded by the Syndicate leader, Sanjiva Reddy.

A member of the upper house, Dewan Chaman Lall, rushed instantaneously to the platform and proposed that Mrs. Gandhi be elected unanimously, only to see that the rest of his sentence was drowned by a chorus of "No, no." The party office in the adjoining room immediately mimeographed the ballot papers with these two names. Kamaraj asked if either of the candidates wished to withdraw, but his question was greeted with silence. The returning officer then proceeded to issue the ballot papers. From 11:30 A.M. the members of the upper house were called in the alphabetical order of their names to three side tables from where the ballots were distributed.

The counterfoil of each ballot bore a serial number, and each member signed the counterfoil as evidence that he had received his ballot. The ballot itself was not numbered so as to protect the identity of the voter, but it was signed by the returning officer to ensure that the ballot box was not stuffed. Kamaraj got up from his seat, held upside down the only ballot box placed in front of him to demonstrate that it was empty, and then personally supervised its sealing. The members then went into one of the three screened booths erected temporarily on the platform from which the President of the Republic addresses joint sessions of the two Houses of Parliament. Each member secretly marked his ballot with a cross against the name of his preferred candidate and dropped it in the box placed in front of Kamaraj. Both Mr. Desai and Mrs. Gandhi refrained from voting. It took two hours until all the names of members of both houses were called. The returning officer then took the ballot box to an adjoining chamber to count the votes in the presence of the polling agents of both candidates.

It took an hour and forty minutes more to count the 526 ballots that were cast. The Chief Ministers, party officials, reporters, and cameramen who were watching the proceedings from the gallery above were now getting fidgety. It was nearing 3 P.M., and the members below had to forego their lunch. "Sing a song," said the hungry Defense Minister to the angry Minister of Parliamentary Affairs, who shot back with a couplet in Hindi: *"Bhookay bhajan na hoye kripala!"* ("One can't sing even a hymn on an empty stomach!"). At 2:58 P.M. the returning officer reached the rostrum and announced: "I declare Mrs. Indira Gandhi elected..." The rest of the sentence was drowned in a deafening applause. The vote was 355 to 169, with two votes declared invalid. As Mrs. Gandhi was being smothered with garlands inside the Central Hall of Parliament, the Minister of Parliamentary Affairs stepped out to convey the glad tidings to the restive crowd outside the hall. Someone from the crowd yelled: "Is it a boy or girl?" "It's a girl," he said, and they responded with the cry: *"Indira Gandhi ki jai!"* ("Victory to Indira Gandhi!")

3

The Ancestral Home

Is it a boy or a girl?" was also the question which the residents of Anand Bhavan had asked forty-eight years ago. The answer then as now was the same as a large and anxious family welcomed into its midst a newcomer on November 19, 1917. The bubbling bard from Bengal, Mrs. Sarojini Naidu, soon dubbed the latest arrival in the Nehru family "the new Soul of India"—not inappropriately, since the tiny baby, weighing only four pounds, had hardly any flesh to speak of. Soon a *nam sanskar*, or christening ceremony, was held, and Jawaharlal Nehru named his daughter Indira *Priyadarshini* (Dear to the Sight). The ceremony occasioned a reunion of the clan which, feasting and celebrating, reminisced about its origins in the green valleys of Kashmir ringed by the snow-capped peaks of the Himalayas.

The Nehrus belonged to an illustrious family of Kashmiri Brahmins who were given the honorific title of pandit, "a man of learning." The first of them to have left his mountain retreat in Kashmir and descend to the plains was Raj Kaul, whose fame as a Sanskrit and Persian scholar had spread far and wide. When the Mogul Emperor, Farruksiar, visited Kashmir, he persuaded the pandit to migrate to the imperial capital and profit from the patronage he extended to the palace's men of letters. Raj Kaul accepted the tempting offer and repaired to Delhi about the year 1716. The Emperor conferred on him a *jagir*, or estate, and since Kaul's house was situated alongside a *nahar*, or canal, he became so closely associated with it in the popular mind that he came to be called Kaul-Nehru, or Kaul of the canal. In time the name preceding the hyphen was dropped, and the family simply were known as Nehrus.

The eighteenth century in India was a time of cataclysmic upheaval, and the great Mogul Empire was on its last tottering legs. The Dutch, the Portuguese, the French, and the English had all swooped down on it in the fashion of vultures circling over a carcass. The Nehrus shared the vicissitudes of the Empire, and their family estate dwindled and disappeared. But the Nehrus were gifted with ingenuity and adaptability and soon acquired the skills of the new age. Lakshmi Narayan Nehru, the great-grandfather of Jawaharlal Nehru, became the first Indian to be employed as *vakil* or lawyer by the British East India Company. He represented the company at the court of the Mogul Emperor, whom the company had already reduced to the status of a mere puppet.

Lakshmi Narayan's son, Ganga Dhar, branched off into another occupation and became *kotwal* or chief of police of Delhi. Then occurred the Great Rebellion of 1857, in which Ganga Dhar was suspected of supporting the Emperor against the British. The last of the shadowy Mogul emperors, in whose name the East India Company ruled the country, was deposed, and India henceforth came directly under the sway of the British Crown.

Deprived of his hearth and home in Delhi, and fearful of retribution, Ganga Dhar joined the stream of fugitives who were pouring out of the old imperial city to seek refuge in Agra. On its long journey the family held its breath as an incident threatened to inflict upon it a sudden and ignominious end. The Kashmiris are a very light-complexioned people, and Ganga Dhar's infant daughter could easily have been mistaken for an English girl. As Ganga Dhar's party trudged down the road, they were stopped by a group of passing British soldiers. The Great Rebellion was an event of such recent occurrence that the soldiers suspected the Ganga Dhar family of abducting an English girl. From an accusation to summary justice and punishment was usually a matter of minutes in those days, and the family might well have found themselves hanging from the nearest tree. Fortunately for them, one of Ganga Dhar's sons was conversant enough with the English language to do some explaining and delay matters a little. Meanwhile an acquaintance of the family happened along and testified to the family's innocence, rescuing them all from the direst of consequences.

For a few years the family lived in Agra, where Ganga Dhar Nehru died. Some three months later, his posthumous son, Motilal, the father of Jawaharlal and the grandfather of Indira, was born on May 6, 1861—the very day on which Rabindranath Tagore, India's Nobel-prize-winning poet, was also born. Motilal's eldest brother entered the judicial department of the British Government, and his service made him liable to frequent transfers from place to place. But a second brother settled down as a practicing lawyer in Agra, and it was under his loving care that Motilal grew up. His mother, too, a proud and imperious old lady who suffered none to flout her will, doted on her youngest son, Motilal.

When the High Court—comparable to a state supreme court in America—was transferred from Agra to Allahabad, Motilal's brother was also forced to move with it. Young Motilal was sent to school, and he soon acquired some proficiency in Persian and Arabic, the first of which had been the court language under the Moguls for two and a half centuries. It was only in his teens that he was initiated into the English language.

Indira's grandfather possessed an intelligent mind and a lively curiosity, but he was no bookworm. Endowed with an athletic frame, he developed a fondness for outdoor sports and was eager to show off his prowess on the wrestling grounds. Anything but a model pupil, he was the moving spirit of rowdy elements that involved him in adventures and escapades. Except in Calcutta and Bombay, which were both highly Anglicized, it was uncommon in those days for Indians in the smaller cities to wear Western dress. But young Motilal was highly attracted not only to Western clothing but also to Western ways and manners, and he was immensely liked by his British professors at Muir College in Allahabad, who were only too glad to bail him out of awkward situations.

Motilal's progress through his college years was neither promoted by any distinction nor arrested by any setback. However, he was ill-prepared for the final-year examination of the university that was customarily held in Agra in those days, and he was thoroughly dissatisfied with the way he had answered the first paper. Dejected, he skipped the rest of the examination and spent his time feeding his adolescent imagination on that poem of beauty in marble, the Taj Mahal. Motilal's professors were annoyed with his foolishness, for he had done well enough in his first paper. Thus ended abruptly his university career.

Fortunately, the leader of Muir College's young toughs gathered his spirits and decided to enter the legal profession. It held out many opportunities, and his brother had already achieved modest success in it. Motilal studied hard and appeared for the High Court lawyers' examination. He not only passed it but topped the list and was awarded a gold medal. After three years' apprenticeship at the district courts, he moved to Allahabad to work at the High Court. While he was at the very threshold of success destiny dealt Motilal a cruel blow. The brother who had brought him up from birth died suddenly at the comparatively young age of forty-two, leaving behind him his wife, two daughters, and five sons. At a youthful twenty-five, Motilal became the head of his brother's large family and its sole breadwinner. He himself had been married off when he was still a teen-ager, and his son, Jawaharlal, was born when he was twenty-eight. This awesome responsibility sobered him down and forced him to devote all his attention to his profession.

He received only five rupees for his first brief, but by the time he arrived in his thirties he was making about two thousand rupees a month—certainly an impressive sum for an up-country colt of an Indian lawyer to earn in the last decade of the nineteenth century. Nearly all his brother's briefs were now his, and the consummation of his career came after the turn of the century, when he was permitted to appear and plead at the bar of the Judicial Committee of the Privy Council in Great Britain.

As Motilal minted money, he very much desired living a life that accorded with his new status. He was residing in the densely populated heart of a town that had a continuous recorded history of at least three thousand years. It had been known as Prayag in ancient times, and the Hindus, who belonged to riparian societies, considered the city sacred because it lay at the confluence of two great rivers, the Ganges and the Jumna. Centuries later the greatest of the Mogul Emperors, Akbar, renamed Prayag Allahabad, "the abode of Allah."

When Motilal was ready to move from his congested surroundings, he discovered that there was a property for sale at No. 1 Church Road. It was situated near Bharadwaj Ashram, a spot sanctified by myth and legend. In Sanskrit, *ashram* means a retreat; and Bharadwaj was a famous hermit around whom gathered thousands of disciples to share his enlightenment. In ages gone by, the *ashram* had been on the banks of the Ganges, and Rama, the hero of the epic *Ramayana*, is said to have visited Bharadwaj here during his exile. But Motilal was less impressed by the estate's holy associations than by its potentialities for improvement. Since it was in a dilapidated condition and required extensive renovation, it was going almost for a song. After reconstruction, its large rooms, long verandas, the high terraces, the rolling gardens and the swimming pool would all make for an impressive-looking estate. What clinched the bargain was the fact that Motilal would be living in the spacious and exclusive neighborhood occupied by English and Anglo-Indian families.

Motilal bought the estate in 1900, named it Anand Bhavan "the Abode of Joy," and promptly went about making it look like one. There was abundant reason for joy, because the baby boy who was born to him on November 14, 1889, had now grown up into a sensitive ten-year-old lad, a chip of whom the old block was immensely proud.

The palatial villa with its high turrets and numerous columns was whitewashed, and the open courtyard in the center was paved. A statue of Siva, the Hindu God of Destruction, stood in the middle and, simulating the flow of the Ganges from his head, a stream of water trickled into a pool below, wafting the cool breeze around. The part of the house in which the family lived was furnished in Indian style—the marble floors covered with Kashmiri rugs, the rooms furnished with wide, comfortable divans to sit on with long bolsters and cushions to lean against. Across the inner court Motilal furnished the rest of the rooms in European style and showed off his Victorian furniture, Venetian glass, Dresden china, Persian carpets, and valuable paintings and sculpture.

A well-stocked general library and a specialized law library and office were built for professional needs. Two separate kitchens were maintained to dish out meals in Indian and Western style for the distinguished guests who graced Motilal's lavish table. In one part of the foreground of the house were ancient trees and a flower garden, and in another were tennis courts and a swimming pool lit by electric lights during the night for the delectation of Motilal's guests. At the rear was an orchard planted with mango, guava, lemon, and orange trees. Beyond were the outhouses for the servants and carriages, the stables for the several horses and ponies, and the garage for his Model-T Ford, the first car bought by an Indian resident of Allahabad. A high wall enclosed the compound, and a pair of large wrought-iron gates protected the entrance.

It was in this house, where Indira was born seventeen years later, that her father spent his early years as a lonely boy. Jawaharlal admired, loved, and feared his father as "the embodiment of strength and courage and cleverness," and he was fond of his mother, Swarup Rani, "because of her excessive and indiscriminating love" for her only son. All his cousins were much older than he, while his two sisters, both of whom were born after Motilal moved into Anand Bhavan, were much too much younger than he to be his playmates.

Aside from his mother, the only other person who was young Jawaharlal's confidant was Mubarak Ali. A scion of a well-to-do Muslim family that had been partly exterminated by British troops during the Great Rebellion of 1857, Mubarak Ali became Motilal's *munshi* (clerk), lived with the Nehrus in Anand Bhavan, and spent his spare time holding Jawaharlal spellbound with innumerable stories he narrated from the *Arabian Nights* and other sources. Averse to sending his son to an ordinary school, Motilal appointed a governess for him and, at the age of eleven, a resident tutor by the name of Ferdinand T. Brooks. Of Irish and French extraction and an ardent theosophist by persuasion, Brooks inculcated in his young charge a taste for discursive reading, a passion for science, and an interest in the mysteries of metaphysics.

In May 1905, at the age of fifteen, Jawaharlal set sail for England, there to enter Harrow and Cambridge and be schooled in the ways and manners of the Establishment that pleased his father so much. At Harrow he studied Latin, played cricket, discovered that most English boys were dull, and smelled a little of the underlying anti-Semitic feeling in the school. He joined Trinity College, at Cambridge, in 1907, and after three sluggish years took his natural sciences tripos, with chemistry, geology and botany. This was a period in which his intellectual horizons widened greatly. Anxious not to betray too great an ignorance to his semihighbrow companions, Jawaharlal read up on Nietzsche, George Bernard Shaw, and Lowes Dickinson.

His friends frequently discussed sex—a subject on which he did not want to be regarded as a back number. So he devoured whatever Havelock Ellis or Krafft-Ebing had to offer and at least talked about the subject bravely if he was rather too timid to do anything about it. He was shy of public speaking and would much rather pay the fine for nonparticipation in the discussions of his college debating society than parade his diffidence. Leading a soft and comfortable life made possible by his father's generous allowance, he subscribed vaguely to some sort of diluted version of hedonism. He toyed for a while with the idea of joining the Indian Civil Service but gave it up because it was neither really Indian, nor very civil, nor much of a service.

The die was cast in favor of the paternal profession—the bar—and he joined the Inner Temple. Getting through the bar examinations "with neither glory nor ignominy" and attracted to such odd ideas or movements as Fabian socialism, women suffrage, and the Irish Sinn Fein, young Jawaharlal landed in Bombay in the autumn of 1912, "a bit of a prig with little to commend me," as he wrote in his autobiography years later.

Back in Allahabad after a stay of over seven years in England, Jawaharlal took up the practice of law and joined the High Court. But he felt stifled by the boredom of legal practice, deadened by the placidity of club life, irked by the incongruity of displaying his English fads and foppery in Indian surroundings, and dejected by the tameness of the Indian nationalists.

This winter of discontent lasted for almost four years, until, on February 8, 1916, the day which heralded the coming of spring according to the Hindu calendar, Jawaharlal Nehru married a tall, slim, pretty, and healthy Kashmiri girl who was soon to mother the first woman Prime Minister of India.

The question of Jawaharlal's marriage had actually cropped up some years earlier, when he was still at Harrow. Although he did not envisage an early marriage for him, Motilal warned his son that the Kashmiri community was a small one, and the few eligible girls might be "booked" by the time he returned from England. Motilal felt that an engagement was desirable and suggested to his son that he could rely on his father's judgment to "book" the prettiest girl. In his reply the son chimed in with his father's romantic impulse: "As for looks, who can help feeling keen enjoyment at the sight of a beautiful creature?" Jawaharlal had little reason to doubt his father's exquisite taste, but since seeing is believing, he preferred to do both the looking and the booking himself. The father checked his impatience and waited for the son's return to India.

Meanwhile Motilal kept his eyes open. Most Indian weddings furnish an excellent opportunity for marriage-brokers and matchmakers to indulge their profession or hobby of picking out eligible boys and girls. This is easier to do at a Kashmiri wedding, since the entire clan is present on the occasion, and their small number can easily be negotiated by a swiftly roving eye.

When Motilal attended one such wedding in Delhi, his fancy caught the radiant face of Kamala Kaul, and he had decided on the spur of the moment that she was going to be his daughter-in-law. After his son's return from England, a high tea was arranged at one of his cousin's to facilitate Jawahar's meeting with Kamala. As if paying implicit tribute to Motilal's taste, Jawahar was all smiles to Kamala, but the proud and sensitive girl responded with dignified silence to the young man's innocent advances. However, both father and son agreed that Kamala it should be.

Kamala's genealogy was as impressive as Jawaharlal's. Her fore-bears, the Thulals, had descended from Kashmir in the eighteenth century and sought service in the plains with the Maharaja of Jaipur. So adamant in purpose were the Thulals that the Maharaja nick-named them Atals, which in Sanskrit means "the eternals." The nick-name stuck to them, and the Atals stuck to successive maharajas as *Dewans* or Prime Ministers. One of their descendants, Jawaharmul Atal, was adopted by a family named Kaul in Lucknow. He became Jawaharmul Kaul and went on to become a successful businessman of Delhi. Kamala was his daughter. Kamala's mother hailed from an equally distinguished family—the Topas—who were lured from their mountain haunts in Kashmir by the Mogul Emperor Shah Alam with an offer of extensive estates.

Motilal Nehru, the self-made man with his newly acquired wealth, gladly jumped at the idea of a matrimonial link with a family of such impressive aristocratic lineage. However, the seventeen-year-old Kamala had been brought up in the background of a traditional Hindu family, and Motilal felt that she was not sufficiently cosmo-politan for his Westernized son. Arrangements were made therefore for Kamala to live with an aunt of hers in Allahabad and visit Anand Bhavan frequently in order to get acquainted with her future home. Kamala's knowledge of English was also inadequate, and her defi-ciency was to be remedied by Miss Cecilia Hooper, the English gov-erness of Motilal's daughters, Krishna and Swarup Kumari, who was later to become Vijaya Lakshmi Pandit.

A week before the wedding day, the Nehru party of about two hundred relatives, friends, and invited guests left for Delhi by an elegantly decorated special train. The large party was accommodated in the Nehru wedding camp—a cluster of tents put up in the open maidan temporarily for the purpose—which soon became the center of festivities. The celebration, befitting a royal couple, was the talk of the town and the sight of a lifetime. After the return to Allahabad, the entertainment continued for several weeks. Indian and European friends of the Nehrus were invited to teas and dinners, badminton and tennis parties, *mushairas* (poetry recitations), and *sangeet sabhas* (musical concerts).

The following summer the entire family left for a holiday in Kashmir—their first visit to that land of lakes, floating gardens, and enchanting house boats since the descent of their ancestors to the plains below. Jawaharlal went mountain climbing with his cousin, who saved him from the jaws of death when he slipped down a precipitous gorge. When the family returned to Allahabad after its eventful holiday it was only to discover that Miss Cecilia Hooper, the Nehru family governess who had come from England with the intention of staying only one year but had lingered for twelve, had been suddenly bitten by the bug of matrimony. Her relatives were all in England, so Motilal gave the bride away at a wedding ceremony across the street in Trinity Church, his two daughters acting as bridesmaids.

A few months hence, on November 19, 1917, the arrival of the first grandchild in Anand Bhavan was celebrated with traditional pomp. According to Kashmiri custom, a pandit was standing in readiness to cast the horoscope of the infant as soon as it was born. Twenty-eight years earlier Motilal had had another horoscope cast, on November 14, 1889. Little did he suspect on either occasion what the portentous conjunction of the stars signified: the birth of a son who would become independent India's first Prime Minister, and the birth of a granddaughter who would become the nation's first woman to grace the same high office.

4

A Child of the Revolution

ALTHOUGH Motilal at fifty-six was past the prime of his life, he was still at the peak of his career when Indira arrived. A journalist who had met him before Indira's birth has left us a vivid pen-picture of the patriarch of Anand Bhavan:

> A tall slender man. . . . A head crowned with coal-black locks, carefully cut and pomaded, surmounted an erect, little figure. His forehead was broad and lofty. Time had lightly pencilled a few lines across it. From under arched brows shone two dark eyes aglow with some fire hidden away back in his brain. The expression changed constantly. Now mirth entered them, and they fairly danced with the joy of life. Again, seriousness crept into them, or, they would become suddenly ablaze with righteous indignation. The nose was perfectly modelled. It nevertheless conveyed a suggestion of strength. The lips were thin. A slight curve betokened that they could utter sharp remarks. They were, however, more often parted in a good-natured repartee. The chin was in harmony with the almost Grecian purity of the other features, but gave an impression of combativeness.

All through Indira's infancy Motilal continued to entertain like a prince. Wines of several varieties and "rivers of champagne," to use his own expression, flowed liberally. The reputation of his kitchens, both English and Indian, was a tantalizing invitation to his guests. With the dessert were brought boxes of cigars and cigarettes and liqueurs. But above all it was Motilal's genial banter, his quick wit, ready repartee, biting sarcasm, and verve of the raconteur which made an evening spent at his table a feast of reason and a flow of soul.

Indira remembers to this day her grandfather's resonant laughter, which was often the topic of impolite conversation in Allahabad's polite circles. She is lucky she is not made to remember anything less pleasant. Children are sometimes eyed as monstrous creatures but grandchildren always as angels of perfection. That is how Motilal must have felt when he recorded: "I am always thinking of Indira— the very thought of a personification of innocence is soothing."

But one of poor Jawaharlal's earliest recollections was of his father's temper. As a five-year-old lad he had noticed two fountain pens on his father's office table and helped himself to one. The father instituted a mighty search for the missing pen and conducted the domestic investigation with courtroom care. Jawaharlal was too petrified to confess. When the pen was discovered, the culprit was given a tremendous thrashing, and the future Prime Minister of India remembered to record in his autobiography that various creams and ointments had to be applied for several days to his battered body and badly bruised bottom. But little Indira was the recipient only of her grandfather's affection, and if she was a victim of anything at all, it was of its surfeit.

By the time Indira arrived, Motilal had learned to control himself to a degree, and few were the unfortunates victimized by his tempestuous temper. Jawaharlal has written of how he "shivered with fright, mixed sometimes with resentment at the (father's) treatment of a servant." A cousin of Indira narrates how Motilal was so overcome by anger that a potential feast ended up as a virtual fast. The Kashmiri clan had gathered in his house, and the dinner was to be in Indian style. Motilal had decreed that the *thalis* (round trays) which held the *katoris* (small bowls) and the glasses and serving dishes used that evening should all be of silver. To his discomfiture he observed two servants carrying the food in tin-plated brass vessels. Incensed, he beat up the servants so badly that all the food was spilled on the floor and the stupefied guests filed out of the house in silence. But it was only moments later that the mercurial Motilal was once again his merry self.

Swarup Rani, Motilal's wife and Indira's paternal grandmother, was a short, petite woman of exquisite beauty, with hazel eyes and amazingly tiny hands and feet, and her rich chestnut-brown hair was just turning gray at the time of Indira's birth. She was an Orthodox Hindu lady who preferred the seclusion of her own inner apartments to her husband's boisterous drawing room. If she was far more tolerant than her husband, she was also much less demonstrative of her affection than he.

Indira's grandmother had a constant companion in her elder sister, who was affectionately called Bibima. She had been widowed in her teens, and her maintenance had also been added to Motilal's burden. It was the wont of very orthodox Hindus in the nineteenth century to be extremely strict—if not cruel—to widows, forcing them to shave their heads, to wear only white, and to refrain from eating meat or spicy food that was suspected of arousing the passions. The young widow decided to devote the rest of her life to the service of her frail and fragile younger sister. The monotony of her routine was broken at long last with the arrival of a grandchild, who would occasionally stray into her separate apartment. This consisted of a spotless kitchen with a small, neat, earthen stove, and a *puja-ghar* (room of worship) from which issued the fragrance of fresh flowers and incense.

When Indira was born, her father was still looking very much the young English country gentleman in manner and dress and attitude. He was, as his father's junior, a practicing lawyer, and an industrious one too. He would sit at his desk in Anand Bhavan and pore over his bulky law reports and work on his briefs as his dinner went cold. No one dared disturb him, because he was as quick to lose his temper as his father was, though he never expressed it violently. His strenuous day at the desk and at court was relieved by gossip at the Bar Library, the daily drink and rubber of bridge at the club, the chatter of women at home, and the lazy lounging on Sunday mornings with the glossy magazines. But inside of him, and yet uncommunicated to anyone, his restless spirit was in rebellion against this pointless pleasantry which had become the practical expression of the Cyrenaicism with which he had toyed at Cambridge, and which he thought could be a viable philosophy for the individual. Indian politics of the time, which he denounced as the politics of petition and prattle, disgusted him; and he was growing increasingly dissatisfied with what he derided as the immoderate moderation of his own father.

But fortunately for Jawaharlal, and unfortunately for little Indira, events were crowding upon one another in such rapid succession that they left the young father full with himself and the infant daughter all to herself. On October 5, 1917, about five weeks before Indira's birth, her father went to the Allahabad railway station to bring home to Anand Bhavan in triumphal procession a venerable-looking lady with snow-white hair, clad in an immaculately white sari. As her carriage came out of the station, a party of young men unhorsed it and dragged it themselves through the floral arches decorating Allahabad's streets as flower petals rained from housetops and the tumultuous crowds rent the air with the cry: *"Besant Mata ki jai"* ("Victory to Mother Besant"). The mother in question was the London-born seventy-year-old Mrs. Annie Besant who, having sallied forth with Charles Bradlaugh and George Bernard Shaw into many a political battle in England, had come to India and immersed herself completely in the theosophical movement, and had now suddenly decided to enliven the politics of servility.

In 1916, when World War I was still in progress, Mrs. Besant established the All-India Home Rule League and proclaimed: "Autocracy is destroyed in Russia, tottering in Germany; only under England's flag it is rampant." Impatient with the snail's pace of constitutional reform promised by England, the fiery old lady warned that "India no longer wants your boons, your concessions, and those offers you make; India wants to be mistress in her own house." Combining the tactics of Irish nationalists and English suffragettes and possessed of the capacity to conjure up vivid imagery, she pleaded, "Let India remember what she was and realize what she may be; then shall the sun rise once more in the east and fill the western lands with light." The spectacle of an Englishwoman, advanced in years but unflagging in energy, in love with India but unafraid of England, inspired the youth of India and, as Jawaharlal wrote later, "The atmosphere became electric." With an assist from the Governor of Madras who, with his native genius for muddling up things, had Mrs. Besant arrested, the Home Rule movement spread like wildfire, and Jawaharlal was in the thick of it.

During the war the British Government feared that the contention of the Allies that they were fighting for freedom and nationality was bound to raise political expectations in India. It therefore declared that its aim was "the increasing association of Indians in every branch of administration and the gradual development of self-governing institutions." It also decided to send Mr. Edwin S. Montagu, the Secretary of State for India, to Delhi to ascertain from the Indian people what steps they desired to be taken in this direction. The visit to India of a member of the British Cabinet in the middle of a global war was unprecedented in the history of the Indian Empire, and many nationalist leaders availed themselves of this opportunity to convey their views to him.

One of these leaders was Indira's grandfather, who met the Secretary of State in Delhi, only ten days after Indira's birth. True to his moderate convictions, Motilal suggested for Mr. Montagu's consideration a compromise between Indian aspirations and British objections. Montagu returned to England, and in June 1918 the British Government published the Montagu-Chelmsford Report, so called because it was the product of the combined wisdom of Mr. Montagu and the Viceroy of India, Lord Chelmsford.

The report was a masterpiece of equivocation. It contained a dispassionate account of India's case for self-government and an impassionate rejection of the case by Britain. It aroused nationwide interest in India, and the Indian National Congress met in special session in Bombay on August 29, 1918. Both Indira's father and grandfather left for Bombay, where the grandfather addressed the 3,845 delegates of his party in plenary session on the main resolution. The Congress resolved that nothing less than self-government would satisfy the people of India and demanded freedom of the press, speech, and association, the right to bear arms, and protection of person and property.

Not long afterward the war ended with the signing of the Armistice on November 11, 1918. President Woodrow Wilson's Fourteen Points, one of which proclaimed the right of peoples to self-determination, fired the imagination of the Indians. The attendance at the regular session of the Congress in Delhi on December 26, 1918, was more impressive than ever, with 4,865 delegates present. The Congress recorded its appreciation of "the heroic achievement of the Indian troops" on the far-flung battlefields of Europe "in the cause of freedom, justice and self-determination" and requested President Woodrow Wilson and Prime Minister Lloyd George at the Peace Conference in Versailles to recognize India as "one of the progressive nations to whom the principle of self-determination should be applied."

Meanwhile, on a smaller scale and in a lesser sphere, little Indira was enjoying her self-determination. As the only child in the house, she was left to her own devices in a world of adults. Even her two aunts—the sisters of Jawaharlal Nehru—were now grown-ups. The first of them, Swarup Kumari, who was named after her mother and was later to become Vijaya Lakshmi Pandit, was now in the last year of her teens, while the second, Krishna, was about to become a teen-ager. If Jawaharlal had been a lonely child, Indira was both a lonely child and an only child. Fortunately for the child, she had a mother who was fond of her and devoted to her. The child in turn grew deeply attached to the mother, and quite early in years there developed between them an extraordinary empathy.

When she was not occupied with her exquisite and expensive dolls which her grandfather was ever eager to buy, she became the object of her mother's personal attention. She was bathed and clothed and fed by her. Her thick, curly brown hair was washed and combed by none but her own mother. Although not Orthodox, Kamala Nehru was a devout Hindu woman who prayed and meditated, and Indira was introduced quite early to the mysteries of the occult. She could indulge her fancy and ask for whatever she liked. She did like all preparations of meat and sweetmeats, especially of the Indian variety. And what a variety! *Halwa* made of wheat germ or carrots or pumpkin; *jalebi*, a twist of butter-fried, gossamer-thin tubes of flour floating in scented syrup; or *khir*, the favorite Kashmiri pudding of rice and cream. She loved fruit of all kinds but, like her father and grandfather, she had an inherited bias in favor of the mango. But with the mango came the summer, and how she disliked the summer and the heat rash with which it afflicted her tender skin.

The ideal Indian joint family has traditionally conferred many blessings on its members. The large number of brothers and sisters and cousins form a kind of natural nursery and kindergarten. The aging grandparents and granduncles and grandaunts play the role of baby-sitters and domestic help. The middle-aged men ply their trade, and the middle-aged women attend to their respective domestic chores and subsidiary occupations. The joint family provides nursing and health insurance to the sick, unemployment insurance to the handicapped, and old-age insurance to the elderly. To the indigent peasants, the struggling artisans, and the lower middle classes the benefits of the joint family usually outweigh its disadvantages. But to the upper middle classes and to the affluent the joint family could be a veritable curse, the more so if its members lack understanding or they are more prone to ordinary human failings.

As a posthumous child Motilal had always remembered with gratitude those long years through which his elder brother steered him from helpless infancy to that first day in court when he stood on his own feet and was affectionately hugged for a case well argued. When his elder brother died suddenly without warning, Motilal never grudged the dependence of his brother's entire family on his own fledgling shoulders. A similar sentiment bound Motilal's wife, Swarup Rani, and her sister, Bibima, because of the latter's dependence on the former ever since her premature widowhood.

No such bonds of understanding or of adversity united the next generation of the Nehrus. This was especially true of the older of Jawarharlal's two younger sisters. Born in the secure world of Motilal's warmth and opulence and brought up in the make-believe world of Cecilia Hooper's cold primness and cautious propriety, she was as yet oblivious of the deeper springs of human feeling. All this was compounded by her young and immature age. When seventeen-year-old Kamala arrived to live in Anand Bhavan, Swarup Kumari was only sixteen. The apple of her father's eye and the cynosure of all other eyes, Swarup Kumari was not used to the thought of sharing the limelight with anyone else. But now all of a sudden, Kamala had become Motilal's favorite, and she was admired by the rest of the world as Jawaharlal's wife. Like the queen in "Snow White and the Seven Dwarfs," Swarup Kumari suddenly found the mirror of life betraying her. Young in years, incapable of deeper understanding, and bereft of guidance, Swarup Kumari was consumed by pangs of jealousy.

It was poor Kamala who became the victim of her sister-in-law's tormenting taunts. Swarup Kumari, fortified by Cecilia Hooper's Anglicizing mission, was often seen affecting an air of superiority toward Kamala. Swarup Kumari was affectionately called *Nannhi*, the tiny one, and Krishna was called *Beti*, or daughter. The overzealous Cecilia transformed the two pet names into Nan and Betty. But Nan and Betty were Anglicized not merely in name. They spoke English extremely well, which Kamala did not; they wore Western dresses, which Kamala did not; their table manners were impeccable, while Kamala's were not; their carriage and deportment were the product of Western sophistication, but Kamala's were not. So at least the girls had been taught to imagine, and little did they realize that Kamala could beat them at their own game of adopting the outward trappings of Western refinement, but without in any way affecting the Indianness of her inner being.

It was not infrequently that Swarup Kumari is reported to have carried her complaints against Kamala to her brother. But Jawaharlal's private inclinations as well as public occupations led him to a posture of indifference toward domestic discord. But this was cold comfort to Kamala who, like her husband, was proud and sensitive, and quick to like and dislike. She was not to be taken for granted in the manner of a pony in Motilal's stable or treated as a rare bird lodged in the gilded cage of Anand Bhavan. Years later, after Kamala's death, Jawaharlal confessed repentingly in his autobiography that "she must have suffered and felt a little neglected," adding that "an unkindness to her would almost have been better than this semi-forgetful, casual attitude."

When complaints of one kind or another against Kamala were carried by the girls to their mother, they occasionally fell on more sympathetic ears than Jawaharlal's. And the conventional deference which the daughter-in-law of a traditional Hindu joint family was expected to display toward her mother-in-law left Kamala at a disadvantage. At any rate Kamala herself was too shy, reticent, patient, and long-suffering to trouble others with her woes. She would spend long hours in the more or less solitary confinement of her bedroom, what with her husband flitting in and out of Allahabad in the pursuit of his political self-education. Indira's relatives recall how she sat by her mother's side during those long evening hours, offering her silent sympathy to a kindred spirit. They attribute Indira's extraordinary sensitivity and perception to her early acquaintance with anguish and suffering.

But life in Anand Bhavan held its minor compensations for the growing child. There were many likable people in it. One whom she might have liked immensely was Mubarak Ali, the aristocratic *munshi* or clerk of Motilal, who had regaled young Jawaharlal with tales of romance and adventure. But unfortunately Indira arrived on the scene too late for it. Although he became a victim of cancer in 1917, he had hung on to dear life hoping to see Jawaharlal's child. A few days after Indira was born, she was carried to the dying Mubarak Ali, who blessed her with tears welling in his eyes and died soon after.

Another person who had held some promise of becoming a permanent part of Anand Bhavan's landscape was Datadin the *mali*, or gardener. He had added considerably to the greenery of Anand Bhavan by planting *Neem, Imli, Asoka, Gul Mohur, Aam, Madar, Bel, Amrud*, and *Dhak* trees. From the sturdy branch of a *neem* tree Datadin hung a *jhoola*, a swing, in which little Indira would swing to and fro, helped by a gentle push from her teen-age aunt, Krishna. Then there was the family tailor, Mohammad Hussain, who would trundle into Anand Bhavan with his antiquated sewing machine, sit unobtrusively in a bright corner of the veranda, and turn out deftly-made clothes for Indira and the others.

Finally, there was Hari, who had strayed into Anand Bhavan as a disheveled urchin, grew up into a barefaced liar and thief, absconded after Motilal's memorable flagellation, and returned repentant to remain in Anand Bhavan for good. Hari was trained to become Motilal's valet, but he often played with Indira and accompanied her for a drive in the family brougham, a four-wheeled closed carriage drawn by a pair of fine horses. In later years Hari became an institution; he traveled abroad with Jawaharlal and Indira, performed the incredible feat of getting elected as a member of the state Legislative Assembly, and then proudly courted imprisonment in the anti-British agitation of the 1940's.

Festivals at Anand Bhavan were always celebrated with great zest, and Indira looked forward to some of them with eager anticipation. One such was *Holi*, in which her father always participated with gusto. Coming sometime in the month of March, it heralds the season of harvest. It is an occasion for pranks and merrymaking, when people smear each others' faces with colored powders or squirt one another with colored water. Soon after *Holi* comes *Navroz*, the Kashmiri New Year. It is a day for donning new clothes, and Indira would always get a choice selection from her grandfather. The ladies in Anand Bhavan celebrated it in the traditional way. A red vermilion mark would be made on Indira's forehead as an auspicious sign, and she would receive fruit, nuts, and sweetmeats, and some raw rice—the symbol of fertility.

Divali was another enthusiastically celebrated festival. The ladies of Anand Bhavan did *puja* or reverential homage to Lakshmi, the Goddess of Wealth. Divali symbolizes the triumph of good over evil and of light over the forces of darkness. Rows upon rows of small earthen bowls containing mustard or gingelly oil and cotton wicks were placed along the verandas, on the terraces, and the parapets of Anand Bhavan, and as the sun set, the servants lighted each earthen lamp. All night long the illuminated outlines of the massive structure twinkled against the night's impenetrable curtain of darkness. There was always a display of the most gorgeous fireworks in Anand

Bhavan, and little Indira watched it till she was weary and tired and was carried off to bed.

In 1919, in the month of March, when Kashmiris celebrate their New Year's Day or *Navroz*, there came to Anand Bhavan a visitor who was to herald for India a new era and for the inmates of Anand Bhavan a new way of life. His name was Mohandas Karamchand Gandhi. He had returned to India from South Africa only five years earlier and had established just recently his Satyagraha Sabha. *Satyagraha* literally means "truth-force," and a *sabha* is a society for its practice. In essence the technique amounted to the deliberate violation of an unjust law, even if it resulted in imprisonment, so that the law itself might be repealed.

Young Jawaharlal, who professed to be weary of the politics of talk, was now enamored of the politics of action. Since Gandhi promised action, Jawaharlal wanted very much to join this newly formed Satyagraha Sabha. On the other hand, Motilal deprecated what he derisively called the politics of agitation. But even more, he dreaded the thought of his beloved son going to jail. He therefore invited Gandhi to come over to Allahabad so that he could size up this strange new figure on the Indian political scene and discuss with him the implications of his technique.

The two elder men did most of the talking, and the young man was seldom present to do even the listening. As Gandhi left, he advised Jawaharlal to be patient a while longer and refrain from doing anything which might disturb his father's sleep. And as Jawaharlal discovered later, he was indeed causing his poor father to lose his sleep. The aging patriarch would arise undetected in the middle of the night from the princely comfort of his bed and lie on the cold stony floor to experience at first hand the perils of prison life which his only son was rashly inviting. For the moment, Motilal was happy that Gandhi had to be content with not winning a convert to his political faith. And Gandhi left happily in the conviction that the time would soon be ripe for conversion.

Constitutionally feeble, mentally self-conscious, and weak in will, Mohandas Karamchand Gandhi was born on October 2, 1869, to the *Dewan* or Prime Minister of the former tiny princely state of Porbander (now part of Gujarat State) in western India. Although brought up in an Orthodox Hindu home, Mohandas flirted briefly with atheism in his young years. Completing his university studies in Bombay, he proceeded to London, where he studied law at the Inner Temple for two years, returning to India in 1891. Tongue-tied and diffident, he was an utter failure as a practicing lawyer and was forced to return to his native town of Rajkot, there to live out in penury and obscurity the precarious existence of a petition writer.

Happy to receive an offer of a modest fee from an Indian firm in South Africa for a year's service, he went there at the age of twenty-four, blissfully ignorant of the degrading condition in which his countrymen lived there. When he appeared in a Durban court, he was ordered to take off his turban. When he was traveling by train, he was thrown out of the first-class compartment by a white man who refused to travel with a colored passenger. He was turned out of hotels which would not take nonwhites for residents. And once he was assaulted so fiercely by a white man that Gandhi came close to death. But all these humiliations had a miraculous effect upon the mouse of a man who seemed determined to demonstrate that he was a man among mice.

Expecting to stay in South Africa for a year, he stayed on for twenty-one, during which he organized his fellow Indians to resist the repressive legislation of the South African Government. It was from his experiments in the laboratory of South African politics that the alchemist in Gandhi discovered the combustible compound of truth and nonviolence. Many indeed were the ingredients which went into its making. To borrow the words of a distinguished biographer: "It was not the product of a sudden impulse; behind it lay a lifelong discipline in which the austere background of Gandhi's home, the influence of his devout mother, the impact of the Sermon on the Mount, the daily meditation on the 'Bhagavad Gita,' the inspiring words of Tolstoy, and the harsh realities of South African politics had all played their part."

When Gandhi returned to India in January 1915, he had no clear conception of what he proposed to do. His countrymen were expecting great things to happen after his return, but they were sorely disappointed. Speaking at an annual law dinner soon after his arrival, he almost proposed a toast to His Majesty the King Emperor: "It gives me the greatest pleasure this evening to redeclare my loyalty to the British Empire." For one thing, he did not wish to embarrass the British Government right in the middle of the war. For another, as in the case of Motilal Nehru, Gandhi's conviction about the inherent goodness of English institutions and his faith in the innate sense of justice of the English people had not yet been shaken.

But as if to suggest that it was the memory of George III that they cherished and not that of Edmund Burke, who had pleaded eloquently for the conciliation of the American colonies, the British preferred to provoke India rather than to pacify her. Soon after the war ended and the people of India were expecting a generous gesture from their colonial masters, a series of repressive measures were proposed by the British Government in 1919 for curtailing civil liberties and curbing political activity. Gandhi termed the proposed laws "black bills" and pleaded for their retraction with the British Viceroy, who also persisted even more tenaciously with getting them passed in the teeth of universal Indian opposition. Gandhi promptly established the Satyagraha Sabha to fight these laws, which he described as "subversive of the principle of liberty and justice and destructive of the elementary rights of individuals." Each member of Gandhi's new society took a solemn pledge to "refuse civilly to obey these laws" and to "faithfully follow truth and refrain from violence to life, person or property." In order to galvanize the mass of the people, Gandhi announced that April 6 would be observed all over India as Satyagraha Day.

The stage was now set for the occurrence of a chain of events which altered irrevocably the course of India's history and disturbed profoundly the even tenor of Indira's life. To Indira's father, who took Annie Besant's words as a pleasant diversion, Gandhi's deeds had become a serious obsession. When Gandhi left Anand Bhavan, he had counseled patience to the younger Nehru and provided reassurance to the older. But this hardly settled the argument between father and son. For eighteen months they discussed, debated, and disagreed, while the rest of the family felt deserted, distressed, and dejected. The heated exchanges at the dining table often ended the meal but not the argument. Resentful that his will was being flouted, Motilal would flare up and ask his son to get out of the house. Oppressed and alienated, Jawaharlal would withdraw from the scene of the domestic skirmish and wander about night after night—as he said later—alone, tortured in mind, and trying to grope his way.

The tension in Anand Bhavan imposed an intolerable strain on Swarup Rani and Kamala. With their deference for the older man and affection for the younger, they had to maintain a scrupulous neutrality lest their seeming intervention should inflame the former or irritate the latter. Kamala's feeling of loneliness was immeasurably heightened, and with it Indira's too. But where the mother could dimly perceive what was in store for her, the child was only moored to her helpless incomprehension. Reminiscing in later years about their tribulations, Jawaharlal wrote poignantly: "In spite of the strength of my family bonds, I almost forgot my family, my wife, my daughter. It was only long afterward that I realized what a burden and a trial I must have been to them in those days, and what amazing patience and tolerance my wife had shown toward me."

It was as an infant that Indira learned that one is never less alone than when alone, and developed that extraordinary sense of self-sufficiency which has sustained her ever since. A new India—the child of Gandhi—was born almost at the same time as Indira was. From now on the two grew up together, and the two lives were as one. Outside Anand Bhavan there was the confluence of the two sacred rivers, the Ganges and the Jumna. Inside Anand Bhavan was the confluence of two streams of life, the private and the public, and of two streams of thought, the personal and the impersonal.

April 6, 1919, was observed all over India as a day of fasting. All business was suspended, and mass meetings were held to protest against "the black bills." As a sequel to this, two popular leaders of the Congress were arrested in the city of Amritsar in the Punjab on April 10. As news of the arrests drifted through the busy bazaars of Amritsar, crowds gathered to protest and demonstrate, which led to minor outbreaks of violence and clashes with the police. Amritsar was put under the control of the military, and all public meetings were banned. April 13 happened to be the Hindu New Year Day, and the occasion was seized by a mammoth crowd of twenty thousand which gathered in the heart of the city in a public park called Jallianwala Bagh to protest against the government's highhandedness. The park was enclosed on three sides by eight-foot-high walls and the only entrance-*cum*-exit—so narrow that not even a carriage could pass through it—was on the fourth side.

As the crowd was listening to a speaker, there suddenly appeared at the gate General Dyer, heading 150 soldiers, and ordered the crowd of twenty thousand to disperse immediately. There was, however, no way out of the park, since the only exit was blocked by General Dyer's soldiers. In two minutes' time the General ordered his soldiers to fire at point-blank range on the unarmed sea of men, women, and children, who were trapped in a virtual graveyard. The hail of bullets ended after sixteen hundred rounds had been fired and General Dyer had run out of ammunition. He had brought an armored car with him, but the poor man could not have it moved into the park through the much-too-narrow gateway. General Dyer had to leave disappointed, his job only half done, while all night the dead and the dying lay helpless.

The British Government appointed a committee to investigate the atrocity perpetuated in Jallianwala Bagh. During its hearing, a justice who was on the committee asked Dyer: "Excuse me putting it this way, General, but was it not a form of frightfulness?" The general had no compunction in replying: "I think it was a merciful thing. I thought that I should shoot well and shoot strong, so that I or anybody else should not have to shoot again. I think it is quite possible I could have dispersed the crowd without firing, but they would have come back again and laughed, and I should have made what I consider to be a fool of myself."

But worse atrocities were to follow. Martial law was imposed on the Punjab, and trigger-happy sergeants committed indignities while timorous magistrates imposed draconian punishments. A "crawling order" was issued, which forced the inhabitants of an entire street to crawl on their bellies to get into and out of their houses as punishment for an attack on a missionary who had, however, been protected by decent citizens of the same street. Whole villages were bombed and machine-gunned from the air with the intent of terrorizing them into subjection. It was an offense for two Indians to walk abreast or for Hindus and Muslims to fraternize in public—a crude device for preventing a concerted Hindu-Muslim revolt against alien imperialism. College students were made to march sixteen miles in the scorching sun to salute the Union Jack. A marriage party was arrested, the bridegroom detained, and the priests and guests were whipped. Hundreds of political workers were rounded up, summary justice was meted out by martial-law courts, and public floggings were staged.

General Dyer acted out of the conviction that what he intended to do was merciful. Ironically enough, his merciful contribution did have the merciful effect of uniting father and son in far-off Anand Bhavan. The shocking events in the Punjab brought about a political alignment between Motilal and Jawaharlal. Firing on unarmed men, women, and children was not exactly playing cricket, and even Motilal's faith in the fair play of John Bull had now been dissipated. The venerable Rabindranath Tagore felt compelled to renounce his knighthood and wrote to the Viceroy: "The time has come when badges of honour make our shame glaring in their incongruous context of humiliation." Even that fine Englishman, Charles Freer Andrews, the lifelong friend of Tagore, Gandhi, and the Nehrus, wrote after a visit to Amritsar: "I feel that if only I could take each single Englishman and show him out of my eyes what I have seen, he would feel the same as I. English honour has departed."

General Dyer's action also had the merciful effect of bringing Gandhi and Motilal into close contact for the first time. The two of them, along with three others, were appointed by the Congress to inquire into the Amritsar happenings. In the course of his labors with Gandhi, Motilal was impressed by the incisive intellect, moral sensitivity, and passion for justice of the man whom he had dismissed until recently as an impractical and starry-eyed visionary.

Later that year, on Christmas Day, when a seething mass of humanity welcomed him at Amritsar railway station and took him in procession to deliver the presidential address of the Indian National

Congress, which had decided to convene there as an act of defiance against British rule, Motilal referred to Gandhi as "the most revered Indian of the day," and to his Satyagraha movement as "a new force with tremendous potentialities." No one was more pleasantly surprised than Jawaharlal himself by this new marriage of minds between the introvert Gandhi and the extrovert Motilal. "It was a strange combination," wrote Jawaharlal later, of Gandhi, "the saint, the stoic, the man of religion, one who went through life rejecting what it offers in the way of sensation and physical pleasure," and his father, Motilal, "who had been a bit of an epicure, who accepted life and welcomed and enjoyed its many sensations, caring little for what might come in the hereafter."

Motilal was also appalled that the Privy Council in England had rejected the appeals of two persons who were accused under martial law in the Punjab—persons who Motilal thought were "as innocent as Indu," as he affectionately called his granddaughter Indira. When the government put out its report on the Amritsar happenings and absolved General Dyer inferentially, Gandhi described it as "thinly disguised whitewash." Motilal, equally astounded, wrote to his son, "My blood is boiling," and said they must "raise a veritable hell for the rascals."

But before the two could join hands to "raise hell," domestic developments distracted them. Motilal had to go east to the province of Bihar to argue for eight long months one of the most celebrated cases he had handled in his distinguished career as a legal luminary. His daughter-in-law, Kamala, was not at all well. The first symptoms of the fatal disease that was to end her life prematurely had already been noticed. Motilal was particular about sending detailed instructions for her treatment. When he reached Calcutta, one of the first things he did was to instruct the English firm of Whiteaway Laidlaw to send a perambulator to his granddaughter, whose health also had become a source of anxiety. She had shown some signs of having contracted rickets, and Motilal warned his son that "Indira has to be very specially taken care of as she is not at all well." By May 1920, Motilal's wife too had taken ill. The doctors advised an immediate change of scene, and Jawaharlal departed from Allahabad with his mother, wife, and daughter for Mussoorie, a hill station which served as a popular summer resort for the ruling classes.

The Nehrus checked in at the expensive Savoy Hotel, and Jawaharlal got busy attending to the numerous problems of his family. A delegation from neighboring Afghanistan, which had come to negotiate a peace treaty with the British after the latter had waged the third Afghan war of 1919, was also staying at the same hotel. Jawaharlal had neither the time nor the interest to meet with any member of the delegation, and a month passed.

Suddenly he was visited by the police one evening and was asked to give an assurance that he would not have any dealings with the Afghans. He replied that he was too busy with his domestic problems to entertain the notion of meeting with the Afghans, but would not give the police any assurance either, on grounds of principle. The secret service men knew that Jawaharlal so far had had no dealings with the Afghans, and yet the superintendent of police served an externment order requiring him to leave Mussoorie within twenty-four hours. Jawaharlal left for Anand Bhavan and telegraphed his father in Bihar of the developments. Motilal happened to be a personal friend of the Governor of the province, and it was on the latter's intervention that the police rescinded the order on Jawaharlal.

When he returned to Mussoorie along with his father, Jawaharlal could not believe what his eyes saw. His three-year-old daughter was doing precisely what the police suspected her father would do, except that she was too young and innocent to enter into political deals. She was having a good time in the courtyard of the Savoy, ensconced happily in the sturdy arms of a Minister and member of the Afghan delegation. Jawaharlal learned from the Afghans that they had read about his externment in the newspapers and that, ever since, the head of the delegation had been sending Indira's mother and grandmother flowers and a basket of fruit every day. They had also ensured that Indira herself had an outsized Afghan playmate with whom to while away her time in the absence of her beloved Papu, as she affectionately called her father.

Early in the following year a major domestic event took place in

Anand Bhavan when Indira's elder aunt, Swarup Kumari, wed Ranjit
Pandit, and acquired her well-known married name, Vijaya Lakshmi
Pandit. Most of the prominent nationalist leaders had come to Allahabad, and Anand Bhavan was humming like a beehive of political
activity. Just as the main ritual of the wedding was about to begin,
the police arrived at the gate and asked for one of the Nehrus. Jawaharlal wondered for a moment why the police were being so nice
and cooperative for a change. At any rate, since the watchman at
Anand Bhavan could take care of all the traffic arrangements, Jawaharlal went toward the gate to tell the solicitous officers of law enforcement that no police help was necessary. But he was in for a surprise. The police had come with the suspicion that some massive
conspiracy was being hatched in Anand Bhavan, and it might as well
be nipped in the bud. In a flash it occurred to Jawaharlal why this
suspicion should have arisen in the minds of the police. The wedding
was taking place, by pure coincidence, on May 10—the anniversary
of the Great Rebellion of 1857!

The decks were all cleared now for father and son to "raise hell
for the rascals." In September 1920, when the Congress met in session at Calcutta, Gandhi proposed his famous resolution on his noncooperation program. Almost all the leading lights of the party lined
themselves up against Gandhi, imagining that the program was either
ill advised or harmful or inappropriate. The only incredible exception was Motilal—the man who, only eighteen months ago, had been
telling Gandhi not to lead his son astray on the untested road of
Satyagraha. Gandhi's resolution was carried by a narrow majority.
It called upon Indians to boycott all elections to the legislatures,
since the real power rested in the hands of the British governors of
the various provinces and ultimately with the Viceroy of India as
representative of the British Crown. Everyone was exhorted to renounce any title or honorary office conferred by the British, refrain
from attending all official functions, withdraw his children from
government-owned or -aided schools and colleges, give up practice
of law and the resort to legal redress, and, most important of all, not
use foreign cloth and foreign-manufactured goods.

When Motilal returned to Anand Bhavan, he had to implement at home the resolution which the Congress Party had passed in Calcutta. He promptly resigned his membership of the provincial legislature and announced that he would not stand for reelection. He wound up his legal practice and withdrew his younger daughter from the government-aided local school. He then disposed of all his horses, carriages, dogs, the valuable china, and the treasured crystal. The horde of servants was disbanded, the two elaborate kitchens gave place to a simple one, and the cellar was cleaned out.

It is one thing to vote for the passage of political resolutions but quite another to permit them to affect one's private lives adversely. It was no easy matter for a man on the eve of his sixtieth birthday to give up a flourishing practice, look with equanimity upon the dismal prospect of a future without any income for a large and growing family, and cut himself loose from the expensive habits cultivated in a lifetime of luxury. But Motilal did all this with his customary zeal.

From a health resort where he was staying, he wrote to Mahatma Gandhi about the possessions and the pattern of his new life: A brass cooker had taken the place of two kitchens; a solitary servant—and a not too intelligent one at that—had displaced the former retinue; three small bags containing rice, lentils, and spices sat awkwardly in the place of muleloads of provisions; a single square midday meal of rice, lentils, and vegetables had displaced the day-long routine of breakfast, lunch and dinner *à l'anglaise;* the *shikar* had yielded to long walks, and the rifles and guns to books and magazines. But Motilal's puckish humor was not dimmed one bit, and he exclaimed in the manner of Mark Anthony, "What a fall, my countrymen!" hastening at the same time to reassure Gandhi, "But, really, I have never enjoyed life better."

Little Indira enjoyed immensely the public bonfires at Anand Bhavan, to which were consigned cartloads of foreign finery. Years later she wrote of the excitement which the first of those occasions had held for her. All day long the terrace had been heaped with piles of rich materials that made a rainbow of colors. The toddler had fun playing hide and seek in them, obscured for a moment by an opaque velvet, exposed for another by a translucent chiffon. And it was a treat to the touch to roll with gay abandon on the warm woolens, the cool cottons, the textured tweeds, the smooth satins, and the sheer silks. The evening shadows lengthened, and it was soon nightfall. But as the hour for lighting the bonfire approached, Indira's parents insisted on putting her to bed. In her first major test of diplomacy she instinctively pitted the two great powers against the superpower. The grandfather overruled the parents, and she was, after all, permitted to witness the bonfire. But the poor child was so drowsy that she dozed off even as live charcoals lit the fire and the gentle breeze fanned the flames which licked the mountain of cloth. "Burn everything British, except their coal," the Irish used to say, and the inmates of Anand Bhavan took them at their word. The coals were Indian.

A few weeks later came a test of will which little Indira passed as admirably as her grandfather had. One day she was playing all by herself—as always, being an only child—but within range of her mother's hearing and vision, as she had been taught to do. A relative of the family who had returned recently from Paris had come to Anand Bhavan with a gift for Indira—an exquisitely embroidered dress. Kamala returned the gift to the visitor politely and said the family now wore clothes made only of homespun and handwoven material called *khadi*. Under Mahatma Gandhi's goading, people in India had just commenced spinning and weaving cloth for their personal use, and few had acquired the proficiency in the art yet, the *khadi* of the times seeming indistinguishable from sacking made of burlap. As the proffered gift was being declined, the visitor was staring at Kamala's coarse sari and could not help noticing the sore red patches it made wherever it ruffled her tender skin. "I think you have all gone mad," the visitor burst out, "but you are adults and if you want to be ill, I suppose that is your business, but you certainly have no right to make the child suffer, and it is for her that I have brought this gift."

Kamala beckoned her daughter and said: "Auntie has brought you a foreign frock. It is very pretty and you can wear it if you like. But first think of the big bonfire we made of all our foreign clothes." The temptation to grab the gift was too strong, and the child looked

at it avariciously, her hand half extended. But the stern command-
ment of duty overcame her, and she declined the gift. "But why?"
the visitor persisted in teasing her. The little girl parroted all the
arguments which she had heard the elders in the house advance, and
which she had by now committed to memory. In Indira's arms was
her constant companion—a doll—and the visitor admonished with
cruel logic: "All right, little saint, but how is it that you play with a
foreign doll?"

"It was an idle remark, thoughtlessly made," writes Indira. "Adults
so often look upon children as playthings and make no effort to
understand what is hidden behind their lack of articulation. I was
passionately fond of the doll; I could not think of it, or indeed of
anything, as lifeless. Everything was given a name, and it immediately
developed its own personality. The doll was my friend, my child."
The offended visitor departed, but the sensitive child was now oppressed by the burden of decision. Her passionate love for the doll
and her pride in its possession conflicted with the dictate of duty
that had been drummed into her. Never much of an eater, she developed a colical dislike for food. Sleep came only because of sleep-
lessness. Her mother was disturbed by what she could not diagnose.
At last, in the solitude of her suffering, the child made a decision
worthy of her grandfather. Quivering with tension, she carried the
doll to the roof terrace and set fire to it. A torrent of tears rolled
down her pale cheeks, and "to this day," she says, "I hate striking a
match."

Right through the year 1921 individual Congress workers who
offered noncooperation were being arrested all over the country
under various provisions of the penal law. Two of the most prominent Muslim leaders were given long sentences for inciting the
Army to disaffection. The words for which they had been sentenced
were repeated by others from hundreds of platforms across the
length and breadth of the country. Jawaharlal was often threatened
with prosecution for alleged seditious speeches. Mahatma Gandhi's
noncooperation movement had almost become a way of life with the
people. The morale of British officialdom in India was pitifully low.

The government then hit upon the bright idea of inviting the highly popular Prince of Wales (who was later to abdicate his throne to marry Mrs. Wallis Simpson and become known the world over as the Duke of Windsor) to India to boost the morale of British officials. Elaborate functions and a right royal reception for the Prince were being planned in many parts of India. The Indian National Congress had nothing against the charming Prince in person, but since the government seemed to have no scruples about exploiting the Prince's popularity for an unworthy end, it decided to announce a general boycott of all functions arranged for the Prince. In each city the Congress workers volunteered themselves for organizing the boycott, and the lists of volunteers were published in the daily newspapers. By the end of the year, a few days before the Prince's arrival, mass arrests began.

In Allahabad, the list of volunteers was headed by the name of Motilal Nehru. On the afternoon of December 6, 1921, while an office secretary was showing Motilal some papers pertaining to his party's program, a servant announced the arrival of a police officer. Motilal asked the officer to introduce himself, which he did with a vigorous salute. The officer then presented tremulously to Motilal a search warrant. Motilal told him he had nothing to hide and his whole house was open for scrutiny, adding with a twinkle: "You wouldn't take less than six months to do justice to my house!"

The police officer concurred sheepishly, but was mortally afraid of the moment when the old giant might stop joking and display one of those paroxysms of rage for which he was so well noted. Motilal smelled that the poor fellow was not mustering the necessary courage to say something he wished to, and put him at ease with the question whether the government wanted to prosecute him. "Yes, sir, I have a warrant of arrest, too," answered the timid officer. "Oh, I am ready for it," countered Motilal, "but why didn't you produce it at the outset?"

Still visibly nervous, and incredulous that the tempestuous titan could be so calm and collected, the officer was wondering how he would make known to him that there was a second warrant of arrest in his pocket for the younger Nehru also. When at last the police officer managed to spill it, both father and son went in to collect a few clothes and books. The servants of Anand Bhavan, who were not yet accustomed to their masters' being taken into custody on the flimsiest of pretexts, were readying themselves to beat up the police officer but were restrained by the mistress of the house.

Word of the arrest spread fast, and the compound of Anand Bhavan was full of friends, well-wishers, and sympathizers. Swarup Rani put on a brave front and told a newsman she "rejoiced in the great privilege of sending my dear husband and my only son to jail." She had a lump in the throat when she uttered the words "my only son," but swallowed it stoically and said, "Mahatma Gandhi told me once that others in the world too have their only sons."

The two Nehrus presently emerged from the house and trooped into the police van, the elder handing to the press a farewell message he had dictated to his countrymen:

> Having served you to the best of my ability, it is now my high privilege to serve the motherland by going to gaol with my only son. . . . I have only one parting word to say—continue non-violent non-cooperation without a break. . . . Let the march of pilgrimage to the only temple of liberty now existing in India—the jail—be kept up in an uninterrupted stream.

As the police van drove out of Anand Bhavan, the frail wife of Motilal and the fond mother of Jawaharlal almost broke down. But four-year-old Indira was quite composed, while her twenty-two-year-old mother, Kamala, held back her tears impassively.

5

The Early Years

THE trial of the two Nehrus opened on December 7, the morning after the arrest, in an improvised courtroom in the jail itself. The magistrate was an Englishman and the prosecuting attorney an Indian, but both long-time colleagues and friends of Motilal, and both very much ill at ease in this strange new situation.

Motilal was the most formidable adversary among members of the Allahabad bar, and the government did not want to take any chances. But it was rather amazing that the one witness whom the government was relying upon to prove Motilal's culpability was an illiterate fellow who testified to the authenticity of Motilal's signature by holding the documents upside down!

But all this hardly bothered him. He was having a grand time with his granddaughter. Four-year-old Indira was taken to attend the trial, and her grandfather seated her on his knees, sat cheerfully throughout the trial, refused to defend himself, and denounced the entire proceeding as a farce. The two Nehrus were sentenced to six months' imprisonment and a fine of five hundred rupees each. As Indira's father and grandfather were marched away to the Lucknow District Gaol, she had to return crestfallen to Anand Bhavan.

If she only had a passing acquaintance with the administration of justice, she was soon to have a stirring experience with its enforcement. The police started frequent visits to Anand Bhavan to collect the fines which had been imposed on the two Nehrus. But it was the policy of the Congress party not to pay fines. So the police came day after day to attach movable property and cart it away in lieu of the unpaid fines. And although the fines amounted to only one thousand rupees, the police had no scruples about carrying away expensive furniture and rugs worth several thousands of rupees.

Jawaharlal records how Indira was greatly annoyed at this continuous process of despoliation and stood her full three feet up to the police to protest to them and express her strong displeasure. The contagion of rebellion did not leave the child's psychology unaffected. From now on even her games became politically motivated. The story has often been told of how she used to order her dolls to join Mahatma Gandhi's protest demonstrations. Her older relatives recall how she was also in the habit of gathering the servants of the house, standing on a tabletop and haranguing them on the virtues of civil disobedience.

Fortunately, the family soon had an opportunity to provide the child with a change of scene and take her away from the fretful fever of the highly charged political atmosphere in the home. Since the menfolk of Anand Bhavan were imprisoned, Mahatma Gandhi had invited the ladies to go down to Ahmadabad in western India to attend the annual session of the Congress in the last week of December. It was also near Ahmadabad that Gandhi had his *ashram* (retreat) on the bank of the Sabarmati River. The ladies accepted his invitation and, in compliance with the new spirit of austerity that was in the air, traveled by third class for the first time in their lives. It was a long and tiresome journey, the discomfort of which was forgotten amid the frequent offers of food and flowers made by grateful admirers at railway stations along the route to the wives of the two men who had come to be lionized by the nation. Indira was too young to have remembered Gandhi's visit to Anand Bhavan in March 1919, and now in Ahmadabad she established her first conscious contact with him.

Life in Sabarmati *ashram* was quite exacting for the Nehru ladies. Gandhi's routine called for waking up at four in the morning, bathing at that early hour in the December cold, assembling for prayers on the bank of the Sabarmati, partaking of tasteless meals, cleaning plates and dishes, washing one's own clothes, relaxing in bare, un-adorned rooms, and sleeping on the floor. The only consolation dur-ing that fortnight's regimen of rigor was that the ladies could see so much of Gandhi. The metamorphosis wrought by him in the style of living in Anand Bhavan was palatable to its ladies only because their religious inclinations made them sympathetic toward the saint-politician. His life of renunciation, his politics of spirituality, and his ethic of voluntary poverty appealed to them.

But to Indira he was at best an affectionate elder, at worst a funny man, a sort of Mickey Mouse—as the poetess Sarojini Naidu called him—come alive. It was nice to get up on his chest and ride athwart it; his shapeless ears were meant for pinching, his ugly nose for pull-ing, and his spectacles for playing with. And his philosophy? Well, it could wait its turn.

Jawaharlal was in jail until January 31, 1923, except for a brief intervening period of six weeks in early 1922. From Allahabad to Lucknow, where he was incarcerated in the district jail, was an overnight's journey by train, and little Indira could see him only occasionally, sometimes only once in three months. When she did see him, her father found her "very pale and weak." The health of his little daughter caused him much concern, but her troubles at the time must have been more psychic than somatic, and medicines could hardly have cured her illness. The sudden separation from her father and, even more, from her grandfather, who at the time was the sheet anchor of her emotional security, had rudely disturbed her psychosomatic balance.

Jawaharlal was also worried about his four-year-old daughter's schooling. "I wish," he wrote home, "some arrangements were made for Indu's lessons. I am confident that I could have managed her easily—but I am in Barrack No. 4." The personal attention which he had failed to give her when he was free he now sought to give, when he was chained. He would write her short letters in Hindi: "To dear Indu, love from her Papu. You must get well quickly, learn to write letters and come and see me in gaol. I am longing to see you."

Her Dadu—as she used to call her grandfather—had sent her a spinning wheel to keep her interested and occupied. Jawaharlal inquired if she had plied the spinning wheel or not and asked her to send him some of the yarn she had spun. But although he himself had sent to Anand Bhavan 10,570 yards of fine yarn he had spun in prison, it hardly served as an incentive for the lonely girl to emulate her father's feat. "Do you join your mother in prayers every day?" That, of course, she did, because anything she did with her mother was unalloyed pleasure.

Indira's health showed no sign of improvement, and she was taken to Calcutta for consultation. And her Papu wrote to ask if she had seen the zoo, what animals had attracted her attention, and then admonished her: "You must get strong and plump before you return to Allahabad." But letters, however personal in content, are only impersonal in form; and if they made her strong in spirit, they certainly did not make her plump in physique.

As soon as Jawaharlal was released from prison, politics came to the fore once again. A month before his release, his father had founded his own party, the Swaraj Party (*Swaraj* means "self-rule"), within the Indian National Congress. Mahatma Gandhi was opposed to the Swarajists, because he wanted to continue his noncooperation movement by boycotting the legislatures. Motilal, on the other hand, wanted to fight the British both from inside and outside the legislatures and was therefore anxious to enter the deliberative chambers. The two of them met in 1924 to thrash out their differences, but their meeting proved fruitless. In fact, it revealed a deepening philosophical rift between them, based largely on temperamental inclinations.

One of these related to Mahatma Gandhi's doctrine of *Ahimsa* (nonviolence). Motilal was outspoken in the declaration of his credo: "In fact I hold that it would be doing violence to the highest and noblest feeings implanted in man, if we ruled out violence in any shape or form under all conceivable circumstances. If I see a bully ill-treating or assaulting a person weaker than himself, I would not merely interpose my body between the assailant and the victim, and thus enable him to have two victims instead of one, but to try to knock him down and thus save both his victim and myself. Again, if I were assaulted, I would defend myself, if necessary, by inflicting violence on my assailant, and that violence under certain circumstances may extend even to the causing of the assailant's death."

To the practicing lawyer that Motilal was, violence could be a legally protected expedient; to the practicing spiritualist that Gandhi was, violence was an offense against the higher law. At any rate, Motilal and Gandhi parted ways, the former to become the leader of the opposition in the Legislative Assembly in Delhi, and the latter to continue as leader of the opposition in open-air assemblies of the people. The British Viceroy's government in India at the time was responsible not to the elected members of the Indian Legislative Assembly but to His Majesty's government in England. All that the Assembly could really do was to harass the Viceroy's government. To that task Motilal now brought all his great assets as a brilliant lawyer—unremitting industry, unassailable logic, undeviating purpose, and unparalleled self-confidence.

In the new controversy between the two giants, Motilal and Gandhi, Jawaharlal kept aloof. From 1923 to 1925 he found a great deal of solace and happiness in family life. His term in prison made him long for the company of his wife and daughter. Reflecting later on how fortunate he had been in his family relationships, and how they had soothed and sheltered him in times of stress and strain, he wrote: "I realised, with some shame at my own unworthiness in this respect, how much I owed to my wife for her splendid behaviour since 1920. Proud and sensitive as she was, she had not only put up with my vagaries but brought me comfort and solace when I needed them most."

Clouds of misfortune encroached intermittently upon the sunlit moments of their brief domestic contentment. In 1924 Kamala gave birth to a baby boy. However, as the fates decreed, seven-year-old Indira, who had looked forward to the belated pleasure of ending her prolonged loneliness, had to share the disappointment of her parents when the baby died in a week's time. But worse was to follow. Kamala's health took a serious turn, and in November 1925 her illness was diagnosed as tuberculosis. During the winter months of late 1925 and early 1926 Kamala lay critically ill in a hospital in Lucknow. Jawaharlal was the general secretary of the Congress in 1925, and its annual session that year was being held in Kanpur. Distracted and depressed, he had to flit continually between the triangular points of the home, the hospital, and the site of the party's annual session.

The most eminent doctors in the land now advised that Kamala should be taken to Switzerland for treatment. Jawaharlal was happy at the suggestion, both for Kamala's sake and his own. He was looking for an excuse to get out of India. Indian politics of the time distressed him. There were dissensions within the Indian National Congress. The distrust between the Hindus and the Muslims was deepening. The nationalist cause itself seemed to be in the doldrums. Jawaharlal was confused, his mind was befogged, and no clear path was visible through the wilderness. He felt that a visit to Europe might enable him to look upon the Indian scene from a distance and with some detachment. A clearer perspective, now dimmed by deep personal involvement, might emerge. As he prepared to leave for Switzerland with Kamala and Indira, difficulties arose over the issue of a passport to him. The British Government demanded an assurance that during his stay in Europe he would not dabble in politics. Jawaharlal declined to give any such assurance, and the British Government refused to issue the passport. It was only on Motilal's forceful intervention that the government reversed itself and the passport was granted.

In March 1926 Jawaharlal, Kamala, and Indira sailed from Bombay by an Italian cruiser to Venice en route to Geneva. They had planned to be away from India for only six months but actually stayed away for almost twenty-two. In Geneva, the family lived in a three-room apartment until all the necessary medical consultations were completed. A Swiss maid took care of the housekeeping, and Indira joined the International School. During the summer, Indira's younger aunt, Krishna, arrived in Geneva, and proved a great help in housekeeping, although she herself had had no experience of it in Anand Bhavan.

After the consultations they moved to Montana in late fall, where Kamala stayed in a sanatorium, and Indira was admitted to another school in Bex. To the former inmates of spacious Anand Bhavan their new accommodations must have seemed suffocating. But there were always the wide open spaces, the fresh air, and the mountains, which Jawaharlal loved so much, and the green slopes enameled with autumn flowers. Kamala showed gradual improvement, although a nagging intermittent temperature persisted.

If Kamala was overcoming the ills of her body too slowly, Jawaharlal conquered the ills of his humor far more rapidly. His prolonged vacation from the frustrations of Indian politics restored his *joie de vivre*. He was able to renew his contacts and establish new ones with persons who satisfied his varied interests—Romain Rolland the celebrated thinker and philosopher, Albert Einstein the eminent physicist, Sir Jagadis Chandra Bose the brilliant Indian botanist, Ernst Toller the precocious Jewish poet, and Roger Baldwin of the American Civil Liberties Union. He also had occasion to meet Frank Buchman, the future founder of the Moral Rearmament movement, who was then sponsoring the Oxford Group Movement. While Buchman tried to enthuse, Jawaharlal tried to think, convincing himself that "sudden conversions and confessions and a revisionist atmosphere in general go ill with intellectuality."

Nine-year-old Indira had the unique opportunity of making her first acquaintance with some of these eminent persons. She also made friends with a large number of colorful Indian revolutionaries and expatriates living in Europe. Whenever Kamala felt better, Jawaharlal would take her, Indira, and Krishna to places in England, France, and Germany. As winter advanced, Indira took to ice-skating and skiing, and also to mountain climbing and tobogganing under her father's inspiration. In November of that year her Dadu was very sorry that for the first time he could not send her a birthday present because he was preoccupied with the elections and no one else had the imagination to think of the date in time. But Indira did not miss much; she was having the gayest moments in a long, long time.

Jawaharlal also managed to mix some politics with pleasure. As representative of the Indian National Congress he attended the Brussels conference of the League of Oppressed Nationalities early in 1927, where he exchanged views with Mme. Sun Yat-sen, the Kuomintang leader of China, and Ho Chi Minh, the future liberator of Indochina from the French. George Lansbury of the British Labour Party was president of the Conference, which was attended by a number of Asian, African, and Latin American representatives. From Brussels Jawaharlal accepted an invitation to go to Düsseldorf to attend one of those numerous meetings which excited Europeans were holding during those days to discuss the celebrated Sacco-Vanzetti case that so agitated the Americans.

By September Motilal arrived in Europe, and the family visited a few more countries, including the Soviet Union, where they were invited for the tenth anniversary celebrations of the Revolution of 1917. Indira stayed back in school and did not join the family for the Moscow trip. Returning to Berlin, the family proceeded to Paris and to Marseilles, from where they sailed for India, reaching Madras in December 1927, just in time for the annual session of the Congress. Motilal stayed in Europe for three months longer.

The father's return to India marked another convulsive collision course with the son and new stresses and strains in family relationships. In May 1928 a conference of all the political parties was held in Bombay to draft a commonly acceptable constitution and to present it to the British as their united demand. Motilal was appointed chairman of the committee to draft the constitution. Not all parties in India were in favor of independence or an American-style breakaway from the British. Some desired dominion status or the position conferred on Canada or Australia, which enjoyed self-government but under the sovereignty of the British Crown. In his eagerness to obtain a consensus so that the conference did not fail, Motilal settled for dominion status.

This infuriated Jawaharlal, who would be content with nothing short of complete independence. The mental conflict between father and son continued for a year. They had always had vital differences of opinion which kept them in different political camps—moderate as distinguished from radical—but never had the tension been so intolerable as now. Both made a conscious effort to abstain from political discussion, but there never was any guarantee that even a

seemingly innocuous conversation would not drift unwittingly into
the hottest political controversy.

A relative of the family, then a very young man just out of college
and staying at Anand Bhavan as a guest, recalls one such occasion.
Breakfast was being served, and Motilal was in one of his irrepressi-
bly uproarious moods. Sitting at the head of the table, he recited a
Persian couplet, "Neither can there be two monarchs in a kingdom,
nor two swords in a scabbard, nor two hermits in a cave," and asked
the young guest to his right to expand on the theme. The young man,
who was neither in an expansive mood nor possessed with any
literary inclination, excused himself from opening his mouth save for
the morsels of food. Motilal then turned his gaze to his son at the
opposite end of the table and prodded him to try. Jawaharlal could
not pretend he had no literary propensities but preferred silence as
the better part of wisdom.

Motilal then sent up a gargantuan guffaw, terribly pleased that the
esoteric meaning of his couplet was beyond the divination of the
two young men. He nudged the guest to take another chance, but
the latter would not chance its possible consequences. Motilal then
goaded his son to try again. Whatever the literary implications of the
couplet, its political overtones suddenly made themselves apparent
to Jawaharlal—dominion status in those days was not dissimilar to
having two monarchs in one kingdom—but he still maintained his
sullen silence. When the triumphant Motilal generously offered his
son a last chance to explore its meaning, Jawaharlal exploded that
one who did not know the difference between dominion status and
independence should not have recited that couplet. This was sufficient
for Motilal to offer a practical demonstration of the couplet's meaning. He gave the table a violent jerk. Plates and cups and saucers and
forks and knives went cascading down to the floor, echoing the cry
that neither could there be two kings in Anand Bhavan.

Soon after the All-Parties' Conference in Bombay, Jawaharlal took
Kamala and Indira to Mussoorie for the summer. Curiously enough,
one of the things which Indira wanted her father to tell her about
was kings, what they were, and why they became kings. To para-
phrase her Papu, this was how he answered:

"They were not called kings to begin with. I have told you already about the formation of tribes. When agriculture came and there was some division of work or labour, it became necessary for some person in the tribe to organise the work. Even before this the tribes wanted someone to lead them to battle against another tribe. The leader was usually the oldest man in the group. He was called the patriarch. When he died all the members of the tribe gathered together and chose another. When the patriarch's office became hereditary, that is, son succeeded father, there was little difference between him and a king. He developed into king. And the king got the strange notion that everything in the country belonged to him. He thought he was the country. A famous French king once said: '*L'état c'est moi.*' But at last the common people could not bear it any longer and in some countries they drove out their kings. In England as you know, there is still a king, but he has no power. He can do very little."

At that point, "Amen!" is what the patriarch of Anand Bhavan might well have said if he had been in Mussoorie, overhearing his son. For was this not what he had been trying to tell his son during the last few months? If India accepted dominion status, the sovereign would technically be the King of England, but then, as Jawaharlal was telling his dear Indu, the King of England "has no power, he can do very little."

Jawaharlal might have warned Indu not to be led away by her Dadu's logic. Her grandfather was a constitutional lawyer, very precise, and used to thinking coolly about abstract legal concepts. The question was not how a people *thought* about freedom but how they *felt*. Independence—complete and unqualified—was what the Indian people wished for with all their heart. But her Dadu would certainly have told Indu, as he had told another young lady of the family for an overenthusiastic public speech she had made: "The heart is always a fool whomever it belongs to. The only safe guide is the head."

In substance, this was exactly how father and son argued with each other all through those months leading up to the December 1928 annual session of the Congress in Calcutta. Motilal, who was honored for a second time by being elected president, was determined that the Indian Congress should adopt the resolution of the All-Parties' Conference demanding not independence but dominion status from Britain. Jawaharlal opposed Motilal's proposal in open session. A compromise was worked out under which the Congress was free to revert to a call for complete independence if Britain did not grant dominion status to India within a year.

For the rest of the family, however, the Calcutta session held many happy moments. For one thing, it amounted to a family reunion, since Vijaya Lakshmi and her husband, Ranjit Pandit, were living in Calcutta at the time. Indira was delighted to see her great Dadu being carried in procession in a carriage drawn by thirty-six horses. No less happy was Swarup Rani, who sat through many hours listening to the proceedings, her eyes lighting up at the sound of applause for her husband. Indira had one more reason to be happy because her Papu was elected general secretary of the Congress.

The political climate of the country in the year 1928 had been highly charged. The conservative government of Stanley Baldwin in London had appointed a seven-man all-British commission under the chairmanship of Sir John Simon—a personal friend of Motilal, both of whom appeared together as professional colleagues before the Privy Council in England—to proceed to India to investigate and recommend further constitutional advances. All over India the "Simon Seven" were forced to face the most effective political and social boycott ever organized by the Congress.

Thousands of members of hundreds of newly established youth leagues waved black flags and carried huge signs which read "Simon Go Back." By the end of the year millions of Indians, kept illiterate for two centuries, had managed to learn at least two words of the English language: "go back." The demonstrators were beaten up by the police so severely in every city which Simon visited that Mahatma Gandhi described the commission as making "blood-red progress." It was during these demonstrations in Lucknow that Jawaharlal experienced for the first time the feel of police *lathis* or long batons and truncheons on his back.

Although the mounted police charged against him and rained a hail of blows, he stood his ground, wincing under the blinding pain of those blows till some of his younger colleagues carried him off his feet, suspecting that the police were attempting to kill him. Mahatma Gandhi blessed his favorite disciple for his bravery, but Jawaharlal's family was distinctly disturbed by this new experience. Motilal came speeding from Allahabad to Lucknow, and to poor little Indira the episode was anything but edifying at her impressionable age of eleven.

If the year 1929 marked a turning point in the history of India, and of the Congress, it also witnessed the consummation of the domestic pride and felicity of Anand Bhavan's inmates. On the outskirts of the historic city of Lahore—now part of West Pakistan—300,000 persons had gathered in the great tented camp pitched upon the banks of the river Ravi during the last week of December. The dominion status which the Congress had demanded a year ago had not been proffered by the British Government. The nation's eyes were now turned to Lahore, where the Congress would decide on the next step.

Jawaharlal Nehru, who was chosen president for the session, rode through the streets the opening day on a white charger, surrounded by a contingent of uniformed volunteers and followed by a herd of elephants. The president of the previous session, Motilal, now passed the scepter of authority to his son, very much in the fashion of a retiring monarch conceding the hereditary claims of an ambitious prince. As he did so, he recited a Persian couplet:

> *Harche ke pidar natawanad*
> *Pesar tamam kunad.*

(What the father is unable to accomplish, the son achieves). Motilal's wish proved a prophecy, although he did not live to see his son become independent India's first Prime Minister.

But there was one person in that vast concourse of humanity who was the proudest—Indira, the granddaughter of the retiring president and the daughter of the succeeding president. She heard the latter declare in ringing tones in his presidential address that the Congress now stood for *Purna Swaraj*—complete independence—meaning "complete freedom from British domination and British imperialism." Nothing short of that goal would satisfy India now. He issued a clarion call for battle, promising nothing but peril and privation: "Success often comes to those who desire and act; it seldom goes to the timid who are ever afraid of the consequences. We play for high stakes, and if we seek to achieve great things it can only be through great dangers."

At the stroke of the midnight hour, as the old year was rung out and the new rung in, the Congress adopted Jawaharlal's resolution on complete independence. The party also decided that January 26, 1930, would be observed all over India as *Purna Swaraj* Day, and everyone would reiterate the pledge which Jawaharlal had drafted in words reminiscent of Thomas Jefferson's in the American Declaration of Independence:

"We believe that it is the inalienable right of the Indian people, as of any other people, to have freedom and to enjoy the fruits of their toil and have necessities of life, so that they may have full opportunities of growth. We believe also that if any government deprives a people of these rights and oppresses them, the people have a further right to alter it or to abolish it. The British Government in India has not only deprived the Indian people of their freedom but has based itself on the exploitation of the masses, and has ruined India economically, politically, culturally and spiritually. We believe therefore that India must sever the British connection and attain *Purna Swaraj*. . . . We hold it to be a crime against man and God to submit any longer to a rule that has caused this fourfold disaster to our country."

On the appointed day, millions of people took the pledge in every nook and cranny of the land. Overnight, as it were, Jawaharlal had become the idol of the masses, the hero of the youth, and the ideologue of the intelligentsia. Songs were written about him, and many a legend grew up around his personality and accomplishments. Thousands of ordinary people would stop by at Anand Bhavan to pay him their humble homage. Wherever he went in India to speak, addresses were presented to him in such ornate terms as *Bharat Bhushan* (Jewel of India) and *Tyagamurti* (Embodiment of Sacrifice).

Jawaharlal confessed later in his autobiography that all this ful-some praise had gone to his head to some extent. Luckily for him, he says, these high-sounding terms were used by his family members also, but always loaded with sarcasm. Noticing that her mother and aunts employed them for good-humored raillery, Indira too joined them in the merry game of pulling her father's leg, although she inwardly admired her Papu's accomplishments. Swarup Rani alone took Jawaharlal seriously. It seems that sons can never do wrong—especially only sons.

Meanwhile, in the fertile soil of Mahatma Gandhi's imagination, the seed of a new movement of civil disobedience had been germinating. The manufacture of salt in India was a government monopoly. Furthermore, there was a tax on salt, an item of consumption which even the poorest cannot do without. The Mahatma decided on Salt Satyagraha, or the violation of the salt law. With his unique instinct for high drama, he set out on March 12, 1930, from his Sabarmati *ashram* near Ahmadabad to walk a distance of 241 miles to the small seaside village of Dandi. As he marched from village to village, other sympathizers joined him—thousands of them in flesh and millions in spirit. On April 6 he boiled some seawater and made salt, and with it he also stirred the murky waters of revolution and made history.

On the same day at Anand Bhavan a little history was made too, but not on Gandhi's grand scale. Within the compound walls that encircled the vast grounds of his estate, Motilal had been building a new house. It was not as large as the existing one, but it was well planned, elegant, and utilitarian. On his last European trip in 1927 Motilal had purchased many furnishings and fittings for this house, which he was building for Jawaharlal's comfort, so that the son might devote all his time to the national struggle instead of frittering it away on making a living. The family had recently moved into the new house, and it was Motilal's desire to make a gift of the old house to the nation. On the morning of April 6 Motilal renamed the old house Swaraj Bhavan (the Abode of Independence), and presented it to the Indian National Congress. At a brief ceremony, Jawaharlal, the president of the Congress, accepted Swaraj Bhavan as a gift from his father to house the national headquarters of the party. The new house was now named Anand Bhavan, and fittingly too, for whichever house Motilal moved into invariably became the Abode of Joy.

To the inmates of Anand Bhavan the joy of the moment was confined to breaking the salt law. The ladies of the house collected all available pots and pans and set up makeshift hearths and fireplaces in the open air. Amid a cacophony of sounds and the crackle of cinders there emerged something which bore the semblance of salt but was hardly palatable. But even less palatable to the government was the breaking of the law, which by now had become the national habit.

Little Indira was only twelve, but she decided she would not be a mere onlooker. Her father, grandfather, and Gandhi were all arrested, as were hundreds of thousands of others who sparked off the prairie fire of revolution that swept the country. Her mother and aunts donned male attire and supervised the picketing of cloth shops and liquor stores, as did waves of women who for the first time went surging into the mainstream of treason. Saltmaking was seditious fun, but Indira wanted to do something more serious. Her age, however, proved a bar to her ambition. Rejected by her party for membership and prevented by her family from joining the picket lines, she ventured out to become a leader in her own right by organizing the Allahabad branch of the Vanar Sena (Monkey Brigade).

The first of these brigades was established in Bombay by a group of volunteer youth leaders. It was named Vanar Sena after the monkey army mentioned in the epic *Ramayana*. According to legend, when Sita, the virtuous wife of the hero, Rama, was abducted by the wicked Ravana, and Rama marched to wage just war against him, the monkey-god Hanuman raised a vast army of sympathetic monkeys to fight alongside of Rama. The creation of the Bombay unit of the Monkey Brigade was soon emulated by other youth leagues which had been established all over India in 1928 for organizing the boycott of the Simon Commission.

In Allahabad it was twelve-year-old Indira's initiative which saw the beginnings of a six-thousand-strong Monkey Brigade. At her first meeting Indira's shrill voice could not even be heard at the periphery of the gathering. She asked a burly Congress member and a family friend, Bishamber Nath Pandey, who happened along, to repeat her words in his booming voice. His words were repeated by other human amplifiers till they reached the last row. Indira's "monkeys" performed valuable services, writing notices, licking envelopes and making flags, thus relieving the older people for more important tasks.

They even undertook intelligence activity, slipping unsuspected through police lines and carrying messages from beleaguered leaders to their coworkers who were still free; hanging innocently around police stations, overhearing police officers talk, and forewarning future victims of the custodians of law and order. When Indira first started organizing the Vanar Sena, she kept her father in the dark about her movements. But as one by one her entire family—father, mother, grandfather, aunts—was arrested, she was much freer to do as she pleased. Her grandmother alone was around to lodge her feeble protest against Indira's daring acts.

However, her exploits soon attracted the approbation of her grandfather from behind bars. He wrote to the granddaughter solicitously: "What is the position in the 'Monkey Army'? I suggest the wearing of a tail by every member of it, the length of which should be in proportion to the rank of the wearer."

In spite of his son's devoted nursing in prison, Motilal's asthmatic condition grew worse, and his health was failing rapidly. Averse to having on its hands the dead body of one of India's most distinguished sons, the government set Motilal at liberty on September 11, 1930. Three days later he was taken by his wife, daughters, and granddaughter to Mussoorie. His daughter-in-law, Kamala, stayed on in Anand Bhavan to look after party activities.

Exactly a month later, his term having expired, Jawaharlal was released. Along with Kamala he rushed to Mussoorie and found his father in a slightly better condition. He spent three delightful days in Mussoorie with the entire family. He would occasionally join his daughter Indira, now in the first year of her teens, and her three younger cousins, to march round the house in stately procession. Led by the youngest of them—a three-year-old tot—and carrying the

Congress standard, all of them sang with full-throated vigor, "*Jhanda ooncha rahe hamara*" ("May our flag ever fly aloft").

In the Nehru household it was a thin line that divided ordinary games from the political game, and so Jawaharlal rushed downhill from Mussoorie to the plains below to play the more serious game of how to land in prison. Traveling by car, he stopped at several places and addressed peasant gatherings, urging them not to pay taxes. The next day the rest of the family returned from Mussoorie, and Jawaharlal went to the Allahabad railway station to receive them. Sending them home, he hastened with Kamala to address another peasant meeting. When he was through with it, the government invited him once more to be its guest, and as he was marched off to prison, Kamala returned home alone to tell the family of the latest honor done to her husband.

Jawaharlal had left instructions early in 1930 that in the event of his imprisonment his father should act as Congress president. Incensed by his son's rearrest, the ailing Motilal took full control of directing the agitation. Jawaharlal's birthday in the middle of November was only three weeks away. Motilal issued orders to observe it as "Jawahar Day throughout the length and breadth of India as a protest against the savage sentence of two-and-a-half years" passed on him.

In Allahabad itself, Indira was at the head of the procession, along with her mother, grandmother, and two aunts, which marched to the city park. There she listened with proud defiance as her mother read out the entire seditious speech for which her father had been convicted. Not long after, on January 1, 1931, Kamala too was arrested. And on that New Year's Day Jawaharlal wrote to Indira: "As I lay in bed, very early in the morning, watching the stars, I thought of the great year that was past, with all its hope and anguish and joy, and all the great and gallant deeds performed. And I thought of Bapuji [literally "father," as Mahatma Gandhi was affectionately called] who has made our old country young and vigorous again by his magic touch, sitting in his prison cell in Yeravda. And I thought of Dadu and many others. And especially I thought of Mummie and you. Later in the morning came the news that Mummie had been arrested and taken to gaol. It was a pleasant New Year's gift for me."

On January 26, 1931—the first anniversary of the declaration of Independence Day—Jawaharlal, Mahatma Gandhi, and all other Congress leaders were released by the government in a tactical reversal of policy. Motilal was now in very serious condition, and many of the leaders poured into Anand Bhavan to pay him their homage. On February 4 he was taken to Lucknow, which had better facilities for deep X-ray treatment than Allahabad. "I am going soon, Mahatmaji," he said to Gandhi as he was being taken away, "and I shall not be here to see *Swaraj*. But I know that you have won it and will soon have it."

The early hours of February 6 are best described in Jawaharlal's own words: "He had had a troublesome and restless night; and suddenly I noticed that his face grew calm and the sense of struggle vanished from it. I thought that he had fallen asleep, and I was glad of it. But my mother's perceptions were keener, and she uttered a cry. I turned to her and begged her not to disturb him as he had fallen asleep. But that sleep was his last long sleep, and from it there was no awakening."

Draped in the national flag, the body was brought by car from Lucknow to Allahabad, thousands of people along that 146-mile route paying their last respects to the departed soul. After last rites in Anand Bhavan, Motilal began his last journey to the Ganges, accompanied by a vast concourse of people. Jawaharlal's words recapture the last scene: "As evening fell on the river bank on that winter day, the great flames leapt up and consumed that body which had meant so much to us who were close to him as well as to millions in India. Gandhiji said a few moving words to the multitude, and then all of us crept silently home. The stars were out and shining brightly when we returned, lonely and desolate."

Lonelier and more desolate than ever was poor little Indira, with the departure of her dearly loved Dadu. Nayantara Sahgal, Mrs. Pandit's daughter and one of India's best-known young writers, recalls that her first clear impression as a child of her thirteen-year-old cousin Indira is of a lanky girl, about four-and-a-half feet tall, standing by the sideboard in solitary suffering, swallowing her tears as they streamed down her cheeks, for she knew she would never set eyes on her Dadu again. Motilal's exit marked the end of the first stage of India's struggle for independence. It also marked the end of the first stage of Indira's search for her own identity.

6

Schooling

IF Indira's childhood bore the scars of loneliness and insecurity, her education carried the stamp of inadequacy and incompleteness. In contrast to the smooth flow of her father's systematic and well-planned education—from Harrow to Cambridge and the Inner Temple—Indira's schooling was sporadic and ill-planned. To the vagaries of an uncertain domestic life which frequently interrupted her education must be added the personal whims, the educational biases, and political prejudices of those responsible for her schooling, all of which conspired to put the helpless girl into the position of an unprotesting guinea pig.

After the arrest of her father and grandfather in December 1921 during the first noncooperation movement, Indira was sent off by her mother to Delhi so that she could at least be protected from the disturbing psychological effect of watching the depredations of the police. She remained in Delhi in the sheltering tranquillity of her maternal grandmother's house, and attended kindergarten till her return to Allahabad after Motilal's release from prison. It was at this time that the first of the perpetual problems in Indira's education had arisen.

The Calcutta session of the Congress in 1920 had recommended the boycott of schools run or aided by the government, and soon after Motilal reached Allahabad he had withdrawn his younger daughter, Krishna, from one such school. But withdrawing students from government schools was a much simpler proposition than getting them admitted into private schools, especially when few existed. New schools had to be established, and money had to be found for doing so. As a result, a number of educational societies and foundations sprang up to establish and operate nationally-approved institutions.

The first of such schools to be established in Allahabad in 1923 was the Modern School, and Indira was in the very first batch of students to be admitted to it. Most of these institutions, beset by paucity of resources and inadequacy of staff, ran classes from the first grade to the last in order to effect economies in plant and equipment. The result was that students of all ages and all divisions from the first year of the primary school to the last of the high school were to be found under one roof.

Motilal felt that his granddaughter might be happier in the congenial company of youngsters like herself. Given his aristocratic preferences and exclusive tastes, he might well have even thought that Indira deserved a better education than she obtained from the rough-hewn ways of hastily founded and yet untested schools. Whatever his reasoning, he withdrew his granddaughter from the Modern School and admitted her to St. Cecilia's School in August 1924. The latter, situated in Allahabad itself, was apparently a private institution operated by three European sisters, the Misses Cameron. Motilal's action immediately caused an estrangement between father and son.

In the 1920's it was customary for foreign correspondents to have a dig at Motilal, Jawaharlal, and Mahatma Gandhi by referring to them as the Trinity of the Father, the Son, and the Holy Ghost. Although intended as a jibe about their political collaboration, it was no less true of their domestic consultations and controversies. Indira's education was one of those topics about which all three got into an argument.

Motilal's contention was that in admitting his granddaughter to St. Cecilia's School he was prompted solely by the desire to give her the companionship of children of her own age. Jawaharlal had apparently bowed to his father's wish but seemed to have nurtured a secret grievance that the kind of instruction imparted by the three

Misses Cameron of St. Cecilia's would not be very different from the one inflicted by Miss Cecilia Hooper on his two younger sisters. Put out by the Father, the Son prayed for the intercession of the Holy Ghost. But in writing to Mahatma Gandhi, Jawaharlal gave a political twist to his argument and suggested that in view of the principles of the noncooperation movement which bound all Congress members, it would be distinctly improper to let Indira attend a school run by teachers alien in their thought and ways.

Averse to adding the fuel of private differences to the fire of political disagreement between Father and Son, the Holy Ghost wrote to the former: "I don't want to be the cause, direct or indirect, of the slightest breach." But he added mildly, albeit conclusively, that his letter "is meant to be a plea for Jawaharlal," since "he is one of the loneliest young men of my acquaintance in India." An infuriated Motilal telegraphed to the Mahatma asserting that the version he was given was "a tissue of lies from beginning to end." He reiterated that the school to which Indira had been admitted was neither operated by the government nor patronized by it, and that Jawaharlal's reservations were based not on the principles of noncooperation but on his own peculiar views about what constituted a proper education. In a fit of intemperate rage Motilal concluded his telegram by saying that if Jawaharlal had given any other version, it was "absolutely false" and "too mean for the proudest father in the world." The net result of Gandhi's intercession on behalf of his "lonely" disciple was to enhance the loneliness of the disciple's daughter too, since she had to stay at home and be trained by private tutors.

Happily for the child, a delightful interlude was soon to begin when she sailed for Europe with her parents in March 1926. While her mother was undergoing medical examination in Geneva, Indira was a student at l'École Internationale de Genève, run by the League of Nations. For the first time she was exposed to a firsthand acquaintance with students of many nationalities and to the influence of such good teachers as Mlle. Hartoch, an excellent friend of the French thinker Romain Rolland. When Kamala was taken to rest at the sanatorium in Montana, Indira was admitted to l'École Nouvelle in Bex—a Swiss boarding school run by a Frenchwoman.

Indira was fortunate to do her traveling at an impressionable age, and doubly fortunate to do it with the help of an extraordinary tourist guide—her father. Sailing through the Suez Canal, he had told her of the existence of the Sphinx and the great pyramids, the ruins of the massive temples at Luxor and Karnak, the wall paintings in the tombs of Thebes and the hieroglyphic writings of Egypt and Babylon. Proceeding from Port Said to Venice they passed Crete, and Indira heard from her father all about the ancient civilization of that island, the remains of the palace in Knossos, its bathrooms and water pipes "which some ignorant people think are modern inventions," the beautiful pottery, sculpture, and the fine metal- and ivorywork of that Mediterranean culture, and the lore of King Minos and the Minotaur.

In Europe Jawaharlal took his daughter on a round of the great museums for a lecture-demonstration of early life on this planet. He showed her the fossils big and small of many species that lived at different times, the replicas of enormous extinct brutes in the South Kensington Museum in London, and the plants in Kew Gardens, and he told her of the interesting experiments conducted by Sir Jagadis Chandra Bose to demonstrate that plants and stones also have life. In Heidelberg he showed her the skull of the so-called Heidelberg man and told her of our kinship with the monkeys and his suspicion that "even now many of us, I am afraid, behave like the monkeys do." In the Geneva Museum he led her through the array of stone axes, spears, and needles to the model of the wooden house built on stilts in the middle of a lake that was the habitat of Neolithic man. And in Paris he took her, of all places, to the Conciergerie prison to tell her of Lord Acton's dictum that power corrupts and absolute power tends to corrupt absolutely, of what happened there to Louis XVI and Marie Antoinette in 1793, and of the similar fate which befell the czars in the very month and year of Indira's birth.

When Indira returned to India in December 1927, the struggle for independence was in low tide. The fervor of the freedom fighters had somewhat abated in intensity, and everywhere there was a partial return to the conventional schools that had been hitherto boycotted. Within Anand Bhavan itself, the imagined nexus between education and political aspiration had obviously come into question. After all, Motilal had studied only Persian and Arabic in the *maktabs* or indigenous schools before he enrolled in Muir College at Allahabad. Yet, this did not prevent him from becoming a social rebel and adopting Western ways. Jawaharlal, on the other hand, was educated by English tutors at home in India and then in a school and a university of the Establishment in England. Yet, this did not obviate his turning a political rebel and adopting Indian ways.

On the contrary, in spite of the veneer of his Western ways and an almost constitutional predisposition toward English constitutionalism, Motilal was an Indian to the core, whereas Jawaharlal, despite his lately cultivated affectation of Indian ways and a visceral proclivity for radical nationalism, remained almost to the end essentially English in thought. If then education bore little relation to educability, did it matter what school Indira attended? At any rate, she was now put in the St. Mary's Convent in Allahabad; and if the old school tie is all that Jawaharlal retained from Harrow, the blue tunic and white blouse of St. Mary's is all that Indira now retains in her memory. The only concession to patriotism which was made at the time was the appointment of a pandit to teach her Hindi at home.

It will be recalled that Jawaharlal had inquired anxiously about Indira's schooling during his first incarceration, and had suggested, somewhat rashly, that he could easily have taken care of it if he were not confined to his prison cell, only to discover that he had even less free time for the family once he was free. Prison at least gave him enforced leisure, time enough for reading and reflection, and even time to spare for writing an occasional letter. If Motilal could expend all the great resources of his wealth for his son's education, Jawaharlal could at least expend the wealth of his vast knowledge for his daughter's education. He therefore hit upon the brilliant idea of giving her a sort of correspondence course in general knowledge.

The first of this series of letters was written in the summer of 1928 when Indira was vacationing in the hill station of Mussoorie and Jawaharlal was battling with the Simon Commission in the plains below. Picking up the threads of the guided tour of European museums which he had given her the previous two years, Jawaharlal enlarged upon the origin of the earth, the origin of life, the origin of man, and the origin of man's social institutions in twenty-seven letters. He wrote her three more letters on the beginnings of Indian history, but Indira returned to Anand Bhavan from her summer resort, and the correspondence course was suspended.

The letters came to the attention of Mahatma Gandhi, who did not agree wholly with the exposition of his favorite disciple but wrote to him: "Your letters to Indu are excellent and should be published." Published indeed they were for the delectation of a million other children in November 1929 as *Letters from a Father to his Daughter*. In including the last three letters in the volume, Jawaharlal explained apologetically in the Foreword that they "begin a new period and are somewhat out of place by themselves. But I have included them as there is little chance of adding to them."

Little did he know that the chance would come in the following year. He was back in prison for 180 days from April 14, 1930, to October 11, 1930; for another 99 days from October 19, 1930, to January 26, 1931; and for a further 612 days in his sixth term of imprisonment from December 26, 1931, to August 30, 1933.

Jawaharlal commenced his second series of letters on October 26, 1930, Indira's thirteenth birthday according to the Hindu calendar, and ended it on August 9, 1933, six months after Hitler came to power in Germany. They were published later as *Glimpses of World History*, which the author described as "further letters to [his] daughter, written in prison, and containing a rambling account of history for young people." He confesses freely that the letters were written more for his own pleasure than for his daughter's enlightenment. The result, however, is that even his daughter must have derived more pleasure than enlightenment from her father's *History*.

Far from being an objective or systematic history, it was a highly personal and subjective survey of the past. Although he wrote his daughter in the very first letter that he must not sermonize, he did so indeed till the very last. More than being merely narrative history, it was a materialistic interpretation of history along the lines of Marxist methodology. Its chief virtue as history was to correct the distortion caused by the Europe-centered view of Western scholars and to reestablish the primacy of Asia, the loss of which Jawaharlal deplored.

In spite of the subtle undertones of its materialistic interpretation, Jawaharlal's *History* did not become the plaything of blind, imponderable forces in the face of which human beings are helpless. Rather, his *History* now appears as the product of the conscious design and endeavor of great men who have the capacity to transcend the limitations of ordinary men. As he wrote to Indira: "Ordinary men and women are not usually heroic. They think of their daily bread and butter, of their children, of their household worries and the like. But a time comes when a whole people become full of faith for a great cause, and then even simple, ordinary men and women become heroes, and history becomes stirring and epoch-making. Great leaders have something in them which inspires a whole people and makes them do great deeds." It is clear that he asked his daughter to aspire for such greatness as he ended his first letter with the blessing, "May you grow up into a brave soldier in India's service."

Jawaharlal's conscious Marxism was also often overshadowed by his unconscious Brahminism, with the result that he sought to inculcate in Indira a number of values. He extolled selflessness and quoted a Sanskrit verse: "For the family sacrifice the individual, for the community the family, for the country the community, and for the Soul the whole world." He emphasized service and cited another Sanskrit verse: "I desire not the supreme state of bliss with its eight perfections, nor the cessation of re-birth. May I take up the sorrow of all creatures who suffer and enter into them so that they may be made free from grief."

He stressed that truth emanates only from our performance of the Socratic function of acting as a gadfly to contemporary civilization, and inscribed the last words of the voice that was stilled by the cup of hemlock: "If you propose to acquit me on condition that I abandon my search for truth, I will say: I thank you, O Athenians, but I will obey God, who as I believe set me the task, rather than you . . . "

He reminded her of the need for tolerance and quoted from an edict issued around 250 B.C. by the great Indian emperor Asoka: "Gifts or honour are not as important as the advancement of the essential doctrine of all religions. This progress of the essential doctrine takes many forms, but its basis is the control of one's speech, so as not to extol one's own religion or disparage another's ... On each occasion one should honour another man's religion, for by doing so one increases the influence of one's own religion and benefits that of the other man; while by doing otherwise one diminishes the influence of one's own religion and harms the other man's. ..."

But prison life had its moods of doubt, depression, and disillusionment. Jawaharlal went through many such moods, and when they were accentuated by external developments, such as Hitler's rise to power, he gave free vent to his bitterness. He wrote to Indira: "Sometimes the injustice, the unhappiness, the brutality of the world oppress us and darken our minds, and we see no way out. With Matthew Arnold we feel...

> For the world which seems
> To lie before us, like a land of dreams
> So various, so beautiful, so new,
> Hath really neither joy, nor love, nor light,
> Nor certitude, nor peace, nor help for pain;
> And we are here, as on a darkling plain
> Swept with confused alarms of struggle and flight,
> Where ignorant armies clash by night."

The dominant mood of the letters, however, was optimism, reinforced by his romantic belief in the nineteenth-century concept of infinite progress. He wrote to Indira of the plethora of ideologies, "feudalism, capitalism, socialism, syndicalism, anarchism, communism—so many isms!" He warned her that "behind them all stalks opportunism!" But he assured her "there is also idealism for those who care to have it," and quoted George Bernard Shaw with approval: "This is the true joy in life, the being used for a purpose recognised by yourself as a mighty one; the being thoroughly worn out before you are thrown on the scrap heap; the being a force of nature, instead of a feverish, selfish little clod of ailments and grievances, complaining that the world will not devote itself to making you happy."

Jawaharlal left his adolescent daughter in no doubt that it was as necessary for her to chart the future course of history as it was to follow its past developments, as imperative for her to make history as it was inevitable to be made by it. So he spurred her to action, reminding her of what their friend Romain Rolland had written: "Action is the end of thought. All thought which does not look toward action is an abortion and a treachery. If then we are the servants of thought we must be the servants of action."

At the time that Nehru was writing his first letter to his daughter, however, all action seemed futile. The British Government seemed entrenched in its Indian Empire. The Labour Government of Ramsay MacDonald had come and gone, suppressing the Indian struggle for freedom with a ruthlessness which the Conservatives might well have envied. Was it demonstrating the truth of another Shavianism about which the optimistic Jawaharlal did not write to his daughter: The one thing that man learns from history is that man does not learn from history? That may well be the reason why history repeats itself. At any rate, Jawaharlal convinced himself that the history we approve of must be *made* to repeat itself and wrote to his sister, Krishna, to send Indira as soon as possible the volumes on Garibaldi that were at the time being read by Motilal.

If Indira was too young to be inspired to revolutionary action by Garibaldi, she was old enough to have her imagination fired by the exploits of the Italian liberator. She recalls that she was reading voraciously and perpetually during this period. "The problem—my mother's greatest problem—was to get me to eat, get me to sleep, because just the minute I finished one book I wanted another. Lots of books, of course, I didn't understand. Some things I understood, some things I didn't. But I developed the habit of reading."

Her grandfather also testified to Indira's new interest in her studies. Fearing the impending arrest of Kamala, Motilal wrote to his son in prison on November 11, 1930, that he planned to take Indira with him to Calcutta, where he was proceeding for medical treatment, since the girl would be quite lonely in Anand Bhavan. But in a postscript which he added to the letter the very next day, Motilal reported to his son: "Indu is now settling down to her studies and I do not propose to disturb her unless she herself is keen on accompanying me."

Indira was settling down not only in her studies but also in her emotions. Just a fortnight before he died, Motilal again wrote to his son: "Indu is quite happy. She has fitted up the old wooden house in which the deer was kept as a sort of a summer house and Betty and she both spend some time in the middle of the day in it." Unfortunately, her grandfather's death once again brought emotional unsettlement to Indira and also resulted, for the first time in her life, in a physical uprooting from Anand Bhavan, as she was sent away to a boarding school in Poona.

Soon after Motilal's death, the Congress met in annual session in March 1931 at Karachi—now in Pakistan. It was there that Jawaharlal made accidental acquaintance with a couple who had founded a little school in Poona, 120 miles southeast of Bombay. Since there was a distinct possibility of their being imprisoned again for participation in the noncooperation movement, Jawaharlal and Kamala decided that they would admit Indira to this school in June. Meanwhile Jawaharlal was advised by his doctors to take a rest and seek a change of scene. So father, mother, and daughter set sail in April 1931 from Bombay to Colombo, Ceylon, on the *Cracovia*—the very ship on which Motilal had sailed to Europe in 1927 and returned to India in 1928. Some of Motilal's fellow passengers were on board the ship now, and they regaled Indira with stories about her grandfather's exploits.

But her father too had many things to tell her. After the conclusion of the Karachi session of the Congress, Jawaharlal had gone to visit the nearby ruins of Mohenjo-Daro in the province of Sind, which is now part of West Pakistan. The ruins, which had been excavated barely ten years earlier by Sir John Marshall, exposed to light one of India's earliest civilizations, approximately five thousand years old. Jawaharlal gave Indira a vivid word-picture of this civilization, as he had done about the civilizations of Egypt and Crete in the course of their voyage to Europe.

What emerged from his description was a great city of high, solid brick houses and wide thoroughfares, public baths, and an underground drainage system. Looking at the statuary, the beautiful jewelry and porcelain jars that were unearthed there, he told Indira he could "almost imagine men and women, decked out in gay attire, walking up and down its streets and lanes, and children playing, as children will, and the bazaars, bright with merchandise, and people buying and selling, and the temple bells ringing."

The three Nehrus were soon in Lanka—as Ceylon was called in ancient times—and it being their first visit to the tropics, they were bewitched by the luxuriance of the vegetation and the limpid waters that lashed against the island shores. They rested for a fortnight at Nuwara Eliya, where groups of laborers, tea-garden workers, and other humble folk walked many miles to bring them daily offerings of wild flowers, vegetables, and homemade butter. By evening they were loaded with so many gifts that Indira and her mother passed them on to the local hospitals and orphanages.

Then began Indira's conducted tour with Jawaharlal through ancient history. Starting at Sigiriya with its great rock fortress, they went on to Pollunaruwa with its extensive remains of old palaces and temples, and the great statues of the Buddha and frescoes of gods set in a pond carved out in the shape of a lotus flower. They then went to see the ruins of Anuradhapura, the city that was built two thousand years ago when the message of the Buddha was taken there by the son and daughter of the famous Indian Emperor, Asoka. There was also the peepul tree, reputed to be two thousand years old, which was planted as a sapling brought from Gaya in India, cut out from the same tree under which the Buddha attained his enlightenment.

But what attracted them most was the seated statue of Buddha, a picture of which became Jawaharlal's constant companion in his prison cells. More than the past, however, what gripped Jawaharlal was the present—and people. So in Kandy, famous for its vigorous dances, he addressed a great gathering in the very shadow of the Temple of the Tooth, and many more such gatherings in Colombo.

One night there occurred a minor mishap. Jawaharlal fell off his bed onto the floor. He was obviously in deep sleep, and by the time he had awakened blood was oozing out of a head wound. He stirred with the unpleasant taste of blood in his mouth and woke up Indira and her mother, who were asleep in an adjoining room. As Kamala was washing her husband's wound, she fainted away, and Indira had to run and fetch Hari, the family's faithful long-time valet. It was now Jawaharlal's turn to carry his wife, and Hari's to dress his master's wound.

Nobody could unravel the mystery of how Jawaharlal could have slipped off from what was literally a great big bed. The only clue to a possible explanation can be found in a little confession he made later in his autobiography. Before Jawaharlal's departure for Harrow, F. T. Brooks, his private tutor, had introduced him to several theosophical works as well as to Hindu and Buddhist scriptures. Thinking consciously for the first time of metaphysical arguments and theories of reincarnation during the day, he used to dream at night of astral bodies and imagined himself flying vast distances. This dream of flying high up in the air, without any wings or other means of keeping afloat in space, was a frequent one throughout his life. The dream was always vivid and realistic, and he could clearly see the countryside lying underneath him in a vast panorama as he soared through the ethereal sky.

It is conceivable that on this night, reflecting upon the transplanting of the peepul tree from India to Ceylon, and upon the spread of the message of the Buddha over countless miles of land and sea and through countless generations of people, Jawaharlal's imagination ran riot, and his fancy made him take off from his bed on one of his wingless flights, only to land him on the floor with a thud. Happily, the wound was far less serious than the dream. A number of eminent doctors came and examined him, including a heart specialist who thumped his chest a great deal, but the most needed, a psychoanalyst, was not around, and Jawaharlal was pronounced fit.

The family returned to India in May, and in June Indira found herself in Poona. As planned, she was admitted to the Children's Own School founded in 1928 by the husband-and-wife team of Jehangir Jivaji Vakil and Coonverbai Vakil. Jehangir had been a brilliant student, having been graduated from Oxford with a first-class first in Greek and Latin at the young age of nineteen. His father wanted him

to join the Indian Civil Service, but the young man resisted the
parental pressure and returned to Bombay, where he took to writing
poetry. The Vakils belonged to the Parsi community in India, which
has been prominent in commerce and banking, and the young man
was now persuaded to take a job with a bank. Fortunately for him,
the Nobel-prize-winning poet Rabindranath Tagore came on a visit
to Bombay at the time, and Vakil tagged along with him to Santiniketan—the school which Tagore had founded near Calcutta. Spending some years there, Vakil returned west to start a school of his
own.

He was now hunting for teachers, and thought of one, Raghubhai
Nayak, along with two others who had studied at Santiniketan. Raghubhai, sharing the fervor of the revolutionary youth of his times,
had attended the famous Lahore session of the Congress over which
Jawaharlal Nehru presided in 1929, took the independence pledge on
January 26, 1930, and was clamped in prison for participating in the
civil disobedience movement which followed soon after. As he sat
behind prison bars, Raghubhai wondered if politics was really his mé-
tier. It was when he was having these second thoughts that Vakil went
to see him in prison and acquainted him with his educational project.
Raghubhai concluded that he was not cut out for agitational politics
and decided to throw in his lot with Vakil.

The Vakils selected house No. 3 on Staveley Road for their school
premises because the dilapidated structure, built in Portuguese colo-
nial-style architecture with its tiled roof, would be inexpensive to
buy, and also because it had extensive grounds enclosed by a compound wall that would suit the requirements of a school. The location was ideal. It was relatively uninhabited, and across the road were
the St. Mary's School for Girls and the Bishop's School for Boys,
both of which were run by the Catholic Church.

But the owner of the house, a Parsi dowager of modest means, at
first refused to sell it for sentimental reasons. A few Parsis were
always very loyal to His Britannic Majesty—so loyal indeed that if
they were entertaining an English guest, they would not serve afternoon tea till one of their children played "God Save the King" on
the piano. The Parsi dowager of Staveley Road declined to part with

her property because it was in this very house that long years ago Lord Wellesley had once slept during his brief sojourn in Poona. And Wellesley was no ordinary man. He was the very resourceful Governor-General who had perfected a variety of land-grabbing techniques and added such a great deal of real estate to the still shadowy British Empire in India that it did become substantially real. However, after some skillful persuasion, the Vakils convinced the old lady that her modest means could not afford an immodest sentiment, and succeeded in acquiring the house. The school was inaugurated by none other than Rabindranath Tagore himself, who was happy that Santiniketan on the eastern seaboard would now have a sister institution on the western seaboard.

The Vakils, together with their two little daughters, occupied but one room of the house, and the other rooms were used for classes. To begin with, there were only eleven boarders—seven Hindus, two Muslims, and two Parsis. They would sleep at night either outdoors or in one of the classrooms, and roll up their camping-style bedding at dawn and dump it in the room of the Vakils, already crammed to capacity with cupboards and cabinets. In addition to the eleven boarders, there were about seventy-five day students. As principal of the school, Mr. Vakil took charge of the upper-grade students, while Mrs. Vakil was held responsible for the lower-grade pupils. The monthly tuition fee was four rupees (roughly equivalent to a dollar in those days) for lower-grade day students, and seven rupees for the upper-grade ones. The boarders paid no fixed fees, but the expenses of the eleven were added up each month and divided equally among them, averaging 111 rupees a month.

Thus thirteen-year-old Indira Nehru moved from the no mean comfort of Anand Bhavan into the Spartan surroundings of her school. She had gone there soon after the loss of her grandfather, and the unfamiliar environs accentuated the anguish of her loneliness. As anticipated, Jawaharlal was imprisoned again in December 1931, and in the same month Kamala had to be moved to Bombay for the treatment of the disease that was gradually gaining the upper hand over her. Coming on the heels of her grandfather's death, these two events added to Indira's insecurity. Jai, the Vakils' daughter (now

Mrs. Jai Dordi), remembers distinctly how often her schoolmate Indira used to stand behind the trunk of a tree, lost in her private world of grief, and shed tears profusely, too helpless to control them and yet too proud to show them.

In January 1932 Mrs. Pandit was arrested, and in the following month the Pandit girls—Chandralekha, Nayantara and Rita—were also sent down to the same school. With the company of these three girls Indira felt much more at home. Besides, the eldest of the girls was just eight years old, the second five, and the last was a toddler of two and a half years. Although Indira herself was now only fourteen she could no longer act as a forlorn teen-ager—not when she was called upon almost to mother the baby cousin. The strength of the school gradually went up to 120, with the influx of the children of other political prisoners. The Vakils, with their penchant for social service, also admitted to their school the children of untouchables. Jai and Indira were assigned the task of bathing, clothing, and feeding many of these dirt-laden, disease-ridden children.

As time passed, Indira grew accustomed to her daily routine. If the politics and prison life of her father retained their imponderability, at least her life in school gained some predictability. The morning would start with a military-style drill or the swinging of a *lathi* or the performance of *lezim* to the accompaniment of a rhythmic beat sounded by a Gramophone record. This was followed by *Dhwaj Vandan* (flag salutation) and the singing either of Rabindranath Tagore's lyric, "*Jana Gana Mana,*" which was to be adopted later as independent India's national anthem, or "*Bande Mataram,*" the revolutionary song composed by that other great Bengali writer, Bankim Chandra Chatterjee. Then started the classes, which were held mostly in open air under large shady trees, except during the season of monsoon rains.

Raghubhai Nayak, who taught Indira history, geography, and civics, remembers her as an attentive and obedient student. Jawaharlal's "correspondence course" was obviously taking effect, and Indira developed a passion for general knowledge. She also had a flair for languages. Besides English, in which her father wrote her his famous letters, she knew Hindi. There were many students at school who spoke Gujarati, and she soon learned to understand it very well and to speak it tolerably well. "Perhaps my thoughts and approach to life are more akin to what is called Western than Eastern," confessed Jawaharlal, and he wanted to make amends for it by giving his daughter a good grounding in Sanskrit, the classical language of Indian thought and culture. Raghubhai, who taught her Sanskrit after school hours, recalls that she took to the language well, learned by rote several *slokas* or verses, and recited them flawlessly.

But she had a deep distaste for Sanskrit grammar—a hereditary failing. Explaining the reason for his own "pitiful knowledge of Sanskrit," Jawaharlal had admitted, "Grammar has had no attraction for me whatever." Indira protested further that Sanskrit, like Latin, was no longer spoken, and she had no desire to learn "a dead language." While in Switzerland she had developed a great liking for French, to which she now reverted in place of Sanskrit. Jawaharlal made certain that Indira received trunkloads of books, and that she kept up her reading habit. This was the period in which he wrote her his historical letters, and when she received them Raghubhai Nayak had her read some of the interesting ones to the entire class.

Indira was a keen participant in extracurricular activities. She took part in most games and sports. An excellent sprinter, she had a free, natural style. She easily beat all the girls and sometimes bettered the boys. Since the school was too poor to buy equipment for Western-style games, the students had a wide choice of Indian games— *Ata Pata, Khokho, Nargolio, Dabadubi,* and *Hututu*—all of which could be extremely vigorous. The only Western game for which facilities existed was badminton, and Indira displayed some talent in it.

The one thing Indira did with great passion, however, was mountain climbing. There are no great mountains to speak of in this region. But an impressive chain of hills, called the Western Ghats, some of which range up to an altitude of five thousand feet, run in a southerly direction all along the west coast of India. In the Bombay-Poona region these hills are studded with a number of forts of historic interest built in medieval times and quite a few caves reputed for their rock carvings executed in the Buddhist period. Indira frequently arranged picnics to these spots because they provided an excellent opportunity to combine physical fitness with cultural enlightenment.

Miss Shanta Gandhi, Indira's schoolmate in Poona and now a professor of dramatics at the National Institute of Dance and Drama in New Delhi, remembers that Indira possessed a perfect sense of rhythm. She took part in all the folk dances which were performed on festival days—a habit that has lingered on and which tempts her even now to join the dance troupes which perform on New Delhi's thoroughfares every year on Republic Day. Although Indira joined singing choruses and dance dramas, she was too shy to give solo performances. There was, however, one memorable exception.

Being a private institution, the Children's Own School never received any grants-in-aid from the government. The fees which the Vakils charged were too meager to meet all the expenses of the school. And there were many who defaulted even in paying these nominal fees. But Jehangir Vakil, who conducted the institution less as a school principal and more as a church father, never dismissed the defaulting students. All he would do was demand statements saying they did not pay their fees, which they gladly signed. He was thus forced to raise money in other ways, and one such was to make his school's dance and drama troupes perform professionally for fund-raising purposes. When the school performed the Gujarati adaptation of Tagore's *Ritu Raj* ("Cycle of Spring") in 1934 in Bombay's then well-known Capitol Cinema, Indira was assigned a prominent solo role in it.

The school had two societies—the Sahitya Sabha and the Samanya Sabha. The first was a literary society, of which Indira was the secretary. The society's chief function was to produce a handwritten monthly magazine, the burden of which, however, fell on its editor, Shanta Gandhi. Indira, whose shyness gave her stage fright, was very averse to taking part in school debates. As if to suggest that this was no disqualification, the school's Samanya Sabha (mock parliament) chose Indira as its *mahamantri* (prime minister)—a mock-serious precedent which even a serious Parliament would not mock more than a quarter of a century later.

In the summer of 1932 Indira returned to Anand Bhavan for a vacation. But it was not much of a vacation, since her father was still in jail. Nor was he in nearby Naini jail across the river from Anand Bhavan. He was being shifted from prison to prison, from Bareilly to Dehra Dun, and Indira had to travel about two hundred miles to see her Papu for a brief while every fortnight. Worse still, the superintendent of the Dehra Dun jail penalized her father by suspending his interviews for a month because of an incident in which Indira was involved. She had gone to see her uncle, Ranjit Pandit, in prison to tell him that his three daughters were faring well in Poona and to hand him a letter from Mr. Vakil, her school principal. When the jail warden objected to the handing of the letter, Indira's grandmother protested strongly. The warden took offense at this, and Jawaharlal was told that his interviews with his family would be suspended for a month as punishment. Jawaharlal was infuriated with the warden's treatment of his mother and wrote to the superintendent that since he wished to spare his family future insults at the hands of insolent jail officials he was asking them not to visit him even after the month of punishment. For almost seven months Jawaharlal went without a visitor, and Indira returned to school dejected.

Two months after Indira's return she heard, along with millions of her countrymen and women, the bombshell which Mahatma Gandhi threw from his cell in Yeravda Central Prison. He declared that he would "fast unto death" in protest against the Communal Award which had been recently issued by the British Government. It was called the Communal Award because each religious community—Hindus, Muslims, Sikhs, Christians—was to be constituted henceforth into a separate electorate. All these communities were to choose only their coreligionists to represent them in legislatures. They could not vote for candidates of other religious communities even if they believed that the other candidates were better than their coreligionists. Mahatma Gandhi felt that this policy of "divide and rule" was a diabolical device designed to pit one religious community against another so that the British could rule India permanently.

This was bad enough, but there was something even worse. The so-called Communal Award had divided the Hindu community itself into two separate electorates—one consisting of all those who belonged to the various castes, and another consisting of the casteless untouchables. The Mahatma declared that "this was the unkindest cut of all." He gave the untouchables the new name of Harijans, or the children of God, and asserted that their welfare was the special responsibility of the caste Hindus. He maintained that if the untouchables were formed into a separate electorate, then the social crime of untouchability would be perpetuated. This would be an offense against God himself, whose children the untouchables were. "I would much rather that Hinduism died," said Gandhi, "than that untouchability lived."

On September 15, 1932, three days before Gandhi was to begin his "fast unto death," Jawaharlal wrote to Indira: "I am shaken up completely and I know not what to do. . . . His picture comes before my eyes again and again—it was the last time I saw him, just over a year ago. . . . Shall I not see him again? And whom shall I go to when I am in doubt and require wise counsel, or am afflicted and in sorrow and need loving comfort? What shall we all do when our beloved chief who inspired us and led us has gone?" On September 18 Gandhi began his fast, and every pupil in Indira's entire school went on a twenty-four-hour sympathetic fast. Indira also took the concrete step of "adopting" one of the untouchable girls in the school as her own. Whether her Papu was destined to see Gandhi again or not, Indira certainly could, because Yeravda jail was on the outskirts of Poona, and she was still a free bird, not a jailbird like her Papu. So she gathered her three young cousins and all of them went to see Gandhi in prison. Talking with them nonchalantly, as if nothing were the matter at all, the fasting Mahatma feasted his eyes on his devoted disciple's daughter and telegraphed him: "Indu looked happy and in possession of more flesh."

Indira's seventy-five pounds of flesh was hardly considerable for her almost five-foot-tall frame. Although Indira was not miserable anymore, Jai Dordi remembers that her friend's big sad eyes and sunken cheeks were constant evidence that she was not really happy either. She was ever concerned about the fate of her parents, and Shanta Gandhi recalls how Indira dwelled dolefully on the sacrifices her family were called upon to make for the country. She was naturally delighted whenever her mother or grandmother visited her at school. They would always come laden with goodies—chocolates, biscuits, and fruit. They would obtain for her ready-made dresses. More often they would get only dress material, since she was a growing girl and measurements were apt to change rapidly. The material was invariably *khadi* or homespun but it was now coming in various pleasing colors and printed designs. If Indira was tired of wearing Western style dresses she would ask the tailor to make her Indian costumes—mostly *churidars* (tight-fitting jodhpurs) and *kurtas* (sheath-like upper garments).

Indira spent her happiest week in school when her father visited her in September 1933. Jawaharlal had just been released from prison and he came hurrying down to Poona to meet Mahatma Gandhi after his recent fast—the third in a year's time. The fast of September 1932 had ended after five days, with the British Government conceding his claim to treat the Hindus and untouchables as a single electorate, although the rest of the Communal Award still stood. Gandhi had undertaken a second fast of twenty-one days in May 1933 for the purpose of "self-purification," which he had observed to the end. Again, in September 1933, he had commenced a fast when the government refused to permit him to work from the prison for the welfare of the Harijans. He was so near death on the eighth day of the fast that he was released unconditionally.

Indira was delighted to meet her father, who had come with a trunkload of books and amusement kits. Jai Dordi remembers how the self-conscious father would squat on the floor and order the curious crowd of children to form a semicircle in front of him. There he would unwrap one of the kits and deftly display his skill in assembling a mechanical model. He would sit occasionally with Indira in one of her classes or meet with her teachers and exchange with them his educational views, not all of which the teachers considered sound. Indira's fleeting joy was shared by the juveniles of her school, who were proud to have in their midst a distinguished delinquent with a fine prison record. Mrs. Dordi recalls that the only thing which marred their happiness was the infestation of the school

grounds by hordes of uniformed and plainclothes men—a spectacle
to which Indira alone among the students was accustomed—who had
arrived to keep an eye on Jawaharlal's subversive activities in the
school. After seven hectic days he left and Indira took to her normal
routine.

But before the end of the year Poona was hit by a severe epidemic
of bubonic plague, and the school had to be shifted to Bombay. It
was renamed the Pupil's Own School, and was reopened early in
1934 in Ville Parle in suburban Bombay, after its formal inauguration
by the poetess and Nehru family friend, Mrs. Sarojini Naidu. In
April Indira finished her final examination and matriculated as a high
school graduate.

The three years of school had made Indira into a new person. The
Vakils—man and wife—were extraordinary individuals, and they influenced Indira profoundly, not by what they said—because they said
very little—but by what they did and how they lived. With his philosophical bent of mind, Jehangir Vakil encouraged his students to
question and probe and not merely accept truth at second hand. He
was an ardent socialist—not one of the armchair variety, but one who
lived his socialism. He owned no private property and gave of his all
to the community of children who were his charges. He spent all
his money to build up an excellent library and he introduced the
youngsters to the great seminal ideas which underlie man's civilization. They obtained much less from his lectures in the classroom
than they did by engaging in discussion with him at the dining table,
on evening walks, and in day-long excursions. Jehangir was an agnostic like Jawaharlal, and this suited Indira's own religious inclination.
She did not possess awareness enough to affirm a god whom she was
not presumptuous enough to deny. The door was always open and
the search was never abandoned.

Vakil was also a strict disciplinarian and character-builder. Indira
intensely disliked drinking milk and had never been overly fond of
eating breakfast. But with the principal at the table, she swallowed
every day mouthfuls of oranges, eggs, toast, butter, and jam, and
drained them down with a glass of milk. Indira would have loved to
eat Kashmiri rice every day, but all she was permitted was a once-

a-week ration of coarse parboiled rice from Kerala. Vakil taught his students never to become a slave of habit or a victim of the affections. He would ask his students which of their possessions they were most attached to. With hardly any possessions worth the name, they would mention a pillow or a pen or a dress or a fruit. But whatever the item was, Vakil would ask them to give it up, just to prove to themselves that they were masters of their own selves.

Years later, when Indira became Prime Minister, famine stalked the land and the people of the state of Kerala were short of rice. When she exhorted them to eat wheat or substitute something else for cereal, there was a hue and cry. She promptly gave up eating rice. The hard-boiled critics said her meager ration could hardly meet the staggering demand for rice in Kerala. Few people knew how much she loved rice, and almost all missed the point she was trying to make. You could live on any diet in an emergency, she was trying to say, because it was just a matter of one's simply willing so. That, at any rate, was what Vakil had drummed into her mind.

Coonverbai Vakil was actually many persons rolled into one— mother, teacher, nurse, administrator, social worker, and musician. Indira developed into an excellent housekeeper for her prime-minister father and a fine mother to her children largely because of Mrs. Vakil's training. Of this unassuming lady with a demonic drive and energy, Indira says, "She had a very great influence on me and it is really through her, I think, that I learned to work on the ground floor, so to speak." She recalls that before going to school in Poona, she had worked with her father and mother for the economically depressed in the countryside and the socially oppressed in the cities. But her parents were both political leaders on the top floor, not social workers on the ground floor. If Indira got a bird's-eye view from her parents, she got the worm's-eye view from Mrs. Vakil. However, the transition from the top floor to the ground floor was facilitated immensely by Indira's parents themselves. They insisted she receive no special treatment at school and she received none. Her teacher, Raghubhai Nayak, testifies that Indira moved with the bulk of lower-middle-class students in school as if she were one of them, displaying not the least trace of upper-class snobbery.

One of the abiding influences of Mrs. Vakil on Indira is to be seen in the loss of her self-consciousness and an accretion of her self-confidence. She thought less and less of herself and of her trials and reflected more and more on others and their tribulations. Like her mother, Indira possessed an innate sense of sympathy and concern for others. Jawaharlal also possessed it. But whereas he expressed it in intellectual terms, Kamala expressed it in human terms. Indira was more like her mother, and this instinct of hers was heightened by the influence of Mrs. Vakil.

Indira had been in the school for close to two years before Shanta Gandhi joined it. Shanta, who until this day continues to be an extraordinarily sensitive and perceptive human being, was a lost soul that Friday evening when she arrived at the Children's Own School. A meeting of the Sahitya Sabha was scheduled for the next morning, and Shanta's teacher asked her to go to the meeting hall and do *alpana*—the art of decorating the floor in pleasing patterns with colored liquids or powders. As her teacher walked away briskly, Shanta stood gaping, not knowing where to find the decorating materials. She felt a gentle tap on the shoulder and heard a warm voice volunteering to help. They were Indira's. Shanta Gandhi also reminisces about a fat schoolmate whose corpulence was caused by some glandular disorder. The poor girl was a target of everyone's missiles—verbal and concrete. Indira alone shielded her from both. The sixteen-year-old Indira who passed out of the portals of the Pupil's Own School was indeed a new person, more self-assured, self-possessed, and self-reliant than the one who entered through them three years earlier.

7

The College Years

INDIRA's last months at the Pupil's Own School in Bombay were hectic and tense. She had to catch up with her studies and be adequately prepared for the final-year high school examination. Shifting the school from Poona to Bombay entailed for the Vakils unforeseen expenditures for which money had to be found. Iagore's *Ritu Raj* was about to be performed for raising funds for the school, and Indira could not miss any of her dance rehearsals.

Tension was high during those weeks, but it was relieved over the weekends which she spent with Mrs. Hoshiben Captain, the wife of a wealthy Parsi and herself a well-known Congress Party worker in Bombay City. The Captains used to let Indira indulge in one of her special delights—swimming. They drove her to Juhu Beach—a winding seashore of white sand fringed by tall, verdant palm trees. After swimming in the clear-blue waters of the Arabian Sea and being carried on the crest of frothy waves which crashed on the belt of shifting sands, she returned from the weekends to school refreshed and reinvigorated.

When Jawaharlal came back to Anand Bhavan by the end of September 1933, after his meeting in Poona with Indira and Mahatma Gandhi, domestic affairs were awaiting his immediate attention. The long-neglected financial problem grew to staggering proportions and now seemed to defy any solution. The continual despoliation of movable property by the police had gone on for so long in Anand

Bhavan that the house was now bare and denuded. The last of the movable items, the family car, had also been attached in lieu of non-payment of fines. Ever since Motilal suspended his fabulous legal practice, there had been no income worth the name. The books which brought Jawaharlal great fame and sizable royalties were yet to be published or still to be written. While there was no income, there was also no manner of curtailing expenditure.

Happily, Krishna, Jawaharlal's younger sister, had been married in October 1933 in a brief civil ceremony without much fanfare, and one possible item of major expenditure was now out of the way. Jawaharlal and Kamala were content with the satisfaction of the simplest personal wants and they hardly needed any money for themselves. But Jawaharlal did not wish to bring any discomfort to his mother in the evening of her life, and she was used to a decent standard of living. She was bedridden and needed to be taken care of well. Kamala's health had shown no improvement since 1931, and a fresh expenditure for a new round of medical consultations loomed large from the ledger books. Jawaharlal also had at the back of his mind the desirability of sending Indira to Europe for her higher education, and some money had to be set apart for that purpose.

To tide over the immediate difficulties, Jawaharlal and Kamala decided to sell the jewelry, silver, and other valuable articles and personal effects. Carloads of odds and ends were also sold. It was with a very heavy heart that Kamala parted with her jewelry. Not that she wanted to have it herself. She had not worn it for over a dozen years, and it had lain idle in the safe-deposit vaults of the bank. But she was hoping to pass it on to Indira as her bequest, and it was this hope that was belied.

By the time these affairs were all settled it was January 1934. On the twenty-sixth of the month the country would celebrate Independence Day. Jawaharlal would surely address public meetings on that day, and as surely, if the past was any guide, he would be arrested. Since Kamala was far from well, it was necessary that the more important medical consultations should take place while her husband was still at liberty. On the fifteenth of the month Kamala and Jawaharlal left for Calcutta, where they stayed for three days.

While she underwent her medical examinations, he wasted no time addressing three public meetings.

Wife and husband went on from Calcutta to nearby Santiniketan, where they wanted to send their daughter for her higher studies. Jawaharlal was dead set against sending her to any of the conventional universities in India. Most of them, receiving as they did government grants, were official and semiofficial institutions. Explaining his dislike of these institutions, Jawaharlal wrote later in his autobiography: "The whole atmosphere that envelops them is official, oppressive and authoritarian. They have no doubt produced fine men and women in the past, and they will continue to do so. But these few exceptions cannot save the universities from the charge of suppressing and deadening the fine instincts of youth." Jawaharlal and Kamala therefore decided on sending Indira to Santiniketan, although they knew that "in some ways it was not so up to date and well-equipped as the other universities."

When Jawaharlal returned to Anand Bhavan, he was confronted with a warrant of arrest from the Calcutta police for the three speeches he had made there on his brief sojourn. He was sentenced on February 16 to two years' imprisonment and put in the Alipore Central Jail.

As he was being taken to jail, Jawaharlal dashed off a telegram to Indira: "Going to the other home." This was sad news to a girl who had hoped to go to her parental home and spend her first summer vacation in three years with her father. Kamala's condition cried for immediate attention, and now that her husband was in jail in Calcutta, and many eminent doctors too were in that city, she decided to move to Calcutta.

Indira's state of mind was thus not very different from what it had been three years ago when she joined the school in Poona. Her mother then was lying ill in Bombay and her father was in the Dehra Dun jail. Her mother now was once again ill, although in another metropolis, and her father was once again languishing in prison, although a different one. On that last school day in April when Indira left there was naturally a great outpouring of sympathy for her from the entire student body. Practically all the students and some of their parents traveled with her on the suburban train from Ville Parle to Victoria Terminus, from where she would catch the cross-country express train to Calcutta, to bid good-bye to her. They all sang old songs, spoke nostalgically of old times, and then departed, their tears mingling with laughter.

In an article she wrote many years later Indira admitted with candor that she had often wished she were a boy. This was certainly understandable, given the anxiety and uncertainty of her life. She might well have felt that in a man's world she could have faced her difficulties with greater confidence if she herself had been a boy. Happily, she says, "at sixteen the delight of being a woman began to unfold itself, and almost overnight the long-legged tomboy in frocks changed into a sari-clad young lady." But the only delight she could look forward to in Calcutta was to be with her ailing mother and "to share with her the unsatisfactory but greatly treasured twenty-minute fortnightly interviews" with her father in Alipore jail. For the first time in her life, the interviews held some meaning for her. Hitherto she had gone tagging along to jail almost in the manner in which a puppy dog would, standing there during the interview wagging its tail silently, or whining occasionally for recognition, periodically petted but always taken for granted. But not anymore.

She was now a person, an entity, full of eager questions and ready responses. And her father treated her as such. Even three years earlier, when the family had been holidaying in Ceylon, Jawaharlal had written to his younger sister, Krishna: "Kamala has often been taken for my daughter. But what do you say to Indu being taken for the mother! This has happened repeatedly." In 1934 the question of a mistaken identity was a recurring one. Once the very picture of healthful vitality, the emaciated Kamala was now a pale shadow of her former self. Indira, in contrast, was filling out, and her angularities were being rounded off. The two of them, looking very like sisters, would spend many hours every day in the Ramakrishna *Math*—a monastery established in the name of the nineteenth-century Bengali saint, Ramakrishna.

Kamala's end was not far, and she had had a premonition of it earlier when Jawaharlal was presented with the warrant of arrest in

Anand Bhavan. She had gone upstairs to collect some clothes for him, and he followed her to say good-bye, and then something very unexpected happened. Writing about it later, he recapitulates the scene: "Suddenly she clung to me and, fainting, collapsed. This was unusual for her as we had trained ourselves to take this jail-going lightly and cheerfully and to make as little fuss about it as possible." She still took jail-going lightly and his departure to prison cheerfully. But it was about her own departure from all that is terrestrial that she wanted to make as little fuss as possible. Sitting for hours on end in the *Math* "peacefully by the riverside," says Indira, "a new world of thought and experience opened out to me." Kamala too must have observed the sluggish flow of the river Hooghly which, not far from there, merged into the illimitable ocean, and contemplated the parallel it held for her.

By the end of June Indira was in Visva-Bharati, the university which Rabindranath Tagore had formally inaugurated in 1921 at Santiniketan. It had a fascinating history, and that was one of the factors which influenced Jawaharlal's and Kamala's decision to send Indira there. Soon after Rabindranath's birth, his father, Debendranath—who was called *Maharshi* (the great sage) because of the spiritual merit he was reputed to have acquired—happened to visit a friend whose country estate was situated about a hundred miles west of Calcutta. Krishna Kripalani, the distinguished biographer of Rabindranath, tells us what transpired on that visit:

> Getting down at Bolpur which was then, as it still is, the nearest railway station, he proceeded by palanquin and as the sun was about to set found himself in an open plain bereft of vegetation, stretching to the western horizon with nothing to break the view of the setting sun except a thin row of wild palms lining the horizon. Such open stretches are not common in Bengal where the characteristic landscape is one of luxuriant vegetation. The Maharshi was enchanted and sat down for his usual evening meditation under a pair of *chhatim* trees. When he rose from his meditation he had already made up his mind that the place would be his. He lost no time in negotiating for its purchase and later built a house and laid

out a garden and named the place Santiniketan, which literally means an abode of peace.

The two ancient *chhatim* trees still stand side by side, enclosed by a railing of red sandstone. Beneath them is a stone tablet on which is inscribed in Bengali the quintessence of the Maharshi's faith:

> He is the refuge of my life
> The joy of my heart
> The peace of my soul.

In ancient India, a good bit of utilitarian education, apart from spiritual instruction, was imparted in the *ashrams* (hermitages). One, the Bhardwaj Ashram of hoary antiquity, was just across Anand Bhavan in Allahabad. Rabindranath's imagination dwelled on an idealized image of those *ashrams* and he desired duplicating one, where teachers lived with the pupils and demonstrated through practice rather than mere precept the pleasures of simple living and the virtues of high thinking.

Tagore discovered that the ancient Indian system of education was decadent if not dead, and the modern English system was soulless and mechanical. He charged that the "educational institutions in our country are India's alms-bowl of knowledge; they lower our national self-respect; they encourage us to make a foolish display of decorations made of borrowed feathers." He also warned that "if the whole world grows at last into an exaggerated West, then such an illimitable parody of the modern age will die, crushed beneath its own absurdity." Tagore was bent upon synthesizing the ancient and the modern, the Eastern and the Western in the new school he established at Santiniketan at the end of 1901. He had to sell his house and a part of his library to find the money to run the school, while his wife gladly parted with her jewelry. It was the couple's devotion to the young and their spirit of self-sacrifice which the Vakils admired while they were at Santiniketan, later to emulate that example in Poona.

Tagore had a cogently argued educational theory. He agreed basically with ancient Indian philosophy "which speaks of fulfillment through a harmony with all things." Such a harmony has "the effect of arousing a great desire in us to seek our freedom." For the achievement of perfect freedom "we have to be vitally savage and mentally civilised; we should have the gift to be natural with Nature and humane with human society." That is why classes at Santiniketan were held in the open, under the trees, and the students were encouraged to study and love nature in its changing moods and phases.

Tagore also believed that the child learns with his limbs and his senses long before he learns with his brains. Children at Santiniketan were therefore encouraged to do things for themselves. It was this idea and practice of teaching through some form of activity or craft which was first developed at Santiniketan that was later adopted by Mahatma Gandhi in his system of Basic Education.

After a tour of the United States Tagore wished to upgrade his little school at Santiniketan to a university. For its motto the poet selected an ancient Sanskrit verse, *Yatra visvam bhavati eka-nidam* ("Where the whole world meets in one nest"). Visva-Bharati literally is a world university.

Tagore's name was a hallowed one in all of India, and it was with some trepidation that Indira arrived at Santiniketan, only to discover that a pleasant surprise was in store for her. What had been a wasteland of barren soil when it was first acquired was now a miniature garden, thanks to the annual tree-planting festival which Tagore had initiated in 1928. The sylvan setting and the cloistered silence of the place almost transformed her into a new being. "I had never been in a quiet place before," Indira explains. "You know, I had always been in crowds and noise and arrests. And this was also partly the reason for the considerable bitterness in me. It was too much for a small child to have the police or the military coming into the house at all hours of the day and night for removing the carpets, carrying off the silver, taking away the car. I built up a lot of hatred and bitterness inside me, and I think it was really at Santiniketan that I washed it out."

There was one other reason for her newfound happiness, says Indira. "For the first time, I was amongst people of my own age. You know, before that I was always with adults, except when I was at school. But even at school, I was the oldest person." However sound Jawaharlal's theories of education may or may not have been, there is no question that Motilal had the much sounder practical sense. He had defended his action in sending his granddaughter to St. Cecilia's school purely on the ground that she would have companions of her own age. He was eminently right. For even in the Children's Own School in Poona Indira had been thoroughly lost. It was essentially a kindergarten school which suddenly experienced an influx of older children of imprisoned political leaders and had to hold improvised upper-grade classes for their convenience. Being much younger than her teachers and much older than the other students, she felt completely out of place in Poona. But in Sri Bhavan Ashram—as the girls' dormitory of Santiniketan was called—living, studying, and playing with students of her own age was a wholly novel and pleasurable experience.

The daily routine at Santiniketan, however, was a rigorous one, although this was nothing new to a girl who at the age of four had been introduced to the discipline of Mahatma Gandhi's Sabarmati Ashram. The school bell rang at four thirty in the morning. After making the beds and washing and bathing themselves, the girls had to sweep and scrub floors, cook and serve themselves breakfast, then do the dishes, and be ready at 6:30 A.M. All the inmates of the *ashram*, young and old, joined in congregation on the open lawns in front of the school and sang a hymn in chorus. There were no compulsory prayers, but twice a day, at sunrise and sunset, the students sat in silent meditation. They were free to meditate or not, but the silence was obligatory.

At seven in the morning began Indira's classes in liberal arts. The greatest pleasure which she derived at Santiniketan was from spending a few engrossing hours everyday in Kala Bhavan, an art center which was then under the directorship of the distinguished painter Nandalal Bose. Indira's great passion during those days was Indian classical dance of the Manipuri School, the fluid style and graceful undulations of which were perfected centuries ago in the easternmost part of India, Manipur.

But no sooner had she become used to her unbelievably happy surroundings than domestic catastrophe beckoned her home. Her father, who had always taken prison days in his stride, was losing weight alarmingly in the Alipore jail. In the month of May he was transferred to the Dehra Dun jail, and the mountain air and the onset of the monsoon cheered him a little. But inwardly he was extremely unhappy. His knowledge that Kamala was again in the grip of her old disease and his inability to be of any service to her, combined with the suspicion that his presence by her side might have made a difference, oppressed him a great deal. It was partly to mitigate this suffering by getting involved in some purposive endeavor that in June 1934 he began writing his autobiography. Toward the end of July, Kamala's condition deteriorated rapidly and Jawaharlal was rushed under police escort to Anand Bhavan.

From the eastern extremity of the country Indira was summoned, on the suspicion that these might be Kamala's last days. To Jawaharlal, who had come from his solitary confinement in prison, and to Indira, who had returned from her nest of song and dance, the atmosphere of crowded Anand Bhavan with its doctors, nurses, and anxious relatives was unbearable. But even more intolerable was the obsession that Kamala might leave them. However, the presence of her husband and daughter somewhat revived Kamala and she showed signs of slight improvement. Jawaharlal was now returned to Naini prison in Allahabad, while Indira brooded her way back to Santiniketan.

The transition from the purely political animal, that young Indira up to this point had been, to a new and many-sided personality was now assured. In his earlier years, Tagore had traveled a great deal both in India and abroad, which meant being away from Santiniketan for long stretches of time. Luckily for Indira, he was well past three score and ten and could not countenance easily the strain of prolonged travel, and she saw more of him than did other students in the past. The poet-philosopher was easily accessible most of the time. His tall and majestic figure in flowing robes could be seen flitting past the dark silhouettes of groves at dawn or on moonlit nights. *Gurudev*—god in the person of the teacher—is how he was addressed reverentially not only by his students but by all his countrymen, for he was indeed a stern remonstrator if he thought his nation was being wayward or mankind errant.

Always painfully shy with strangers, Indira was at first quite overawed by Tagore's towering presence. He would sometimes address the school congregation, comment upon some transitory development of the week or enlarge upon one of man's perennial concerns. In the evening, after he had had his afternoon tea, Tagore would sit alone in quiet on his terrace. Students venturing out on an evening walk had to pass by his quarters. Sometimes they would drop in and get him to talk. "Never would I have dared to encroach upon his time," recalls Indira, "had he himself not complained of negligence." In spite of the impression of lofty aloofness which he gave, avers Indira, "he kept a close watch on all of us and seemed to be aware of all the crosscurrents in the institution." Of the time she spent with him she reminisces nostalgically: "Many were the evenings when a small group of us sat at his feet and talked on various subjects, or silently watched him paint. Often he would recite or read aloud. These were moments of serene joy, memories to cherish."

In distant Allahabad domestic events were heading to a crisis again. Early in October, when Jawaharlal was taken home by prison officials, he found Kamala in a daze with a high temperature. He immediately had arrangements made for having her moved to a sanatorium in Bhowali, a health resort nestling high up in the foothills of the Himalayas. Jawaharlal was also moved up from Naini prison to a nearby jail in Almora district so that he could visit Kamala once every three weeks. His mother's ailment grew worse in the meanwhile, and she was taken to Bombay for treatment. There, in the middle of January 1935, she suddenly had a stroke of paralysis. There was talk of Jawaharlal's being taken to a prison in Bombay so that he could be by his mother's deathbed. A seesawing fortune raised Jawaharlal's mother's hopes but plummeted his wife's. In May 1935 the doctors advised that Kamala be taken from Bhowali to Europe for further treatment. However, since His Majesty's government was reluctant to part company with its illustrious prisoner, Indira had to be summoned from Santiniketan to accompany her mother to Europe.

The feelings of all Santiniketan's inmates were expressed by Tagore in his letter to Jawaharlal:

> It is with a heavy heart we bade farewell to Indira, for she was such an asset in our place. I have watched her very closely and have felt admiration for the way you have brought her up. Her teachers, all in one voice, praise her and I know she is extremely popular with the students. I only hope things will turn for the better and she will soon return here and get back to her studies.

The poet's hope was belied, but Indira took away from Santiniketan, even after that short stay of nine months, a lasting legacy. Krishna Kripalani, who taught Indira literature at Santiniketan, and later wrote his fine biography of Tagore, says that the poet-philosopher's greatest contribution to his country was his message of humanism and internationalism. He adds, however, that this message was preached equally eloquently by Jawaharlal, so that Indira drank at the fountain of thought of two great world citizens of India in the twentieth century. But there was one thing that Tagore alone could have given Indira: a harmonious conception of life and a wholesome concern for the development of the whole man. If Indira acquired in Anand Bhavan a passion for politics, she developed at Santiniketan a passion for life in all its multiplicity. She confirms this view with a confession: "I had always regarded poetry as something separate from life; Tagore showed that all the arts were integrated." She says she was tightly bundled up and her emotions bottled up before she went to Santiniketan. But there she opened out. As she puts it: "I think it was a sort of unfolding of my personality, and I was very deeply influenced by Gurudev. In fact, I would say he completely changed my life."

Indira took her mother to a sanatorium in Badenweiler in the Black Forest of Germany. The doctor's medicines and her own ministrations had little effect on Kamala, whose condition grew progressively worse. Indira cabled her father late in August about her mother's worsening condition, and the prison authorities released him suddenly on September 4. He took a plane immediately and joined his wife and daughter at Badenweiler on the ninth. Jawaharlal's presence had a temporary stabilizing effect on Kamala, and her condition took a turn for the better. Indira and her father even managed a short trip to England. As Christmas approached, Kamala suffered another marked deterioration but fought it off successfully. Jawaharlal managed one more side trip to Paris and London after Christmas.

At the end of January 1936, Kamala was removed to another sanatorium in Lausanne and Indira was admitted to school in nearby Bex. One more month passed. On the morning of February 28, Kamala breathed her last in the presence of her daughter, husband, and a relative and physician, Dr. M. Atal. A few friends of the family arrived from neighboring towns in Switzerland and the body was taken to a crematorium in Lausanne. Father and daughter collected the ashes in a small urn and retired to Montreux to spend a few quiet days together before parting their ways.

On one of his visits to England before Kamala's death, Jawaharlal had made arrangements for Indira to continue her education at Oxford. Landing in England, the first hurdle which Indira had to clear was the entrance examination in order to become eligible for admission to the university. One of the compulsory subjects she had to take for this qualifying examination was Latin—a language for which Indira could whip up no more enthusiasm than she had been able to show in her Poona school for that other "dead language," Sanskrit. While she was struggling on her own, she accidentally met the principal of a girl's school in Badminton, who said imperiously: "Well, in half an hour I am going back to the school. Why don't you come with me?" Indira rushed to pick up her bags and scurried after the principal.

Her stay in Badminton was all to the good, and on her return she passed the entrance examination and was admitted to Somerville College, Oxford. Her major interest was in History, Economics, and Political Science. However, she evinced great enthusiasm for "Modern Greats," a composite course in the development of human thought. As in the past, she supplemented all this by a good bit of independent reading. She enrolled as a member of the Left Book

Club, something of a misnomer because it attracted members not so much with Leftist sympathies as with empty wallets. The club published inexpensive editions of a number of excellent works which Indira lapped up eagerly.

Indira's years in England were most eventful, politically speaking. There was the civil war in Spain, the formation of the Axis, the humiliation at Munich, and the outbreak of the Second World War, during the course of which Indira returned to India. Above all, there was the question of Indian independence. Being both by nature and nurture a political animal, Indira found in these issues a good amount of ammunition to feed her political artillery, which she trained against the enemy camp. She was actively involved with an organization which enrolled volunteers for the International Brigade that was fighting for Republican Spain—a logical step for a veteran of the Monkey Brigade to take.

Shanta Gandhi, Indira's old schoolmate from Poona, was also in England at the time. In fact, the two of them had shared an attic apartment before Indira left for the school in Badminton. Shanta, who was an accomplished dancer, used to perform for the "Aid Spain Committee" to raise funds, while Indira would speak occasionally from the platform. Once she offered, on an impulse, her black *meenakari* bracelet to be auctioned for raising funds for Spanish relief. Shanta recalls that it fetched fifty pounds from an enthusiastic buyer. Dr. M. Atal, the Nehru family friend and physician who was with Kamala to the very end, was also in London at the time and was preparing to join an ambulance unit for the Spanish Republicans. He finally ended up with taking an ambulance unit to China, where he lost his life. Indira herself was extremely active in the China Committee and its numerous programs to aid beleaguered China in the Sino-Japanese war.

Most Indian students at the time became involved one way or the other in domestic British politics, and so did Indira. Given the predispositions of the two main political parties toward the issue of Indian independence, it was largely Labour that invited the sympathy of the Indian student in England. Indira was not a member of the Labour Party as such but of its youth movement. Its main activity was to sponsor speakers to acquaint young men and women with Labour's policies and principles. There was close liaison between the Labour Party and the India League in London, which was then headed by Mr. V. K. Krishna Menon. Menon was later to be rewarded by Prime Minister Jawaharlal Nehru with the portfolio of Defense in independent India—in recognition of his long service in the cause of Indian freedom and the battles he had fought in England single-handed in spite of great personal privation. Indira, along with most other Indian students, volunteered to work for Menon's India League during her spare time.

Although politics coursed through her veins, Indira was never obsessed by it—at least not after her coming under the influence of Tagore. She gave of herself liberally to numerous political causes, including that of Indian independence, but she never flaunted any kind of self-righteous patriotism or looked askance at those whose absorbing interests were mainly nonpolitical. Both Jawaharlal and Mahatma Gandhi had argued that Indians must give up all professions, including study, in favor of the sole occupation of jail-going until independence was achieved. Tagore decried the neglect of other fields and harped on the pursuit of excellence in all of man's endeavors. Indira shared this view of Tagore's. Muriel Wasi, another Indian girl studying at Cambridge at the time, recalls that Indira was an extremely fair-minded person who never belabored others for not taking part in politics, although she was proud of the sacrifices her own family was making for India's freedom.

Tagore had kindled many another craving for self-fulfillment in Indira's unfolding personality. Shanta Gandhi remembers well how she and Indira used to save up their money to buy inexpensive seats for opera, ballet, and the theater. Once in a while, when the temptations of the palate could not be resisted, they would forego aesthetic enjoyment for gastronomic satisfaction and enjoy a meal in an Indian restaurant in Piccadilly. It was on one of these occasions that Indira's friends dared her to eat in the Indian style, using her fingers, which she did without batting an eye and without bothering about the offense it might give to English squeamishness concerning table manners. Finally, Indira always found time for her outdoor interests

—swimming, skiing, mountain climbing—and Shanta Gandhi recalls that it was Indira who took her to the German-speaking part of Switzerland and gave her the first unforgettable glimpse of the glistening white snow.

In the four years which Indira spent in England she never felt as lonely as her father had. For one thing, she was a little older than Jawaharlal had been when he first went to Harrow. For another, there were many more Indian students in England in her time than in her father's. Finally, she was extremely fortunate in feeling free to call upon the large circle of distinguished friends her father had made in England. "I was especially privileged," she says, "that my father was friendly to and known and loved by such a wide variety of people—scientists, artists, literary people—in many countries abroad, and because of him I was able to meet them and know them also." Indira was constantly invited to lunch or dinner at their homes, and she felt relaxed in their company because they were friends of India and her cause.

Edward Thompson, poet, critic and man of letters, had assured Jawaharlal: "You Nehrus have been very lucky in many ways, and lucky most of all in your charming and splendid women. . . . If she [Indira] will regard my wife and myself as friends we shall feel honoured." Indira did visit the Thompsons and the friendship flourished. Ernst Toller, the sensitive German-Jewish poet, whom Indira had met on her first European visit in 1927, and his wife Christianne had been hounded out of Nazi Germany, and they were now in England. Indira liked to visit them, and after one of her visits Christianne wrote to Jawaharlal: "Yesterday your daughter Indira came to us for lunch. . . . I only want to tell you how delighted I was to have met her. Not only that she is so beautiful, but so pure which makes one feel very happy and very little against [sic]. She seemed to me like a little flower which the wind might blow away so easily, but I think she is not afraid of the wind."

The list of people whom Indira visited either by herself or in the company of her father when he came to England in 1938 reads like a catalog of celebrities. There were the well-known Labourites—Ellen Wilkinson, Aneurin Bevan and his wife Jennie Lee, John Strachey,

Herbert Morrison, Reginald Sorensen, Sir Stafford Cripps. There were other visits of a nonpolitical nature to the Very Reverend Hewlett Johnson, Dean of Canterbury, the English writer H. N. Brailsford, and the famous American Negro singer Paul Robeson and his wife.

Very occasionally she would visit someone in the enemy camp—but much against her will. She recalls one such incident. Jawaharlal had sailed from Bombay to Genoa in June 1938. From there he proceeded to Marseilles and by land route to Barcelona to have a first-hand acquaintance with the Spanish Civil War. When Jawaharlal reached England, he had a standing invitation from Lord Lothian, the well-known Conservative leader. Indira recalls that Lord Lothian had promised her and her father many alluring attractions over a weekend visit to Aylsham in Norfolk. Blickling Hall, where Lord Lothian lived, was almost the most beautiful Elizabethan house and garden in England. He had invited Lady Astor and others of the so-called Cliveden set to interest and amuse the Nehrus, and also General Ironside, who was, true to his name, one of the best soldiers in England.

"I was very violently opposed to the Tories at that time," says Indira, and so she had declined Lord Lothian's invitation on the pretext that she had a prior engagement. "No, this is very wrong," her father said in disagreement, and added: "You should go." Indira retorted: "I know I am going to lose my temper there and I am not going," to which her father countered, "You must control your temper and learn to mix with all kinds of people, so that you get to know how these people think." Meanwhile, Lord Lothian had written to Indira again, renewing his invitation and asking her to put off her previous engagement for another day, which she reluctantly agreed to do. As she puts it: "And so, much against my grain I did finally go, but in a very fighting mood."

Disagreements, however, were not reserved only for political opponents. Indira wanted to accompany her father on his European tour of 1938. "Munich" was soon to be in the making, and Jawaharlal wrote later of the way he "went to Czechoslovakia and watched at close quarters the difficult and intricate game of how to betray your friend, and the cause you are supposed to stand for, on the highest moral grounds." The itinerary appeared interesting and so Indira told her father she would go along with him. However, Harold Laski, the high priest of British socialism and the indoctrinator of many a doctrinaire Indian socialist got wind of Indira's intention and objected vehemently: "Look, you're just developing your personality, and if you tag along with your father, you'll just become an appendage. So you'd better not go with him. You must now strike out on your own." Little did Laski know he was talking to someone who did not want to be her master's echo any more than she wanted to be her father's appendage. Says Indira: "I listened very attentively, but of course I went along with my father! And Laski was very angry. He complained he had given a lot of time to me and I just didn't take his advice." Did he make her read any of his classics, such as *The Grammar of Politics?* "Well," she asserted, "I read them. He didn't make me read them!"

Indira's stay in England also did not make her feel lonesome because she had two opportunities to visit home in those four years. Her father could return to India only once during his seven years in England. Indira was forced to return to Bombay in the summer of 1937 for a minor operation. Again, since she had accompanied her father all the way from London to Cairo on his European tour of 1938, he suggested that she come home for a holiday, so Indira spent the winter months of 1938 in India. This November she received the best birthday gift of her lifetime. She was twenty-one and the Indian National Congress was delighted to enroll her as a full-fledged member. Her visit to Anand Bhavan made her grandmother happy; it was the last time she would see her.

Indira left for Oxford in March 1939. The year was an unlucky one for her and she was badly stricken. Her aunt, Mrs. Sheila Kaul, who was in England at the time, recalls that Indira had gone hiking into the woods in Penn Village. It rained heavily and she was completely drenched, catching a nasty cold soon afterward. She was admitted to Brentford Cottage Hospital in Middlesex, where it was diagnosed that she had developed pleurisy. Dr. P. C. Bhandari, a friend of the family and advisor to the Ministry of Health in England, looked after her. She improved gradually, and by December Edward Thompson could report to Jawaharlal: "I have seen Indu. She looks well, and she *is* well. She is thin, of course, and there seems no doubt that just now she is what used to be called 'delicate' and will have to go carefully. But she is wiry underneath, and when she is past these difficult days that end adolescence she will pull into real strength." Thompson confirmed what Indira herself had reported to her father in a cable she sent him on his birthday a fortnight earlier— that for the previous nineteen days she had had no temperature, that the inflammation had subsided, and that she had gained five pounds.

In the middle of December Indira went to Leysin in Switzerland to recoup her health. In a very short time the change of air helped her immensely. Before the first week of January 1940 was over, Jawaharlal was writing to Thompson: "I have heard from Indira from Leysin. She seems to be happy there and likes the place. The doctor has told her that he proposes to transform her into a Diana in the course of three months. Naturally this has cheered her up immensely."

By November 1940 she was well enough to move. Neutral Switzerland was a haven of refuge in the armed camp of Europe. But even Swiss neutrality was entirely at Hitler's mercy, and prudence demanded that Indira leave as soon as possible. From Geneva she traveled to Marseilles and from there flew to Barcelona, Lisbon, and London, stranded at each place for a few days in order to obtain a connecting flight. From war-ravaged Spain to London during the blitz was indeed like jumping from the frying pan into the fire. Undaunted, she enrolled as a volunteer for the Red Cross and drove an ambulance right through Hitler's raids.

During her stay at Oxford, a new constitution had gone into effect in India. The Government of India Act which the British Parliament passed in 1935 came into operation in 1937. It gave India a federal form of government. Elections were held, and the Indian National Congress, which swept the polls in eight provinces, formed the new provincial governments. Congress Party members who had been in jail not long ago were now holding ministerial positions. Theoretically at least, the British governors of the various provinces were responsible to the elected legislatures in specified subjects.

Unfortunately, this encouraging experiment in self-government came to an abrupt end. On September 3, 1939, when His Britannic Majesty's government declared war against Germany, it was announced that India was also automatically at war with Germany. The Indian National Congress was quite willing to fight Nazi Germany to save the democracies of the world. But the Congress insisted that Indians must first enjoy democracy before they fight for it. It also maintained that the unilateral declaration of war by Britain without consulting the wishes of the elected representatives of the Indian people was an affront to Indian democracy. In October 1939 the Congress ministries in all the provinces resigned. Individual Congress members started offering *Satyagraha,* and Jawaharlal was among the very first to return to jail.

Indira on her part felt that political developments at home should be given precedence in any calculation of her future course of action. The purpose for which she had come to England—higher education—was now being jeopardized by the steady extension of war. And even if that purpose still stood a fair chance of achievement, Indira had very little interest left in it. She had never been taught to regard formal education highly. And if, as Robert Louis Stevenson said, a year of downright loitering is an essential element of liberal education, Indira deserved to be graduated, for she had had four such years! These years in England also stood witness to the steady flowering of her romantic love. She had come to understand and admire her future husband, who had been passionately fond of her for some years past. Both of them felt that their salad days now ought to be steadied, and were seriously studying the prospect of matrimony. Boarding a steamer in London, the two of them sailed around the Cape of Good Hope, to avoid German submarines in the Mediterranean, and reached Bombay in March 1941.

8

Love and Marriage

On Thursday, March 26, 1942, Indira Nehru wed Feroze Gandhi. The marriage of the very personable daughter of the most popular leader of the country should have produced unmixed joy. But it actually elicited a mixed reaction both in the family and in the nation.

Feroze was the youngest of five children born to a middle-class family of the Parsi community in Bombay. The Parsis are so called because they originally came to Persia, from where they fled in the eighth century after that country had been invaded by the Arabs. The first wave of Parsi immigrants landed on the west coast of India in 706 A.D. in what is now the state of Gujarat. They took to the local language, Gujarati, which they speak to this day. The Hindu ruler of the region at the time received them warmly and assured them freedom of worship. But although the Parsis continued to follow the teachings of Zoroaster in matters of religion, they became acclimatized to Indian culture in their manner of living.

In the course of time the Parsis branched out to several urban centers in India. Their community in Bombay, which dates from 1640, is the largest and most flourishing in India. Highly enterprising and sagacious, the Parsis took to business of various kinds and proved very successful. The founder of the first steel mill in India, Jamsetji Nusserwanji Tata, who was later knighted by the British monarch, was a Parsi. Since then the House of Tata has expanded consistently into several industries and now holds the preeminent place in the sphere of private enterprise in India.

Extraordinarily versatile as the Parsis are, they entered other fields also, and in proportion to their miniscule population have produced an astounding number of eminent men. Dadabhai Naoroji, who wrote a masterly indictment of the British performance, entitled *Poverty and un-British Rule in India,* was one of the earliest presidents of the Indian National Congress. Another Parsi, Sir Pherozeshah Mehta, a towering liberal politician of Bombay, was also elected president of the Congress.

Dr. Homi J. Bhabha, who died in an air crash almost at the same time Mrs. Indira Gandhi became Prime Minister, was one of the world's well-known nuclear physicists and was primarily responsible for making India a leading developer of atomic energy for peaceful uses in the underdeveloped world. Minoo R. Masani, a brilliant Parliamentarian, is one of the founders of the Swatantra (Freedom) Party, which is now the largest opposition party in the Indian parliament. Another Parsi prodigy whom the Western world has come to know well and admire is the young music conductor, Zubin Mehta. Parsi women have always enjoyed equality with their men. Since the first principle of their religion is benevolence, Parsi men donate liberally to many worthy causes and their women turn out to be energetic social workers.

Indira's husband, Feroze, was born on September 12, 1912, to Jehangir Fardoonji and Rattimai Gandhi. Although Parsi first names are generally Persian and their last names Indian, they belong neither to the Muslims nor to the Hindus, unless related by marriage. The Parsi Gandhis were not related to the Hindu family of Mahatma Gandhi. Jehangir was a marine engineer and was the first Parsi to be appointed warrant engineer by the King's Commission during World War I. With the outbreak of war, Jehangir had to hop with his naval craft from one Indian coastal city to another. So in 1914 he sent his children away to Allahabad to be taken care of by their aunt, Dr. S. H. Commissariat, the first Parsi woman to become fellow of the Royal College of Surgeons. The five Gandhi children lived with their aunt in the spacious quarters allotted to her in the Lady Dufferin Hospital in Allahabad.

Since their aunt was away at work most of the day, the care of two-year-old Feroze fell to the eldest children, Tehmina the daughter, and Faredun the son. They could not take this onerous task for longer than two years. Feroze was a devilishly mischievous tot, and at four he was put into the boardinghouse of a girls' school, where he stayed until he was seven. He was then brought home to live, and was admitted to the Anglo-Vernacular School in the city. Tehmina and Faredun still found the lad's restless energy unmanageable and later let him join the Boy Scouts. Twelve-year-old Feroze joined the troop of Scoutmaster Keshav Dev Malaviya, who was later to become the Minister for Oil, Mines, and Fuel in Jawaharlal Nehru's Cabinet. Feroze was also given a bicycle so that he could roam the streets and get rid of his excess energy. At fifteen he matriculated from the Anglo-Vernacular school and then joined Allahabad's Ewing Christian College.

The next year, when he was sixteen, an incident occurred which was to change his life completely. It was 1928, the year of mass demonstrations, when the Simon Seven visited India and were greeted with black flags and the annoying slogan, "Simon Go Back." Feroze was terribly amused one day by these marching and shouting demonstrators, and as he stood silently by the sidewalk with his bicycle, the police swooped down on them all and gave the innocent bystander also a severe thrashing. When he revealed his identity, the police escorted Feroze home and reprimanded his aunt, a government employee, for permitting her young nephew to join subversive elements. At home Feroze received one more thrashing at the hands of his brother Faredun, but the Empire could not prevent the loss of yet another loyal subject to the nationalist movement.

The sensitive lad was now full of tempestuous rage and was bent upon teaching His Majesty's police a lesson. Ewing Christian College saw less and less of Feroze and the police saw more and more of him. Since Dr. Commissariat was a very respected and law-abiding citizen of Allahabad, the police were hesitant to beat up her young nephew. They would take him home handcuffed only to release him there and register another warning with his nervous aunt. At home, Faredun, who is even now a somewhat excitable lawyer in the High Court of Allahabad, took on the role of policeman and beat up his younger brother mercilessly.

Reminiscing about these beatings, Faredun says he was so filled with tender compassion after each flagellation of Feroze that he himself always burst out into tears. Feroze would quietly disappear again, very often to the house of Mrs. Uma Nehru, the wife of a cousin of Jawaharlal's, who gave solace and comfort to the emotionally orphaned boy. When asked what it was that must have driven Feroze to the point of no return, Faredun says, "Well, it couldn't have been love of country. Patriotism and sacrifice are adult impulses, and Feroze was just a teen-age kid. I think it was circumstances and personalities. He was wronged by the police, and Feroze, being a very determined sort of fellow, was out to defy them. Then, of course, he had this extraordinary fascination for the Nehrus. He hero-worshiped them."

When Faredun's intimidation failed to produce the intended effect, Tehmina tried her entreaties. She pleaded with Feroze to calculate the consequences to the family of his persistence with subversive activities. They were now living in a fine house at 16 Stanley Road. Their aunt was a well-paid government employee who was certain to be penalized for his indiscretion. Tehmina was just about to qualify for her Master's degree in education, and Faredun was still studying for his law degree; both of them could be disqualified because of Feroze's mulish obstinacy. All of Tehmina's entreaties fell on deaf ears and she met with no greater measure of success than had Faredun. She then tried hiding away Feroze's clothes and shoes to prevent him from getting out of the house, but he only walked out barefoot and in his underclothes.

Feroze had now become a frequent visitor to Anand Bhavan. Rallies, demonstrations, and picketing had become the staple of his political activity, and in 1930, when he was still a teen-ager, he was sentenced to imprisonment. When Motilal died in February 1931, Anand Bhavan was full of political leaders from all over India, including Mahatma Gandhi. Feroze's mother, Rattimai, made one last desperate attempt to disentangle her son from the politics of sub-version. She approached the Mahatma directly and begged him to advise her son to stop his erring ways and take to his studies seriously. Speaking in his native Gujarati, which is also the language of the Parsis, the Mahatma said to her: "Sister, in the future no one in India will ask whether your son has a B.A. or M.A. degree. They would only like to know how many times he has courted imprisonment. Give me seven boys like Feroze and I shall achieve Swaraj [independence] in seven days. Don't be afraid for Feroze's safety. Not a hair of his will be touched. I assume personal responsibility for him."

Assured of the support of no less a person than the Mahatma, Feroze was now emboldened to do as he pleased. He became an active worker in the Allahabad City Congress Committee and a lieutenant of Mr. K. D. Malaviya, his former Scoutmaster. In 1931 Feroze organized, with a meticulous eye for the smallest detail, a corps of two hundred volunteers for the impending Civil Disobedience movement. Mr. Malaviya recounts a story which establishes Feroze's demonstrated organizational ability. On one occasion there was some rank indiscipline in the volunteer corps which appeared to have been abetted by the captain of the corps himself. Unable to control the situation, Mr. Malaviya, who was then the secretary of the Allahabad City Congress, ran to Jawaharlal Nehru, the President, to come and reprimand the captain. By the time the two leaders arrived on the scene, the situation was completely under control, the captain had apologized and given assurance that he would obey the orders of the secretary of the City Congress. It was all accomplished by Feroze's swift and effective intervention. Within a few months after that, every one of these disciplined soldiers went to jail during the Civil Disobedience movement of 1932. Feroze himself ended up in prison for the third time, with a fifteen-month sentence, to be followed by a six-month sentence in 1934.

All through the years that Feroze made Anand Bhavan his home, he had harbored a secret teen-age crush on Indira. But after Motilal's death, Indira was sent away to Poona for schooling and Feroze lost his playmate. Jawaharlal was in prison, and Kamala was in Anand Bhavan stricken with illness. To Feroze, Kamala was the concretized representation of the idealized version of Indian womanhood, with all its supposed tenderness, compassion, strength, and self-effacement. Her helplessness in the face of a dread disease that was all the time getting the better of her endeared him the more to his "Kamala auntie," as Feroze called her fondly. Kamala in turn was very grateful for the boy's personal devotion and showered all her affection on him.

When he came out of prison in 1933, it occurred to Feroze that he had attained full adulthood and he promptly made use of his legal eligibility to declare to Kamala his serious intentions of marrying Indira. As is the wont with old Indian women, Indira's grandmother was anxious to get her married off, but Kamala stood firm in her conviction that it was too early. Indira has written of a second proposal received from another admirer of hers at this time. But whoever it was, he must have been more daring than deserving, for he sent the entire family into peals of laughter for weeks after he had dispatched his proposal. For the moment, Feroze also fared no better. Kamala's conviction that her daughter was too young to marry, and her suspicion that Feroze might yet outgrow his puppy love, somewhat cooled the young man's ardor.

His devotion to Kamala, however, never abated in intensity. He visited her frequently when she was in the Lucknow Hospital, and nursed her patiently in the Bhowali sanatorium while Jawaharlal was in prison and Indira was at Santiniketan. Later, in 1935, when Kamala was in Badenweiler and Feroze was in London awaiting entry into the London School of Economics, he used to travel that long distance by boat and train to see her as often as he could. It is believed that it was at this time that Kamala yielded to Feroze's desire to marry Indira. Young Indira, however, had always possessed a will of her own, and it was highly unlikely that she would have done anything she herself did not desire. What actually happened was that Indira's own attitude toward Feroze had matured considerably. The more she observed him the more she grew to admire some of his qualities —his devotion to loved ones, his humane concern for all the world's oppressed, his personal involvement in impersonal causes, his great gusto for all the good things of life, and above all his urbanity of manner and spontaneity of wit. She fell deeply and indubitably in love with him.

Soon after Indira landed in England in 1936, she moved in with Shanta Gandhi. The girls were living in an attic room on Fairfax Road. One day Indira told Shanta that she was to meet someone very special and suggested that Shanta too should meet him. Feroze obligingly purchased an extra ticket and the three of them attended a ballet performance. Shanta recalls that Indira was earnestly and seriously in love. It was no lighthearted affair, no sudden impulse, and there was no bravado about it either. The psychology of Feroze's love was simple. He saw in Indira the image of Kamala. For her part, Indira believed that her mother would have approved of her decision and would have felt happy to see her marry Feroze.

Life in England became pleasanter for both Indira and Feroze because they had each other's company. Of the two, Feroze had a greater interest in purely academic pursuits, and did manage to bag a Bachelor of Science degree from the London School of Economics. Feroze had a clearer mind and a keener perception of current affairs than Indira, recalls Muriel Wasi. This was certainly likely and for a very obvious reason. Thanks to her father, Indira had had a fairly good introduction to history, politics, and economics. As for practical politics, they constituted the very breath of the Nehru family. In England Indira therefore turned away from politics and sought fulfillment in other things. In contrast, Feroze had had an ordinary school education in India and no college education at all; consequently, in the London School of Economics, he was seeking an intellectual justification for his visceral politics. The subjects of his major interest there, however, were international law and diplomatic relations. For the purpose of gaining experience, Feroze worked with the Royal Institute of International Affairs at Chatham House, and also with the London County Council as an apprentice in Public Administration.

If Indira and Feroze did not find much in common on the campus, they found plenty of it off the campus. Both were active in the India League of Mr. Krishna Menon. Feroze was as involved in the popular political causes of the day as was Indira. In fact, he was even more deeply committed to some of them. Indira recalls that Feroze was all set to leave for Spain and join the International Brigade to fight for the Republic. Intelligence services got wind of his intentions, and Feroze was sent for by the police and his passport impounded. However, he did manage to get to Spain later on, where he spent a few months. He also traveled in Russia and took some excellent pictures of what he saw.

In 1938 he went to France as the special correspondent of *The National Herald* of Lucknow with an assignment to cover the French general strike. The touchy gendarmes snatched away his camera, destroyed the film, and put him in a prison cell. The following day the budding photographer himself became the object of photography —a transformation which titillated him and became his stock story for long afterward. In the version that was related to Mrs. Jai Dordi, Feroze was stripped naked and made to stand on a revolving stool. As he rotated, the police photographer shot from different angles. Feroze was quivering with uncontrollable laughter. He wondered if the police found him a suitable subject for the celebrated "Frenchie" picture cards. He was sternly ordered to behave himself, which he tried to the best of his ability, clothing his naked imagination in more decent thoughts about his indecent exposure. He was let off after a few days' detention along with other journalists.

Feroze's courting of Indira was quite hectic. With his exquisite taste he always bought her the finest of flowers. But neither of them had money to spend extravagantly. Jawaharlal's remittances to his daughter were not as generous as were those of Motilal to his son. Feroze hardly ever wrote home except for money, of which Tehmina and Faredun did not have much, but they were always glad to send him what they could because they preferred to see him thrive on the streets of London rather than languish in the jails of India. Indira and Feroze made, as often as they could afford, the rounds of Soho, Covent Garden, and the West End to satisfy their thirst for the theater, ballet, and opera, and of the Indian restaurants in Piccadilly to satisfy their hunger for Indian curry. But when there was no money, the deficiency was always made up by Feroze's wealth of anecdotes and his saucy humor.

Mrs. Jai Dordi, still unmarried at the time, was among those who had gone to receive Indira and Feroze at Bombay Harbor in March 1941 after their long voyage together from London via the Cape of Good Hope. Finding them full of each other, Jai asked Indira if something were brewing, and she responded with an affirmative whisper. Feroze and Indira reached Allahabad but could not make known their intentions to Jawaharlal, who was in prison at the time. Their romance flourished all through the spring and summer of 1941, although they could not always be together. Dr. B. C. Roy, an eminent physician and the future Chief Minister of West Bengal, invited Indira to Calcutta for a "thorough overhaul," as he put it. She then spent the summer in Mussoorie, recouping her health at St. Cecilia's Cottage, which her father had reserved for her. Her romance did not therefore arouse public suspicion or domestic misgiving initially, since both Indira and Feroze happened to be childhood friends, and Feroze was for all practical purposes a resident of Anand Bhavan. By the time Jawaharlal was released from prison, whispers about the alleged romance between the Kashmiri Brahmin girl and the Parsi boy were getting more audible, and rumor and innuendo fed on themselves in the absence of a confirmation or denial from the family itself.

When Indira made known her intentions to her Papu, there was solid opposition from the immediate family. The instinctive reaction was to think the way the Kashmiris have always thought subconsciously about the subject of marriage. As Jawaharlal recorded in his autobiography: "The objection to intermarriage with others is not based on religion; it is largely racial. There is a desire among many Kashmiris to preserve our group identity and our distinctive Aryan features, and a fear that we shall lose these in the sea of Indian and non-Indian humanity. We are small in numbers in this vast country."

Yet, in the immediate family itself, there had been instances of intermarriage prior to Indira's. Her elder aunt, Swarup Kumari, had married Ranjit Pandit, a Maharashtrian, while her younger aunt, Krishna, had married Raja Hutheesing, a Gujarati. But both Ranjit and Raja were at least Hindus. A cousin of Indira's, Shyam Kumari Nehru, went further and married a Muslim, while still another married a Muslim who now lives in Pakistan. Indira's most distinguished cousin, Braj Kumar Nehru, who is India's Ambassador to the United States and one of the country's ablest diplomats, had also married a girl who was both a non-Hindu and a non-Indian.

The opposition from the ladies of the family to Indira's proposed marriage was based more on class than on caste consciousness or religious considerations. Both Vijaya Lakshmi's and Krishna's husbands were men of more than modest means, befitting the patrician lineage of Motilal. But poor Feroze hailed from a plebeian background, although he was every inch an aristocrat by temperament. Jawaharlal's socialistic homilies had not yet permeated the female consciousness of his family, which still held stubbornly to the belief that, although all are born equal, some end up more equal than the rest. But in fairness to the ladies it must be said that to Jawaharlal himself egalitarianism thus far was good political theory but not desirable social practice. As Indira says, her father was flamingly revolutionary in many ways but surprisingly traditionalist in others.

Aside from political doctrine or social philosophy, the subject of matrimony naturally aroused a purely paternal concern to which Jawaharlal, as any other human being, was not immune. He was not going to hand down to Indira the kind of patrimony he had inherited from his father. Feroze had put in some attendance at the Inner Temple but had returned to India without qualifying as a barrister-at-law. Jawaharlal was quite unconvinced of Feroze's ability to earn a living sufficient to maintain Indira at the standards to which she had grown accustomed in Anand Bhavan. Those standards no doubt had been diluted by a self-imposed simplicity under Gandhian influence, but they were still above those of the ordinary middle class. Mahatma Gandhi, of course, had assured Feroze's mother that jail-going would become the surest qualification for success in the future. But back in 1941 that future seemed distant, and for the present, Feroze's hard-earned qualification in the Faizabad jail promised no dividends.

One other matter which troubled Jawaharlal was the question of compatibility. He was no bigot to put undue store by racial or religious considerations. But his long scientific training would not permit him to ignore the fact of different upbringings which Indira and Feroze had received. In the diversity of their social backgrounds might lie concealed the seeds of some incompatibility that would sprout through the surface romance in the unknown future.

After all, his own father had felt a similar concern about him. When Motilal heard of the rumored romance of a Kashmiri youth in England, he wrote to his sixteen-year-old son, who was then at Harrow: "You must not confuse real love with a passing passion or a feeling of pleasure in the society of a girl.... You know all the arguments against Indians marrying English women.... You must know that I hold you too dear to think of coming between you and real happiness.... In everything that concerns you, do not look upon me as your father, but your dearest friend in the world, who would do anything for you to make you happy."

Jawaharlal too was equally concerned about his daughter in matters of the heart. On her thirteenth birthday he wrote her a letter with which his famous series on world history began. All commentators have seen only political significance in this letter because of the following passage:

> If we are to be India's soldiers we have India's honour in our keeping, and that honour is a sacred trust. Often we may be in doubt as to what to do. It is no easy matter to decide what is right and what is not. One little test I shall ask you to apply whenever you are in doubt. It may help you. Never do anything in secret or anything that you would wish to hide. For the desire to hide anything means that you are afraid, and fear is a bad thing and unworthy of you. Be brave, and all the rest follows. If you are brave, you will not fear and will not do anything of which you are ashamed. You know that in our great Freedom Movement, under Bapuji's [Gandhi's] leadership, there is no room for secrecy or hiding. We have nothing to hide. We are not afraid of what we do and what we say. We work in the sun and in the light.

But what is of greater significance, in the context of love and marriage, are the lines immediately following:

> Even so in our private lives let us make friends with the sun and work in the light and do nothing secretly or furtively. Privacy, of course, we may have and should have, but that is a very different thing from secrecy. And if you do so, my dear, you will grow up a child of the light, unafraid and serene and unruffled, whatever may happen.

Indira was on the threshold of adolescence, and it is quite apparent that Jawaharlal wanted to encourage her to take him into confidence and share with him her private hopes as well as her public aspirations. If he had not been in prison he might have had an opportunity to exercise some vigilance about her private excursions. But incarcerated, the least he could do was give her some sound advice and hope for the best. If the nature of the advice is not more obvious than it is, it is because of the temperamental differences between Motilal and Jawaharlal. The practical and blunt Motilal was direct in his approach and broached the subject of sex and marriage with forthrightness in his letter to his son. But the sensitive, and a little devious, Jawaharlal came to the same point in a circuitous way. He gave his daughter the impression that he was talking about her public conduct whereas he was actually dropping gentle hints about her private comportment. Motilal and Jawaharlal had, however, one quality in common: not to impose their will on their progeny. Both were to their children not merely stern disciplinarians but also sympathetic friends.

Indira stood like a rock in her unyielding determination to marry the man of her choice against the concerted opposition of her entire family. When Jawaharlal realized that his daughter's decision was the product not of impulse but of deliberation, he yielded gracefully. Indira's maternal relatives were more sympathetically disposed to her than were her paternal relatives. Some of them impressed upon Jawaharlal the inconsistency of compelling Indira not to act upon the thoughts which her father had expressed for two decades. Was it not he who had preached that the peoples who inhabited the subcontinent, extending from the snowy peaks of the Himalayas in the north to the peninsular tip of Kanya Kumari in the south, where the waters of the Arabian sea mingled with those of the Bay of Bengal, were all one nation, whether they were fair-skinned Kashmiris or dark-skinned Tamils, merchants from Sind or peasants from Bengal, and whether they were Hindu, Muslim, Buddhist, Christian, Parsi, Jew, atheist or agnostic? Could Indira be blamed for acting upon that belief in her private life as much as in the public? The argument was superfluous because Jawaharlal had already understood. He was now her friend, and a staunch one at that, because he soon took up cudgels on her behalf to battle a hostile and vocal public opinion.

News of the forthcoming wedding had leaked out prematurely to the press. *The Leader*, a daily newspaper of Allahabad, scored a scoop when it published on page one of its issue of February 21, 1942, a cryptic announcement under the heading, "Miss Indira Nehru's Engagement":

> The marriage of Miss Indira Nehru, daughter of Pandit Jawaharlal Nehru, has been settled, it is understood, with Mr. Feroz Gandhy, brother of Mrs. Tehmina K. Gandhy, personal assistant to the Chief Inspectress of Schools, United Provinces.
>
> The wedding may take place shortly. A date for the ceremony will be fixed on Mr. Nehru's return to Allahabad.

The family was entirely unprepared for handling the leak. On the day the news item appeared, Jawaharlal was busy in far-off Calcutta, escorting two distinguished guests. They were Generalissimo and Mme. Chiang-Kai-shek, who had come on a goodwill visit to India to seek Indian sympathy for their war effort against Japan and to pledge Chinese support for India's freedom. Jawaharlal had taken them to Santiniketan because it was the first university in India to have established an institute of Chinese studies. The three of them had just returned to Calcutta and were having a meeting with Mahatma Gandhi when the news broke.

Hastening to Allahabad, Jawaharlal issued a statement to the press on February 26 confirming the report which had appeared earlier in *The Leader*. Among other things, the statement said:

> A marriage is a personal and domestic matter, affecting chiefly the two parties concerned and partly their families. Yet I recognize that in view of my association with public affairs, I should take my many friends and colleagues and the public generally into my confidence.
>
> I have long held the view that though parents may and should advise in the matter, the choice and ultimate decision must be with the two parties concerned. That decision, if arrived at after mature deliberation, must be given effect to, and it is no business of parents or others to come in the way. When I was assured that Indira and Feroze wanted to marry one another I accepted willingly their decision and told them that it had my blessing.
>
> Mahatma Gandhi, whose opinion I value not only in public affairs but in private matters also, gave his blessing to the proposal. The members of my family as well as the members of my wife's family also gave their willing consent.

The statement which was intended to assuage adverse public opinion by taking the public into confidence had precisely the opposite effect. Thousands of protests were sent to Anand Bhavan, warnings dispatched, and dire consequences threatened if the proposed intermarriage were consummated. Jawaharlal had claimed in his statement to the press that the engagement had Mahatma Gandhi's blessing. Countless irate fanatics and members of militantly revivalist Hindu religious bodies addressed abusive communications to Gandhi. To them, the Mahatma, clad in loincloth and walking staff in hand, munching nuts and gulping down goat's milk, claiming that there is no politics other than religion, asserting that God is truth and non-violence, preaching that renunciation is the path to God-realization, advancing such nostrums as sexual abstinence, the ban on intoxicating drinks, and the prohibition of the slaughter of that "poem of pity"—the cow—had appeared to be the very embodiment of the quintessence of the Hindu ethos. How could such a man now advocate the impure union of a Hindu girl with a non-Hindu boy? The Mahatma

pored over these communications with increasing consternation, and
on March 8, 1942, he printed a rejoinder to them in his weekly newspaper, *The Harijan*. The statement, which deserves to be reproduced
in full for its subdued anger and for its exposition of his meaning of
Hinduism, reads as follows:

> I have received several angry and abusive letters and some
> professing to reason about Indira's engagement with Feroze
> Gandhi. Not a single correspondent has anything against
> Feroze Gandhi as a man. His only crime in their estimation
> is that he happens to be a Parsi. I have been, and am still, as
> strong an opponent of either party changing religion for the
> sake of marriage. Religion is not a garment to be cast off at
> will. In the present case there is no question of change of reli-
> gion. Feroze Gandhi has been for years an inmate of the
> Nehru family. He nursed Kamala Nehru in her sickness. He
> was like a son to her. A natural intimacy grew up between
> them [Indira and Feroze]. The friendship has been perfectly
> honourable. It has ripened into mutual attraction. But neither
> party would think of marrying without the consent and bless-
> ing of Jawaharlal Nehru. This was given only after he was
> satisfied that the attraction had a solid basis.
>
> The public knows my connection with the Nehrus. I also
> had talks with both the parties. It would have been cruelty to
> refuse consent to this engagement. As time advances such
> unions are bound to multiply with benefit to the society. At
> present we have not even reached the stage of mutual tolera-
> tion. But as toleration grows into mutual respect for religions,
> such unions will be welcomed. No religion which is narrow
> and which cannot satisfy the test of reason will survive the
> coming reconstruction of society in which the values will have
> changed, and character, not possession of wealth, title or birth
> will be the sole test of merit. The Hinduism of my conception
> is no narrow creed. It is a grand evolutionary process as an-
> cient as time, and embraces the teachings of Zoroaster, Moses,
> Christ, Mohammed, Nanak and other prophets that I could
> name. It is thus defined: Know that to be true religion which

the wise and the good and those who are ever free from passion and hate follow, and which appeals to the heart.

If it is not that, it will perish. My correspondents will par-
don me for not acknowledging their letters. I invite them to
shed their wrath and bless the forthcoming marriage. Their
letters betray ignorance, intolerance and prejudice—a species
of untouchability, dangerous because not easily to be so classified.

Just before his rejoinder appeared in print, Gandhi wrote to Jawaharlal: "I have seen your statement about Indu. I liked it. I receive
letters concerning her marriage every day. Some are dreadful. I have
destroyed all of them. In reply to all these, I have sent a note in *The
Harijan*, a copy of which I am sending herewith. Since yesterday,
letters from Moslems are pouring in, revealing their intention to
attack. . . ."

The Parsis could not be left out of the reckoning either. Many
Orthodox Parsis were opposed to the match and Feroze's own aunt
and former guardian, Dr. Commissariat, did not approve of it. Since
the domestic fence had to be mended first, Jawaharlal had already
sent for Rattimai, Tehmina, and Faredun—Feroze's mother, sister,
and brother—before he issued his press statement. Jawaharlal told
them that Feroze and Indira seemed determined to get married and
asked them if they had any objections to it. They replied that objections usually came more often from the girl's side but if Jawaharlal
had no reservations, nobody on Feroze's side had any either. Jawaharlal then told Rattimai that he feared a demonstration by the Parsis
of the city on the wedding day and that this distasteful possibility
must somehow be averted. Rattimai promised to meet the elders of
the Parsi community and take care of that problem.

Tehmina then expressed a very natural apprehension. She wondered if Indira would be happy, or could be happy even if she
wanted to be, with Feroze's ways, which were essentially those of
a humble Parsi family of modest means. This was the fear which had
made Jawaharlal himself hesitant initially, but by now he had overcome it. So he told her reassuringly: "I certainly am aware of that

aspect of the problem, but I have watched Feroze a good deal, and whatever he does I am sure he will always land on his feet."

One other question remained, and this was the type of wedding ceremony to follow. This question, in turn, was bound up with legal complexities, and Jawaharlal said there was only one way out of this whole web of intricacies. The discussion now revolved at length around this question.

In India, most questions pertaining to family relations—marriage, divorce, adoption, inheritance, etc.—were exclusively decided by the personal law of the individual concerned. On each of these questions, for instance, a Hindu would be governed by Hindu law, and a Muslim by Muslim law. As long as the bride and bridegroom belonged to the same community, no legal problems of any kind arose. But if they belonged to different communities, two legal alternatives were open to the parties. The first was for one of them to be converted to the faith of the other, so that they could be married according to the personal law, which then became common to both. The second alternative was for both bride and bridegroom to renounce their respective religions and declare on oath that they did not follow any religion. They could then enter into a civil marriage under the provisions of the Special Marriage Act of 1871. (The Act, which has been amended since the achievement of Independence, now permits intermarriage between persons of any faith, without their having to renounce it.) Both alternatives were unacceptable to the Nehru family. Happily, however, there was a third way, and a precedent in that direction had already been established in the Nehru family itself; to this Feroze and his family had no objection.

The problem had first arisen when Indira's cousin Braj Kumar Nehru wanted to marry Magdalena Friedman, whom he had met while they were both studying in England. Miss Friedman was Hungarian in origin and Jewish by faith. Brijlal, Braj Kumar's father, disapproved of the proposed union and sent his wife, Rameshwari, to England to dissuade the son from proceeding any further with his foolish infatuation. But the mother was so charmed by the girl that she was eager to become her mother-in-law. Flabbergasted by this unexpected turn of events, the elder Nehru now put what he thought was an insuperable obstacle. He said he would be agreeable to the marriage if the girl came to India first and lived for a year the life of Orthodox Kashmiri Brahmins and still wanted to marry his son despite the rigors of that experience. Miss Friedman came out of the test in such flying colors that the older Orthodox Kashmiri ladies now held her up as worthy of emulation by the young westernized Kashmiri girls!

But while this happy denouement might have promoted domestic harmony, it still did not cut through the legal tangle. Since both Hinduism and Judaism are, strictly speaking, nonproselyting religions, the conversion of one to the faith of the other was impossible. The other alternative—renunciation of religion by both—though possible, appeared ludicrous to them. They argued that a formal renunciation of religion hardly meant anything, since even an atheist has a religion of his own, even if it be nothing more than the religious denial of God.

It was at this point that a scholar of great repute, *Mahamahopadhyaya* (a great one among great teachers) Lachmi Dhar Shastri, Professor of Sanskrit at St. Stephen's College, Delhi, came to their rescue. Professor Shastri was the author of a handbook called *Vedic Paddhati* or "The Way of the Vedas," which incorporated all the Hindu *samskaras* or sacraments from the *Grihya Sutras*, as well as some rituals of later growth. The learned professor had included in the handbook certain marriage rites which he contended were applicable to all people, irrespective of caste, color, or creed. He also asserted that these were time-honored rites and not an innovation of his fancy, and that individuals belonging to different faiths could resort to them without changing or renouncing their respective religions.

Since this appeared a highly attractive solution, the family wanted to have the advice of some eminent lawyers. One of those consulted was Sir Tej Bahadur Sapru, a legal luminary and a colleague of the late Motilal Nehru. Sapru dismissed Professor Shastri's marriage rites as nothing better than legal mumbo jumbo. He pointed out that Hindu law was not what Professor Shastri chose to interpret it to be, but what the courts of law construed it to mean. The judges construed the ancient texts literally and no gloss could be put on them.

However, since "custom was king," the courts ruled that a deviation from the literal meaning of the texts was valid if it was sanctioned by custom. And custom was nothing less than a clearly established practice of long standing, easily ascertained. Sapru said that Professor Shastri's marriage rites were not sanctioned by custom, were the result of his own exegesis, and that they could not stand the scrutiny of the courts which would declare the marriage null and void. But notwithstanding Sir Tej Bahadur's strictures the Nehrus decided to go ahead with the Shastri prescription for a wedding ceremony, and Braj Kumar and Magdalena were finally wed.

Once again, the Nehru family faced such a situation. One is simply born a Hindu or a Parsi and cannot artificially be processed as one such through formal conversion. And neither Indira nor Feroze was agreeable to a ludicrous denunciation of their respective faiths. So once again the valued services of Professor Lachmi Dhar Shastri were utilized for the wedding.

Indira's marriage came as a bright but brief dash of lightning in a murky political sky. After the Congress governments in the various provinces of India had resigned in October 1939 as a protest against the unilateral British involvement of India in the war, individual members of the Congress commenced offering Satyagraha. As a result, Jawaharlal was asked to go to his "other home" in Gorakhpur prison in October 1940, where he remained until December 1941. Days after his release a scene occurred at Pearl Harbor which marked another act in the drama of World War II. In rapid succession the Japanese overran Hong Kong, the Philippines, and Malaya. Indochina and Thailand had come under their control. Then, on February 15, 1942, that great naval bastion of the British Empire in the east, Singapore, fell. But disaster did not stop there. On March 8 the Japanese occupied Rangoon and were at the doorstep of India— the brightest jewel of the British Crown. In London the War Cabinet panicked, and on March 11 Churchill announced in the House of Commons that Sir Stafford Cripps, leader of the Labour Party's Left wing, a sympathizer of India and an admirer of Mahatma Gandhi, was being sent to India with new proposals to enlist the colony's cooperation in the prosecution of war.

After years of neglect, in the month of March 1942, Anand Bhavan started wearing a gay appearance. Appropriately, the festivities commenced with *Holi*, which fell that year on the sixth of the month. No other festival could lend itself better to mischievous pranks and tomfoolery by young lovers than this one. Indira and Feroze had their fill of squirting colored water and smearing each other with oily pastes. By evening they had washed and cleaned themselves to attend a lavish dinner which was being given by a friend of the family, Pandit Triloki Nath Madan, in his residence at 13 Elgin Road in the fashionable Civil Lines area. The dinner was attended by a large and distinguished gathering. Preceding the gathering was a fancy-dress competition, the results of which were very edifying to the inmates of Anand Bhavan. The first prize for ladies was carried away by Miss Rita Pandit, the youngest of Mrs. Pandit's daughters, and the second prize was won by Miss Indira Nehru.

Although cranks and fanatics had opposed Indira's engagement to Feroze, thousands of decent citizens all over the country applauded their mutual choice as progressive and forward looking. All through the month of March, a steady stream of gifts and parcels poured into Anand Bhavan. Mrs. Nayantara Sahgal records how Indira's room was filled with rustling tissue paper and satin ribbon from which emerged exquisite silverware, expensive crystal, gorgeous saris, and occasionally a velvet-lined casket containing a jeweled ornament. Most of the presents had to be carefully rewrapped and returned to the senders, many of whom the family did not know.

Indira was married, as were her parents, on an auspicious day. Jawaharlal and Kamala were married on *Vasant Panchami* Day, the Hindu festival which heralds the coming of spring. Thursday, March 26, 1942, the day on which Feroze and Indira were married, was *Ram Navmi*, the birthday of Rama, the virtuous hero of the epic *Ramayana*—a day given to prayer and rejoicing among Hindus. Simplicity was the keynote of the entire wedding, in keeping with Jawaharlal's wishes and the exigencies of the national and international situations. The *mandap* or canopied square under which the ceremony took place was very simply decorated with trunks of banana trees at the four corners and strings of mango leaves and cowries embellishing the canopy. There was no ostentation of any kind, and even the traditional music of the *shahanai* quartet was absent. Indira wore a plain sari of shell-pink *khadi* embroidered with a narrow silvery border that had been especially ordered for her from the Gandhi Seva Sena in Bombay. The matching short-sleeved blouse she wore and the handkerchief she carried were both made of yarn spun by her father. She had no jewelry to wear, since all of Kamala's jewelry had been sold to straighten out the family's financial situation. However, instead of the conventional jewelry of gold, Indira was adorned with armlets, bracelets, necklace, and earrings, all made of fresh leaves and flowers by Coonverbai Vakil, her old schoolmistress from Poona. Feroze was dressed in an *achkan*, a long coat with a Russian-type closed collar, *churidars*, or tight-fitting jodhpurs, and a narrow cloth cap, all made of white *khadi*.

The ceremony took place in the eastern wing of the open circular veranda outside the room that was once used by Indira's grandmother. In the center of the *mandap* erected here was a tiny enclosure in which the sacrificial fire would be lit. On one side of it were two mats for seating the bride and bridegroom and two more mats on the opposite side for the bride's parents. The invited guests sat on carpets spread all around. There were hundreds of uninvited guests who could not be turned away. The more enterprising of them perched themselves on treetops to get an unhindered view. And there was the inevitable scene, which Nayantara records, of "a photographer from an American fashion magazine struggling with his equipment, beads of perspiration trickling down his temples and glistening on his upper lip."

It was a pleasant March morning, and the fragrance of incense was wafted along by a gentle breeze. At 9 A.M., as the priests commenced the chanting of Sanskrit *slokas* (verses), Jawaharlal came and seated himself on his mat, and Feroze sat opposite him. The mat intended for Kamala was vacant, a poignant reminder of the absence of the person who might have been the most pleased with the day's events. Indira came next and sat beside her father. The priests applied *tilak*—a round mark the size of a nickel, made of a paste of vermilion and saffron—on the foreheads of Indira, Feroze, and Jawaharlal.

Then began the two-hour-long marriage ceremony (mercifully a shortened version, according to Professor Lachmi Dhar Shastri) which was itself a subtle marriage of custom and innovation, and a blend of marital desire with nationalist passion.

The ceremony began with obtaining the bride's consent to the marriage. Then came the *Jaya-Homa* (literally, a sacrifice to victory) which was an ancient ceremony symbolizing the love of freedom and the determination to preserve it. In a voice quivering with emotion, Indira recited the Sanskrit *sloka* which meant:

"If there be any in the four quarters of the earth who venture to deprive us of our freedom, mark! Here I am, sword in hand, prepared to resist them to the last. I pray for the spreading light of freedom; may it envelop us on all sides!"

Notwithstanding his creed of nonviolence, Mahatma Gandhi had justified the resort to violence by women for protecting their honor. Professor Lachmi Dhar Shastri's inclusion of the above passage in a wedding ceremony was apparently intended as a concession to the prevailing mood of national defiance. He was obviously not bothered that the expression "sword in hand" constituted a thin dividing line indeed between marital desire and martial adventure!

The second part of the ceremony commenced at 9.30 A.M. It began with *Kanya Dan* or the giving away of the daughter, which is considered the most exalted gift a man can make, because there is no more precious possession than a daughter. Indira now rose from her father's side and went over to sit beside Feroze. Reciting a *sloka*, the bridegroom promised to act according to the bride's wishes and never to neglect her. Then began the *Mangalya-Mala*—a flower offering to the couple, invoking upon them good auspices. This was how the sloka read:

"Adorn yourselves with the grace of divine providence and accept this offering of the first flower, that of nonviolence; this second flower of self-control; this third of compassion for all living things; this fourth of forbearance; this fifth of enlightenment; this sixth of purity; this seventh of profound meditation; and this eighth, that is, the flower of Truth. May God bless you."

Then began the *Homa*, the lighting of the sacrificial fire, into which the chanting priests poured clarified butter with a silver ladle. The couple now performed the most crucial part of the ceremony, the *Sapta-Padi*, or walking hand in hand around the fire seven times, upon which the seal is set on the wedding. Feroze and Indira ate a symbolic meal off each other's hands. The ladies of the house performed *Posh-Puja*, showering flower petals on the couple to the accompaniment of marriage songs. The ceremony concluded at 11 A.M. with the married couple standing before the assembly and the priests reciting the *sloka* from the *Rig Veda:*

> May our projects be common
> And common the assembly of our people
> May our people be of like mind and purpose.

When Vijaya Lakshmi was married to Ranjit Pandit on May 10, 1921, the police had suspected that Anand Bhavan was celebrating the anniversary of the Great Rebellion of 1857. No such suspicions were aroused on the occasion of Indira's marriage with Feroze. The reason was that Sir Stafford Cripps had arrived in New Delhi on March 22 bearing an olive branch from none other than Winston Churchill. Only the day before Indira's wedding Cripps had commenced negotiations with Maulana Abul Kalam Azad, the president of the Indian National Congress. Azad arrived for the wedding, as did scores of other leaders.

If only Churchill had known that in four months' time the greatest civil disobedience movement of all history would be launched by these very leaders he would never have let go the opportunity of getting so many arrested in so short a time with so little effort. Besides Maulana Azad, the president of the Congress and India's future Minister of Education, there were among the distinguished guests Dr. Rajendra Prasad, who was to become independent India's first President, Pandit Govind Ballabh Pant, the future Home Minister, Dr. Syed Mahmud, the future Minister of State for External Affairs, Dr. Rafi Ahmad Kidwai, the future Minister of Food, Hafiz Mohammad Ibrahim, the future Minister of Irrigation, Dr. Kailash Nath Katju, the future Minister of Defense, the Honorable Babu Purshottam Das Tandon, a future president of the Congress, Mrs. Sarojini

Naidu, "the Nightingale of India" and a future Governor of Uttar Pradesh, Acharya J. B. Kripalani, a future president of the Congress, Babu Sampurnanand, a future Chief Minister of Uttar Pradesh, Dr. B. C. Roy, a future Chief Minister of West Bengal, Dr. Jivraj Mehta, a future Chief Minister of Gujarat, and Lal Bahadur Shastri, independent India's second Prime Minister. In the immediate family itself were independent India's first Prime Minister, her first woman Prime Minister, and her first woman Ambassador to Moscow, Washington, and London, and first woman president of the General Assembly of the United Nations. What a lot of subversives to catch under one roof!

Jawaharlal gave a buffet supper to the guests the same evening at 7:30 P.M. at Anand Bhavan. On the twenty-eighth Feroze's mother, Rattimai Gandhi, held a high tea for the guests at 5:15 P.M. at her residence in George Town.

In between the morning ceremonies and the evening supper Jawaharlal was in a huddle for some hours with the Congress president, Maulana Azad. Azad gave him a rundown on the proposals which Cripps had brought from London for enlisting India's cooperation in the war, as if to highlight the confluence of the public and the private, and the personal and the political, in the lives of Anand Bhavan's inmates. And as if to emphasize the same point, Jawaharlal himself left Allahabad hastily on the evening of March 28 to have breakfast with Sir Stafford in New Delhi the next morning, as the fate of many a nation involved in the war hung in the balance.

9

A Taste of Prison

For days after the wedding, the gifts poured in and the guests came to offer their felicitations. Indira was still in a state of thrill and excitement. A distinguished guest at dinner one evening in Anand Bhavan was Britain's war-time emissary, Sir Stafford Cripps. Indira's tongue slipped, Nayantara Sahgal records, as the nervous newlywed at the table offered Cripps some "potato cripps." It was no small mercy she did not say to the departing guest: "Good-bye, Mr. Chips!"

In April Feroze and Indira took off to Kashmir for their honeymoon. It was spring, the season of eternal youth and hope, and the two of them shared their dreams for the future. Before returning to Allahabad, the couple visited a princely state in western India. There, according to Faredun Gandhi, they went through the formality of a civil marriage. Sir Tej Bahadur Sapru's opinion that Professor Lachmi Dhar Shastri's wedding ceremony was not legal appears to have disturbed Feroze and Indira. Feroze's inquiries had revealed that one of the princely states had a Civil Marriage Act under which individuals professing different faiths could marry without renouncing their religion. To safeguard the legal status of their offspring, he and Indira appear to have decided on a civil ceremony also. Having done that, they returned to Allahabad with lighter minds.

Feroze rented a small bungalow at 4 Fort Road in Allahabad's George Town. The couple still had no definite plans for making a

living. Feroze had with him a number of fine photographs he had
shot on his European travels, which he now used to good purpose,
writing illustrated articles for Indian magazines. In his spare time he
also sold insurance. This short experience with selling insurance must
have provided him with an insight into the rank malpractices then
prevalent in the business. At any rate, it was his investigation of
some of these malpractices more than a decade later which catapulted
him into political fame.

But selling insurance does not ensure one against political up-
heavals; and little did Indira and Feroze know that their marital happiness would be cut short by an almost earth-shaking political event
in India. The Cripps mission failed, and this was a disappointing
blow to the Indian nationalists. Not long before coming to India,
Cripps had served as Ambassador to Russia, arrived at an understanding with Stalin, and returned triumphant to London. Sir Stafford was a sympathizer of the Indian cause, and his visit naturally
heightened the mood of expectation in India. Unfortunately, the
Cripps offer had several limitations. Its first defect was a lack of sin-
cerity. Only a year ago, Churchill had declared: "I have not become
His Majesty's first minister to preside over the liquidation of the
British Empire." If he now sent Cripps in great haste to India, it was
only in the hope that India may be persuaded to fight the Japanese
and save the British Empire. That was what the Indian nationalists
thought.

The second defect of the offer lay in its attempt to please everyone. It tried to please the Indian National Congress by conceding
its claim to draw up a constitution of India by the Indians and for
the Indians. It also tried to please the Muslim League by conceding
its claim to carve out a separate state from India. But the major defect
of the Cripps offer was that all these proposals were in the nature
of a promissory note which would be due for performance only after
the war ended. While the war lasted, Britain would transfer precious
little power to India. Mahatma Gandhi damned the Cripps offer as
"a post-dated check on a failing bank." Mr. Mohammed Ali Jinnah,
the leader of the Muslim League, also rejected the offer, and Sir
Stafford returned to London empty-handed.

Mahatma Gandhi now seized the initiative and demanded that the British quit India immediately so that the country might organize its own national defense against the Japanese, who were now on India's doorstep. The two words, "Quit India," gained as wide a currency in the country as had those other two words, "Go Back," which were addressed to the Simon Seven in 1928. On August 7, 1942, the national committee of the Indian National Congress met in Bombay to endorse Gandhi's stand. It was a historic meeting, which both Feroze and Indira attended. Jawaharlal Nehru made a stirring speech, charging that the British "have made the Indians miserable, poverty-stricken wrecks of humanity" and asserted that the Indians do not propose to be treated any longer as "a benighted backward people." The resolution which Nehru proposed asked for the ending of British rule and the immediate recognition of Indian freedom "both for the sake of India and for the success of the cause of the United Nations." However, if the British Government did not respond to this plea, the Congress authorized Mahatma Gandhi to commence a mass civil disobedience movement. On August 8 the historic "Quit India" resolution was adopted by the Congress.

It was a tiring two-day conference, and the Nehru family, which was staying with Jawaharlal's sister, Mrs. Krishna Hutheesing, in Bombay, returned home and engaged in a late-night discussion of recent happenings. Guests were going in and out of Mrs. Hutheesing's apartment, and the central theme of much of the talks was the possible repressive reaction of the government to the "Quit India" resolution which the Congress had just adopted. Around midnight the guests departed, and Jawaharlal, Krishna, and her husband, Raja Hutheesing, continued their discussion for another hour before retiring. Four hours later, while everyone was in deep slumber, the police knocked at the door. Mrs. Hutheesing knew instinctively it was none other than the police coming at that ungodly hour and rushed to her brother's room. Poor Jawaharlal could hardly open his eyes and wondered what was afoot. Within minutes all the lights were on and everyone was up. As Nehru's clothes and a few other personal articles were gathered, his brother-in-law hastened to get him a few books—Jawaharlal's best companions in prison. Indira then asked her uncle, Hutheesing: "Why aren't *you* getting ready?" Her aunt Krishna naturally wondered why Indira was so anxious to dispatch her uncle to prison. Indira told her unsuspecting aunt that there was a warrant of arrest for him too.

The British Government had obviously decided to strike, and strike before it was too late. Rather than let Mahatma Gandhi and the Congress start a mass civil disobedience movement which might go out of hand, the strategy of officialdom was to stop the movement before it even began. Its first step was to put out of circulation the first-ranking leaders of the Congress. Mahatma Gandhi and the members of the Congress Working Committee were all rounded up before dawn and were taken from Bombay in a heavily armed special train to Poona. Gandhi was detained in the famous Aga Khan Palace near Poona, while the Working Committee members were packed off to the Ahmadnagar Fort, a massive sixteenth-century enclosure two hundred miles southeast of Bombay. And it was here that Jawaharlal began his ninth and the last and longest term of imprisonment —1,040 days—before he was released on June 15, 1945.

If the government struck like lightning against the front-rank leaders of the Congress, the second-rank leaders of the party disappeared from sight like the sun behind monsoon clouds. Going underground and playing hide and seek with the police, they took over the direction of the civil disobedience movement. Since Gandhi was arrested even before he could map the outlines of the movement or issue detailed instructions, the lesser leaders and their followers were left to their own devices. There were spontaneous mass demonstrations all over India, which were repressed with unprecedented severity. The police firings were brutal and indiscriminate, and it was inevitable that violence should breed violence. When the Mahatma was locked behind prison bars, nonviolence was also locked up with him. Students took the lead everywhere and organized campaigns of sabotage—derailing trains, cutting telephone and telegraph wires, instigating peasants not to pay taxes. Police stations were burned and post offices razed to the ground. Workers went on strike and factories were locked out. Whole villages declared their "independence," expelled officials and ran their own affairs for months. In time, the rebellion was suppressed, thanks largely to the greatest concentration of British troops in the history of the Indian subcontinent.

The day after her father's arrest, Indira left Bombay and reached Anand Bhavan late in the evening of August 11. Tired from the long journey, she went to bed early. The eleventh of August was a day of nightmarish experiences for Mrs. Pandit and her two daughters, Chandralekha and Nayantara. The students of Allahabad had stumped in procession, but the military, which had been put in control of the city, fired on them not only to see them dispersed but also terrorized. All day Mrs. Pandit was picking up the battered students and rushing them frantically to various city hospitals.

With the sound of gunshots still ringing in their ears and the faces of young men in agony still haunting them, Mrs. Pandit and her daughters had retired to bed. Mrs. Pandit could hardly sleep, "utterly weary in mind and body and more than a little dazed" as she was. At 2 A.M. she heard a servant knock on her bedroom door and announce that the police had arrived to get her. When she stepped out on the porch, she recognized the city magistrate, the deputy superintendent of police, and dozens of armed policemen and plainclothesmen posted on the grounds and on the veranda. Ordering them off the veranda, she exploded: "Why is it necessary for so many armed men to come to arrest one unarmed woman at this amazing hour?" They presented her with a search warrant and a warrant of arrest. Mrs. Pandit rushed to Indira's room, gave her a few hurried instructions, bade her three daughters good-bye, and sat in the police van. Driving along the familiar road over which she had ridden many times to visit her husband, her father, or her brother, she reached Naini jail for her third imprisonment.

Just before Indira left Bombay for Allahabad, Feroze had decided to go underground. He grew a moustache and dressed in khaki. Because of his fair and ruddy complexion, he could pass off for an Anglo-Indian soldier. Entraining at Bombay, he got off at a small wayside station before reaching Allahabad, where he feared he would easily be recognized even in disguise. Finding no means of transport to Allahabad, he hitchhiked on a military truck full of British and Anglo-Indian soldiers, who took it for granted that Feroze was one of them. As Indira recalls he told her the soldiers "were scared stiff and almost refused to let him get off again, saying that the damned natives would hack him to pieces if they found him alone and un-armed!"

Feroze's skillful generalship was now at the disposal of Allahabad students who were eager to carry on sabotage activities. The police had issued a warrant for his arrest and the intelligence branch was hounding him out. Feroze, however, was quite safe in Yehiapur, one of the oldest localities in the ancient city of Allahabad. Its narrow, congested lanes and winding, obscure bylanes constituted an ideal hideout. Since he had implicit faith in the loyalty of Yehiapur's residents, Feroze moved about freely and openly in that area. Congress volunteers stood guard at all the entry points of the locality and sent out danger signals to Feroze the moment they spotted a uniformed policeman or a suspected plainclothesman, and in the twinkling of an eye he would disappear into the nearest house.

Indira remained aboveground, and her activities seemed above-board—at least for the time being. She lived in Anand Bhavan and was in fact the head of the household, since Jawaharlal and Vijaya Lakshmi were in prison and Ranjit Pandit was still in Bombay. However, life in Anand Bhavan was anything but pleasant. Neighboring Swaraj Bhavan, the national headquarters of the Congress Party, was occupied by the military, who trained their guns on Anand Bhavan. While Indira and the three Pandit girls learned to take this brutal invasion of privacy in their stride, the servants of the house, who were mostly unlettered rustics, were terrified each time they heard in the darkness of night the curt, "Halt! Who goes there?"

The girls in Anand Bhavan were also frightened of one other thing. A warrant had been issued for the arrest of Lal Bahadur Shastri. The police naturally assumed that Shastri would never be so foolish as to stay in Anand Bhavan. Wily Lal Bahadur thought it wise to do precisely what the police assumed would be foolish for him to attempt. He remained incognito in Anand Bhavan and continued with his management of the logistics of the rebellion. He never stirred out of his upstairs room until it was completely dark, and Indira slipped the meals into his den surreptitiously. She pretended she was putting up an ailing relative in one of those rooms. The pretense could not be sustained for long, since there was always the danger of fifth-column activity even within Anand Bhavan. The police themselves could come unannounced any time and carry out a thorough search. Shastri therefore decided to move out and was arrested not long after.

Indira never failed to meet Feroze periodically. The meetings were arranged in the houses of mutual friends who were completely non-political. And it was at these clandestine meetings that Indira passed on to Feroze money and literature to continue the underground civil disobedience movement.

Although Indira's movements seemed as inconspicuous as possible, they started arousing the suspicion of the police. When an arrest appeared imminent to her, she hastily collected some clothes and books and herself went underground. When she next met Feroze she told him of her intention to give herself up to the police and spare herself the strain of remaining underground. A public meeting was arranged for September 11, 1942, at five in the evening. News of the meeting was whispered throughout Allahabad by word of mouth. The police, who swarmed all over the place, were terribly intrigued. They came to know everything about the forthcoming meeting except the venue!

At the appointed hour, the crowds poured from all directions: a neighborhood cinema house, the cluster of surrounding shops, and the houses beyond, where they had been collecting for the past few hours. Of a sudden, Indira appeared on the scene and began addressing the people. She had spoken for hardly ten minutes when truck-loads of armed British soldiers sprang upon the scene and formed a cordon around the speaker and her audience. Feroze knew he was of some value to his party only as long as he continued to remain underground. So he had decided not to become involved in this incident and was observing it through the shutters of a first-floor window of a nearby house. Within a few seconds Feroze noticed the barrel of a gun only a yard away from Indira's face. She remembers how "excitement and anxiety got the better of him and he came charging down, yelling at the sergeant to shoot or lower his gun." He was promptly arrested and thrown into the police van.

Meanwhile, the sergeant made the mistake of grabbing Indira by the arm to lead her also to the van. This served as a cue for the crowd to cause pandemonium. Some women volunteers of the Congress grabbed Indira's other arm and started pulling her in the opposite direction. Her clothes were torn into shreds, and for a moment she was afraid her arms would come out of their sockets if the tug of war went on longer. As the scuffle continued, Feroze freed himself from his captors, climbed out of the van to its roof, and proceeded to harangue his audience. Indira and five other women were arrested along with numerous men and the police trucks were now full. It was not until then that the police discovered Feroze was still free and captured him once more. The caravan of captors and captives finally rolled on to Naini central jail.

It was six thirty and still bright in the evening when they reached the outer gate of the jail. Since the time for lock-up was already past, the gate was opened only after loud bangings on it. Indira was led to the barracks in which her aunt, Mrs. Pandit, was detained, and the other five women were lodged in the opposite barracks. Surprised though Mrs. Pandit was, she was happy because it was a family reunion of sorts. Only twelve days earlier, her eldest daughter, Chandralekha, had been brought to the same barracks on some trumped-up charges. Now came her niece. Mrs. Pandit asked Indira if she had any news of her father or Mahatma Gandhi. Gandhi's detention in the Aga Khan Palace was known to the nation and Indira told her aunt about it. But the place of detention of the members of the Congress Working Committee was a well-guarded secret which no one in the country except a few in authority knew, and Mrs. Pandit had to content herself with the news blackout about her brother.

Indira's barracks was a longish rectangular room which normally held a dozen prisoners. But because of the great popularity which His Majesty's prisons enjoyed in 1942, it had to accommodate twenty-two women. In the same yard was another barracks which was also full of political women prisoners. In the adjoining ward were some forty-four hardened women offenders serving sentences of various lengths for assorted crimes ranging from murder and kidnapping to simple but habitual theft. The two yards were separated by a wall, but when the door in the wall was opened occasionally, the "politicals" and the "criminals" exchanged greetings and friendly smiles. Mrs. Pandit had become acquainted with some of them during her previous internment, and she was happy that her "friends" were still there. Indira too would soon be honored by such friendship. At regular intervals along each wall of the barracks were gratings, and there was one door, which was bolted and locked up at night. At one end inside the barracks on a raised platform was an indoor latrine for use during the night after lock-up time. For daytime use, however, there was a small outdoor bathroom and latrine.

Although it was one of the better-run jails in the province, the structure was in sad disrepair and chunks of plaster fell from the ceiling during the night and decorated the prisoners' chests by the morning. The tiles on the roof were hardly in position, and sun and rain found unhindered entry into the barracks. The floor was uneven and the prisoners stumbled and fell in the darkness of the night. The seasons and the time of day determined the kind of company the prisoners would have. During the monsoon rains, quite a navigable little lake formed outside the barracks. It was full of black, slimy frogs. One of which would begin to croak at night, and soon there was a crescendo of collective croakery. The monsoon also permitted the insect population to flourish and the prisoners enjoyed the company of mosquitoes along with their special gift—malaria. Summer was the time for house mice and field rats and the explosive multiplication of flies. The day was for chirping sparrows, and the night for circling bats.

Each prisoner was given a jail cot for sleeping and individual rations daily. The food cooked in the jail for ordinary convicts was —as admitted by jail authorities—unpalatable and the "politicals" were given raw rations which they themselves had to cook. However, they were allowed daily rations worth only nine annas, or fifteen cents! Little wonder that the rations were mildewed with stones and grit. Black ants crawled into and out of the sugar, tea leaves looked more like dried twigs, and the milk tasted like chalk mixed with water. Mrs. Pandit had built a tiny earthen stove for cooking, but the firewood, soaked overnight in the monsoon rain, belched clouds of smoke before burning.

On the day Indira landed in prison, she was running a high temperature. Although it came down in the following days, it remained constant at 99.2 degrees every morning and evening, and went up a few points during the day. By the end of September it was rumored that she had been recommended for release on grounds of health. It was nothing more than a rumor, and Indira stayed in prison for eight months longer. Her fever persisted, and there was public concern over her ill health. In the third week of October, the Governor of the province sent the civil surgeon to examine her and report to him on her condition. Indira recalls that she was not bothered about her health and "was determined to bear all privations and insults smilingly." She was not eager to get out of prison, and had "no yearning for the outside world, for no one worthwhile was there." The civil surgeon's visit was unexpected, she says, and for that reason remained all the more vivid in her memory. She recollects the scene: "He prescribed a tonic and a special diet including delicacies such as Ovaltine. But hardly was his back turned when the superintendent tore up the prescription and tossed the pieces on the floor. 'If you think you are getting any of this,' he said, 'you are mistaken.' This was surprising for I had not asked for anything."

Writing about her jail experience years later, Indira described what a world of difference there was between mere hearsay and the actual experience:

> No one who has not been in prison for any length of time can even visualize the numbness of spirit that can creep over one when, as Oscar Wilde writes, "each day is like a year, a year whose days are long," and when day after day is wrapped up in sameness and in spite and deliberate humiliation. Lord Pethick-Lawrence has said that the "essential fact in the life of the prisoner is that he takes on a subhuman status." Herded together like animals, devoid of dignity or privacy, he is debarred not only from outside company or news but from all beauty and colour, softness and grace.

But even in jail, life could become bearable for the cheerful in spirit. Quite early it was decided that Mrs. Pandit would cook the midday meal, and Indira and Chandralekha the supper. Breakfast posed no problem, since all they were entitled to was tea. The girls were free to do a lot of reading during the day. Indira helped Chandralekha with her French, and Lekha, as she was called for short, asked the jail authorities for permission to get her books to prepare for her examination. The girls also kept themselves busy cleaning and beautifying their corner of the barracks. Indira named her section "Chimborazo" while Lekha named hers "Bien Venue" because she had a view of the jail's main gate. For obvious reasons, Mrs. Pandit was obliged to call hers the "Wall View." Mrs. Pandit had brought along with her to the prison an old blue rug which had lain on the floor in the children's nursery in Anand Bhavan. It now occupied the central space in the Nehru family section of the prison barracks. The girls dubbed it the "Blue Drawing Room," and it was in this delightful spacious apartment that they ate their delicious meals and read at night by the blinding light of a dim kerosene lantern.

Nothing in their jail apartment was an anonymous item. Everything was given its name and assigned its place. The lantern, for instance, was "Lucifer." A bottle of hair oil, the top of which was lost, became "Rupert, the headless Earl." Indira named the jail cat "Mehitabel." The cat challenged Indira's fertile imagination with its own fertility—it produced four kittens. And the five felines invited themselves to the daily milk ration of the three ladies.

People in jail are human too, and could be as interesting as humans outside prison. In her diary of prison days, Mrs. Pandit has left interesting descriptions of the strange collection of wardresses in charge of Naini jail:

Zohra—a fat, placid woman; very talkative and full of anecdotes of her past; her sense of humour is quite delicious.
Vishnudei—tall and strapping; ideal wardress in size and physique; looks imposing in her uniform; reticent.
Shyama—an altogether negative person, the type one hardly ever notices.

Mrs. Solomon—the nicest of the lot; gentle in manner; lives beyond her means and is in constant financial difficulties; the poor dear seeks relief in speaking about them; has a fine face, soft eyes and grey hair; pity she is connected with a jail!

Indira narrates an incident in which Zohra was the central figure.

One night we were all startled out of our sleep by a blood-curdling shriek. Although Zohra was the nastiest and most un-popular of all the wardresses, we could sympathize that night with her terror and agitation, for there was an enormous cobra only a yard away from our bars, coiled under one of the clocks which the wardresses had to punch on their rounds.

Poor Zohra was in an awful dilemma. If she didn't punch the clock she might lose her job. But if she punched the clock she might die of snake bite. Since we were locked inside the barracks and she within the outer wall, we couldn't go to her aid. There wasn't any stick or other weapon around. Zohra's shouts, now frightened now exasperated, now bullying, now entreating, did nothing to disturb the calm of the sentry out-side. He wanted detailed information about the exact location of the snake, and specifications of its length and girth!

Zohra was now at her wits' end. *"Aray Kambakht!"* ["O you wretched creature!"] she yelled back to him. "Do you think I have a tailor's tape with me to measure it from head to tail?"

Anyway, it was several hours before the sentry could be persuaded to call the matron. Her house was three furlongs away and she in turn had to walk to the Superintendent's house to awaken him, before they could go together to the main office to fetch the key to the women's prison. By the time this little procession entered our enclosure, we had long since fallen asleep philosophically, and the snake had glided away.

Prison walls are no bar to the enjoyment of festivals. October 18, 1942, was *Vijaya Dashami*, the day on which, according to the epic

Mahabharata, the Pandavas won their mighty victory over the Kauravas on the battlefield of Kurukshetra. Indira's barracks played host to their companions in the adjoining barracks and served them lunch. The nonpolitical convicts in the other yard did not want to be left out of the celebrations. They begged the matron to permit them to sing and dance on the occasion, which the matron did in a rare mood of generosity. Had Indira known that a quarter of a century later she would become Minister of Information and Broadcasting, she might have looked upon the performances of these convict women with the eager eyes of a talent scout. But whether she might have ventured to broadcast their songs and telecast their dances is another question. There was, quite naturally, a hint of vulgarity in their songs and a trace of obscenity in their dances.

November 8, 1942, heralded another festival—*Divali.* The previous day, one of the inmates in Indira's barracks bought red glass bangles for all of her companions, and everyone felt very gay. On the evening of the eighth the ladies performed *Puja* and made some sacrificial offerings out in the open yard and lighted a few earthen lamps. Then there were birthdays galore to celebrate. August 18 was Mrs. Pandit's. September 12, the first morning that Feroze spent in jail, was itself a birthday present. November 14 was Jawaharlal's birthday, November 19 of that year was Indira's twenty-fifth birthday, and October 2 was Mahatma Gandhi's.

Indira was extremely happy on her twenty-fifth birthday. On that day she had her fortnightly interview with her husband in the prison office and returned to the barracks full of cheer. The granting of regular interviews between husbands and wives detained in the same jail materialized only after a long duel with the jail authorities. At the time of Mrs. Pandit's arrest, her husband was away in Bombay. From there he had applied for permission to interview her in Naini jail. He never received a reply. He returned to Allahabad on September 17 and two days later he himself was imprisoned and brought to Naini jail. Mrs. Pandit pressed on the superintendent of the prison her claim to see her husband regularly. The prison official referred the question to the district magistrate, and he to higher authorities. At long last it was decreed that husbands and wives in the same jail were permitted to see one another once a fortnight for half an hour.

Gardening was one hobby which the Nehru ladies could freely indulge in in prison. Across the wall which divided their barracks from his, Ranjit Pandit had raised a flourishing garden. On one of his interviews with his wife and daughter, he had given them some cuttings which they planted in the yard outside their barracks. On New Year's Day 1943 Mrs. Pandit could record in her diary: "Our flowers are looking up. The morning glory is climbing well and there are several deep blue and mauve flowers. We have some pansies and nasturtiums also, and a row of cosmos which stand against the wall and look quite pretty. The larkspurs and several other flowers have not done at all well in spite of the care from Indu and Lekha. Sometime ago we persuaded the matron to plant a few vegetables and the tomatoes, chillies and *dhania* (coriander) are all coming up. Yesterday we picked nearly a dozen really good tomatoes."

In contrast to these later times, Indira's early days in prison were quite miserable. Political prisoners were usually classified into three categories, and their treatment and privileges depended upon their classification. For instance, Jawaharlal was classified as an "A" class prisoner, Mrs. Pandit as a "B" class prisoner initially and then upgraded to "A," while Feroze was given a "C" class status. Either due to an oversight or some other undisclosed reason, the magistrate simply made a cross where the letters *A, B* or *C* should have appeared on Indira's prison card. The prison superintendent apparently interpreted this to mean that she was not entitled to privileges of any kind, such as receiving foodstuffs from outside, letters, or visitors. Once when her father had arranged for a basket of mangoes to be delivered to his daughter, the prison superintendent helped himself to them, in the belief that Indira was not entitled to any! Jawaharlal, however, never gave up and would always write to his younger sister, Krishna, in Bombay to send his daughter some mangoes of the *Alphonso* variety, reputed to be the "king of mangoes." One of Mrs. Krishna Hutheesing's parcels did reach Indira at last. On May 14, 1943, Jawaharlal informed Krishna: "Indu wrote to me that she had received the fruit sent by you. She was quite excited about the

Alphonsos, and smelt them and touched them and almost hugged them. She loves mangoes and getting good fruit and especially good mangoes, after long being deprived of them, was an exhilarating experience. I hope the fruit will continue being sent to her." There was, however, no need to continue, since Indira was actually released from prison the day before Jawaharlal wrote that letter to Krishna.

Similar misunderstandings occurred about receiving letters. For months Indira never knew the whereabouts of her father. On New Year's Day 1943 Indira was informed that "the Government of India has permitted the members of the Congress Working Committee to correspond with members of their families on personal and domestic matters only." However, Jawaharlal appears to have remained in the dark about this decision of the government. In the middle of February 1943 he was writing to Krishna about his having "read in a newspaper that Indu had been given permission to write to me," and also "that I had been allowed to write to her." In March he complained to Krishna: "Today I am writing also to Indu . . . I have not heard from her yet." At last he was informed officially of the rules of correspondence, and it was not before the middle of April that he managed to hear from Indira, who assured him that she was "keeping well so far."

During the first ten months of Indira's incarceration the prisoners were not permitted to receive any newspapers. This regulation was relaxed on April 20, 1943, when political prisoners were permitted to receive newspapers at their own expense. However, notwithstanding the earlier restriction, there was no blackout on news in the prison. The male prisoners could always rely on Feroze's ingenuity to get around prison rules. He noticed that an old man who supplied victuals to the prison came regularly with a basket on his head and bamboo staff in hand. Feroze arranged to receive his newspaper every day, neatly rolled inside the hollow of the old man's bamboo staff. When the men were through with reading the papers, they passed them on to the women. Feroze's companion in prison, Bhabani Prasad Banerji, who is now in charge of the international affairs section of the Congress Party secretariat in New Delhi, was assigned this task. The agile Bengali would slither up a drain pipe, hold on to the para-

pet wall of the barracks with his left hand, and hurl with his right
the newspaper into the yard of the women prisoners' barracks. Once
Banerji had perfected his art and began hitting the bull's eye with
never a miss, Feroze slipped into the newspaper an occasional billet-
doux to Indira. The men then felt grieved that the women were
getting something for nothing. They threatened to stop the supply
of newspapers unless they were given a feed. With no choice left
in the matter the women saved up on their skimpy rations for a few
days and gave the illicit newspaper dealers a "home-cooked" meal.

The plight of the habitual female convicts and their children was
something the political prisoners could not bear to see. During her
earlier imprisonment, Mrs. Pandit had converted a small room adjoining the second barracks into a nursery for the babies of convicts.
When she returned she found to her dismay that the nursery had been
reconverted to an office-*cum*-storeroom. The friezes she had painted
on the walls were now faded, the clay toys she had molded were reduced to rubble, and the blackboard was broken to bits. Mrs. Pandit
also discovered that the convicts were not being given their regular
Hindi and Urdu lessons. The prison teacher conducted a class in the
morning for the children of warders, which was open for attendance
by the children of convicts. But the afternoon classes were completely skipped. The female convicts hated the thought of learning,
while the teacher loved her siesta. When Mrs. Pandit returned to
prison, she resumed her educational chores. As other political prisoners joined her, they too shared in her reformist zeal.

Indira discovered that some political prisoners, although they made
excellent noncooperators, proved to be awful mothers. The 1942
movement was noteworthy for the large number of college girls and
young women who courted imprisonment. Among the five volunteers arrested along with Indira on September 11 were a twelve-
year-old adolescent and a sixteen-year-old pregnant teen-ager. Every
other day a new girl joined the inmates of Naini prison. Three weeks
after Indira's arrest, another young girl with a two-month-old baby
was brought in as a "C" class undertrial prisoner. Her husband had
already been arrested and the teen-age mother had little choice but
to take the infant along to jail. The child was her third, and yet the

girl knew precious little about mothering. She was obviously a rich bearer but a poor rearer of children. Being a newlywed, Indira had glanced through some books on child care prior to her imprisonment. She had also acquired considerable practical experience, having attended on untouchable children in the Poona school. She took over the care of the infant, bathing, feeding and clothing it. Since the mother was barely literate, Indira gave her regular classes and had the satisfaction of seeing her become a primary schoolteacher after leaving prison. The baby thrived under Indira's care and became "more and more adorable every day," as Mrs. Pandit recorded in her diary. Indira wanted very much to adopt the baby, but was dissuaded from doing so by the advice of her relatives and the complexity of the legal procedure.

As at the time of Indira's schooling in Poona, Mahatma Gandhi now determined again to observe a twenty-one-day fast. Gandhi wrote to the Viceroy contending that the preventive detention of Congress leaders was unjustified, since at its Bombay session the Congress had *not* outlined any specific action. The Congress had no doubt authorized Gandhi to initiate such action as might become necessary in the future; but at the time of the arrest there was no clear and present danger of imminent action. Gandhi also wrote to Lord Linlithgow, the Viceroy, what monstrous folly it was for him to have arrested a man like Jawaharlal who was eager to support the Allied war effort against the Axis Powers, provided India had some hope of enjoying democratic rights. Linlithgow replied he would consider sympathetically what to do with the imprisoned Congress leaders if Gandhi disowned the August 1942 proceedings of the Congress in Bombay. Gandhi refused and planned his twenty-one-day fast. The Viceroy was disturbed and called Gandhi's threat "political blackmail." Gandhi was now seventy-four, and it appeared doubtful if he could survive another prolonged fast. Linlithgow, averse to having Gandhi's corpse on his hands, offered to release him from detention in the Aga Khan Palace at least for the duration of the fast, but Gandhi declined the offer.

He commenced the fast on February 9, 1943. All the men in Naini prison observed a twenty-four-hour sympathetic fast, and the women too followed their example. Indira joined her companions in signing a letter to the superintendent of the prison asking him not to send them any rations. They fasted all day and held a prayer meeting in the yard at dusk just before lock-up time. Newspapers were not yet permitted freely in prison at the time of the fast, and the women kept an anxious vigil for any information about Gandhi's condition. Everyone was relieved when Gandhi's fast ended on March 2 and he was still alive and on the road to recovery.

On one occasion Indira spent a few anxious moments in prison when its inmates hovered between life and death. Allahabad had become an important center for stationing troops in wartime. Rangoon had fallen to the invading Japanese Army, and it was feared that Calcutta might be its next target. The reconnaissance mission of Japanese planes over Calcutta only strengthened this suspicion. In such an event, Allahabad would become the front line of defense for the Allied forces. The city's Cantonment area was a major center for the concentration of British, American, and Canadian troops. The Allied planes took off constantly on their missions and were a dazzling sight when they flew in formation at night, their twinkling green and red lights taking on the aspect of emeralds and rubies set in a constellation of starry white diamonds in the dark cloudless Indian sky.

Indira narrates the tale of a romance which barely escaped ending up as a colossal tragedy. An ace pilot of the Royal Canadian Air Force was smitten by love. The object of his passionate attention was the voluptuous daughter of the Anglo-Indian prison superintendent. As the superintendent's house was not far removed from Indira's barracks the pilot dipped low over his beloved's house in salutation every day, before landing at the nearby military aerodrome. Pilots were under very strict instructions not to do this over residential areas, since it endangered the life and limb of civilians. But like the peacock parading its plumage to its love-mate, the ace pilot found himself incapable of desisting from his aerial acrobatics. One day his wing got entangled in telegraph wires and his plane immediately burst into flames. Indira and her companions stood breathless as the ball of fire came hurtling down directly in the line of their barracks. Luckily for them, the flaming missile just skirted the prison wall and crashed into an adjoining half-built bungalow.

On May 5, 1943, Indira and her aunt, Vijaya Lakshmi, were summoned to the prison office and were informed they would be released the next morning if they agreed to abide by certain conditions. An externment order would be served, requiring them to quit Allahabad and proceed to Almora district, to which their movements would have to be confined until further advice. Ranjit Pandit had acquired a beautiful country estate at Khali, in Almora district, and it was there that Mrs. Pandit and Indira were told to stay at their own expense. Both the ladies turned down the offer. They insisted that they should be wholly free to do what they pleased once they were released from prison, but if their unrestricted movement did not please the government they would much rather stay behind bars than enjoy a fictitious freedom outside. However, a week later, on the morning of May 13, 1943, Indira and her aunt were released, suddenly and unconditionally.

Hardly a fortnight elapsed when the police arrived at Anand Bhavan and served an externment order requiring Indira and Mrs. Pandit to proceed to Almora. They refused to comply with the order, and poor Mrs. Pandit was dragged back to Naini prison. Luckily, there was no warrant for Indira, and it was just as well, since she lay in bed with fever and a virulent cold.

Although Indira's 243 days in prison were fewer than her father's 3,262, the conditions under which she spent her imprisonment were probably far worse than anyone in the Nehru family faced. Motilal was a distinguished elder statesman, and was treated as such even in prison. During his first imprisonment in Lucknow jail he enjoyed the pleasant company of his son and two nephews. He was permitted to obtain wholesome food from outside, to write letters and receive books and newspapers. The Lieutenant-Governor of the province, Sir Harcourt Butler, was a personal friend of Motilal's of thirty years' standing, and the rumor was that Sir Harcourt through an aide-de-camp sent his friend in prison every day a half bottle of champagne wrapped in a napkin! The awe in which prison officials stood of Motilal is illustrated by an amusing anecdote his biographer narrates. His nephew, Brijlal Nehru, was on a short visit to India from Burma, where he was posted on service.

> Accompanied by his wife Rameshwari, son Braj Kumar, and brother Kishenlal, Brijlal arrived at the prison gates, but was informed that not more than three visitors could be admitted. Brijlal decided to stay out, and the rest of the party went in. Motilal, furious when he learned that his nephew had been kept out, sent for the prison superintendent and demanded to know why the number of visitors had been restricted without his—Motilal's—approval. The superintendent did not wait to contest the propriety of this remarkable query from his distinguished prisoner but issued orders that Brijlal should be admitted at once and the new rule should not be applied to the Nehrus.

Motilal and Jawaharlal had fundamentally different attitudes toward jail-going which naturally affected their moods and activities within prison. One of their coprisoners in the 1930's, Dr. Syed Mahmud, who was later to become independent India's Minister of State for External Affairs, records the difference:

> Jawaharlal did not idle away his time but would keep himself engaged in studying and exercises, while Motilal, on the contrary, would relate anecdotes to his companions. After Motilal arrived, food was daily sent from Anand Bhavan. Quite a troop of prisoners would bring our food from the jail gates to our cell. Jawaharlal did not like so much food being brought to the jail from outside. He would not say anything to his father, but would angrily turn to me and say: "This is not a hotel. This is a jail. We shouldn't get so much food from outside." But this continued in spite of him. When Motilal was released because of weak health, Jawaharlal returned to Anand Bhavan all articles of luxury, like the fan and the ice chest. Motilal wrote an angry note to Jawaharlal and sent back the ice chest with the remark that if he did not like to use cold water in that hot season, "Mahmud was there to use it."

Going to jail was, to Motilal, nothing short of having fun. But to Jawaharlal it was a deadly serious business. The father even ridiculed his son for his overly serious attitude. Dr. Mahmud recalls another occasion in Yeravda prison when the superintendent, Mr. Martin, came to ask Motilal what food the party of three would like to eat.

> He replied with an air of unconcern that some porridge, eggs and fish, and bread and butter and some soup, and a fowl between Mahmud and himself, and some pudding would be enough. And, to his son, Mr. Martin could give any "grass-like" things, meaning vegetables—since Jawaharlal was then a vegetarian. Mr. Martin must have wondered at the kind of prisoners he had, but he quietly obeyed.

Indira's attitude to jail-going was more like her father's than her grandfather's. She was, first of all, only twenty-five years of age when imprisoned, and she burned with youthful enthusiasm for "the cause." Even within Anand Bhavan, she came to live under increasingly austere conditions after her grandfather's death. She felt, as her father did, that one courted imprisonment in order to impress the British that the noncooperators were willing to undergo any amount of privation rather than to suggest that they would be completely lost if they were deprived of certain ordinary amenities. She had her mother's capacity for suffering and patient and uncomplaining endurance. Lastly, unlike her father, who always received the treatment of an "A" class prisoner, she was classified as an "X" prisoner, which signified nothing and left her to the not too tender mercy of the prison superintendent. Temperament and circumstance alike forced her while in prison to withdraw into a shell, wipe the past out of her memory, and subsist only in the present. Not being an intellectual like her father, she could not engage in writing or reflection. She had to snuff out all thought as much as she had to smother all feeling. To reconcile herself stoically to her lot in prison would have involved an act of conscious reasoning. She preferred to banish all consciousness and merely vegetate rather than live.

It was not unnatural that when she was released, freedom came to her somewhat as a shock. Recalling that experience, Indira wrote years later: "My unexpected release was like coming suddenly out of a dark passage. I was dazzled with the rush of life, the many hues and textures, the scale of sounds and the range of ideas. Just to touch and listen was a disturbing experience and it took a while to get adjusted to normal living."

The return to normalcy was helped a great deal by the release of Feroze in August 1943. Whereas no charges were preferred against Indira, Feroze had been tried and sentenced to one year's rigorous imprisonment and a fine of two hundred rupees. He was released for good behavior a little earlier than the expiry of a year. Indira and Feroze were still the only regular inmates in Anand Bhavan, as most others were still in prison. To both of them, tasty food, silence, privacy, and companionship had become, of a sudden, something to savor.

10

Her Father's Understudy

THE year in which Indira came out of prison witnessed the most calamitous famine in all of Indian history. The province which bore the brunt of it was Bengal, but in the country as a whole some 3,500,000 people perished. Before the Japanese invasion of Burma the surplus rice of that country had been exported for consumption in Bengal. Once Burma fell, the rice supply was cut off, and the British Government of the day was tardy in finding substitute sources. Available surpluses from other parts of the country could have been rushed to Bengal, but the railways, the only means of communication, were busy transporting men and material for the war.

The lackadaisical attitude of the government—Lord Linlithgow returned to England after seven years of his viceroyalty without even once visiting the famine-affected province—left the people no alternative but to organize famine relief voluntarily on a national scale. Indira was among the thousands who busied themselves with raising money, finding grain, and keeping the pipeline to Bengal filled with supplies. The celebrated Indian dancer Uday Shankar, himself a Bengali whose performances had enchanted so many Americans of an older generation—just as those of his younger brother, Ravi Shankar, now draw crowds of younger Americans—toured all over India with his ballet troupe to raise funds for famine relief. Indira sold as many tickets as she could for Shankar's performance in Allahabad.

Things settled down somewhat in Anand Bhavan by the end of the year before death paid a call again on the family. Ranjit Pandit was released from prison in October 1943 because of serious ill health. When he arrived at Anand Bhavan, he discovered his wife was away in Calcutta, engaged in famine relief. Ranjit and Vijaya Lakshmi joined each other later at their mountain home in Khali. But since Ranjit's health showed little improvement, his wife took him to Lucknow Hospital, where he died an unexpected death during the early hours of January 14, 1944. Indira and Feroze rushed to Lucknow and helped bring Ranjit's body back to Anand Bhavan. By evening the body was consigned to flames and the ashes were mingled with the perennial stream of Mother Ganges.

"What's the point of your marrying if you don't want children," Indira had once argued vehemently with Shanta Gandhi, and added with obvious determination: "I'll have lots and lots of children." To that task Indira now turned diligently. When she conceived, however, there was no one at home to care for her during her pregnancy. Her elder aunt, the recently widowed Mrs. Pandit, had left for the United States to join two of her daughters at Wellesley College. Her younger aunt, Mrs. Krishna Hutheesing, was living in Bombay. Although she had volunteered as a noncooperator during earlier civil disobedience movements, Mrs. Hutheesing kept away from prison during the 1942 movement because she had two young children to look after. Indira finally repaired to Bombay to live with her aunt. Bombay was the ideal place in India to have children, for the city had a number of excellent centers for prenatal and postnatal care and boasted of many an eminent gynecologist and obstetrician. One of them was Dr. Vithal Nagesh Shirodkar, and it was in his Surgical Nursing Home and Lying-in Hospital that Indira delivered her older son, Rajiv, on August 20, 1944.

Although Shirodkar was a top man in his profession and could have competently handled any situation that might have arisen, Indira was eager to obviate all complications. She never missed out on her daily constitutional, adhered to a strict diet, and performed with her customary perfectionist zeal the prescribed exercises during her entire pregnancy up until the very last day. The result accorded with anticipation. She had an extremely easy delivery. Krishna was all excited and wrote to her brother congratulating him on becoming a grandpapa. Jawaharlal wrote back to her:

"I was happy to get the news—not so excited as you must have been, for excitement is less in my line. I was particularly pleased to learn of the easy delivery Indu had. I hope that she and the baby have kept up to the mark during the days following the confinement."

Indira was indeed more than up to the mark. She was completely relaxed, was in perfect condition, and surprised everyone who ever thought sneeringly of her strength by breast-feeding Rajiv for the first few months. Although Jawaharlal says he was not particularly excited about the arrival of his grandson, he was quite meticulous in instructing his daughter to follow a hoary family tradition. He wrote to his sister Krishna:

In my letter to Indu I suggested to her to ask you to get a proper horoscope made by a competent person. Such permanent records of the date and time of birth are desirable. As for the time, I suppose the proper solar time should be mentioned and not the artificial time which is being used outside now. War time is at least an hour ahead of the normal time.

After Indira returned to Anand Bhavan, events occurred both in India and in the world at breakneck speed. The war in Europe ended. Churchill resigned and new elections were pending in England. On June 15, 1945, Jawaharlal was released from prison. On July 26, 1945, Labour was returned to power in England and Clement Attlee became Prime Minister. Early in 1946 the Labour Cabinet decided to transfer power to Indian hands, and in March of that year a Cabinet Mission arrived in the subcontinent to discuss with Indian political parties the future governance of the country. The Indian National Congress had not held a presidental election since 1940. An authorized representative of the party was now required to conduct negotiations with the British, and in July 1946 the Congress elected Jawaharlal Nehru its president. The Viceroy then invited Nehru, as the Congress president, to form an Interim Government, pending final transfer of power from British to Indian hands.

The Muslim League, headed by Mr. Mohammed Ali Jinnah, however, boycotted the newly-formed government. In 1942, when Gandhi asked the British to "Quit India," Jinnah had countered with the cry, "Divide and Quit." The Cabinet Mission's new proposals, like Sir Stafford Cripps' old ones, were unacceptable to the Congress because it feared they would ultimately lead to the division of India; they were unacceptable to the Muslim League because they did not propose the immediate division of India. With the Cabinet Mission's offer rejected and the impasse between the Congress and the League continuing, Attlee invited the chief spokesmen of the two parties to a conference in London. The conference did not bring the two parties any closer. In December 1946 a Constituent Assembly was formally convened in New Delhi to draft a new constitution for independent India. This too was boycotted by the Muslim League. The stalemate was complete, and the Gordian knot was finally cut only six months later when India, as it was known historically, was partitioned into the two new states of India and Pakistan.

Feroze, now a married man with a wife and an infant to support, had to think of ways and means of making a living. Luckily, while he was in search of a job, there was also a job in search of the right man. The Nehrus had a sort of Jeffersonian interest in newspaper publishing. Back in 1909 Motilal was associated with the inception of *The Leader*, the first daily newspaper in Allahabad. Motilal became its first chairman of the board of directors, resisted vainly all official attempts to muzzle the paper, and turned it within the space of a decade into the most articulate organ of nationalist opinion in his province. In 1918, however, when Motilal pressed for a more forward editorial policy, the paper's editor resisted. Thereupon Motilal decided to launch his own paper, and on February 5, 1919, *The Independent*, also an English daily, saw the light of day. He became the chairman of the board of directors of the new newspaper, but not all of Motilal's money or idealism could sustain it forever, and it folded three years later.

Jawaharlal also tried his hand at publishing when he became a founder of the English daily *The National Herald* of Lucknow in 1937. From the very start the paper had to put up with the government's incessant bullying. Securities were demanded from the paper, and when the doings of the government were depicted in an unfavorable light, the security was forfeited and a fresh deposit demanded. The provincial government imposed a prior censorship and required the paper to clear its headlines and leading articles with officials before publication. When officialdom tampered with the leading articles, the *Herald* chose to leave the editorial columns blank. Subsequently, when the 1942 civil disobedience movement commenced, the paper suspended publication completely. With the release of all political prisoners, *The National Herald* resumed publication in November 1946. Unfortunately, it was at this very juncture that the paper's chairman of the board of directors, Jawaharlal Nehru, was invited by the Viceroy to form the Interim Government. He had accepted the Viceroy's invitation, and to obviate any charge of a conflict of interests, he resigned as chairman of the board. It was thus that Feroze Gandhi came to the *Herald's* rescue and became its managing director.

Feroze and Indira moved from Anand Bhavan in Allahabad to a neat little bungalow in the Hazratgunj area of Lucknow. Feroze started literally from scratch and brought the paper virtually to a self-supporting position by a careful husbanding of its resources. He used the idle hours of his press to print *The Listener*, the Indian counterpart of the BBC's official organ, and soon the paper was on its feet again. Its editor, Mr. M. Chalapathi Rau, says: "Feroze had the common touch. He often worked in the press day and night. He loved machines; he did not mind the ink and the soot. This endeared him to the workers. They carried great influence with him. He could not think of taking disciplinary action against anybody, even in moments of great irritation."

Feroze, however, was not the kind of man to be content with small achievements. He was dreaming constantly about the future enlargement of the enterprise and planned assiduously for a Delhi edition of the paper. He had ordered the finest machinery from Europe for installation in Delhi. But when the machinery arrived, the requisite capital was not forthcoming. Jawaharlal Nehru's political intimate and a power in his provincial politics, Rafi Ahmad Kidwai, was supposed to have raised the necessary capital and given it to Feroze "without any strings attached." But Kidwai was too preoccupied with politics, money was difficult to find, and Feroze was forced to sell all the newly-acquired machinery. Dejected with this depressing development, he resigned in 1952 as the *Herald's* managing editor.

He then went over to New Delhi and joined another English daily, *The Indian Express*, as its general manager. One other factor which influenced his decision to shift from Lucknow to Delhi was the proposed General Election of 1952. The Constituent Assembly of India had drafted a new constitution for the country, which was adopted on January 26, 1950, exactly twenty-one years to the day when Jawaharlal Nehru as president of the Indian National Congress first read out the independence pledge. Under this new constitution, free India's first election was proposed to be held in 1952. Although the Constituent Assembly was dissolved after the adoption of the new constitution, it continued to function as a provisional parliament until the General Election. Feroze had been attending the sessions of this provisional parliament in New Delhi since 1950. He now wanted to contest the election to India's regular Parliament as the Congress candidate from the Rae Bareli constituency of the state of Uttar Pradesh.

Feroze's political ambitions converged with Indira's personal inclinations and prompted both of them to shift their scene of operations from Lucknow, the provincial capital, to New Delhi, the national capital. Ever since Jawaharlal Nehru had become Vice President of the Viceroy's Executive Council and Member for External Affairs and Commonwealth Relations on September 2, 1946, he had lived in a modest two-story house in New Delhi. Indira had been forced to flit between Lucknow and New Delhi, distributing her time evenly between devotion to her husband and care of her father.

On one such excursion to the capital her second son, Sanjay, was born. On the evening of December 14, 1946, Lady Cripps had dropped by at Nehru's house and requested Indira to go shopping with her. She wanted to buy a Kashmiri shawl and pleaded with Indira: "There isn't anyone who knows just what's right for me the way you do." Indira obliged Lady Cripps and went along, although she was feeling faint and not fit enough for an outing on that winter evening. "That night," Indira later recalled, "my second son was born prematurely. We put up a tent, and my husband was put out in that, and the nanny and the baby and I stayed in the bedroom, as we couldn't risk the outdoor chill."

Indira had not yet regained her full strength when Mahatma Gandhi asked her to tour the Muslim residential areas in old Delhi to comfort and reassure the helpless victims of the bloody and savage riots which had preceded and followed the partition of India. Cholera had broken out among the already terrified Muslim communities, who preferred to put up with the terrible affliction in their hovels rather than venture out on the streets and face the Hindus and Sikhs thirsting for revenge. Indira hired a delivery van and carried the frightened doctors into the beleaguered quarter. She first tried to get the hoodlums and the rowdy elements arrested, but her deterrent approach did not work. She then tried the human approach. She ascertained from the Muslims, Hindus, and Sikhs the names of the leaders of the rival communities in whom they had faith and trust. Some five hundred such leaders with decent instincts were brought together at a social gathering. They in turn carried the message of fraternal feeling and communal harmony to their coreligionists, and tension between the rival communities eased a little.

When the frenzy of communal rioting was still at its peak, a new Viceroy, Lord Louis Mountbatten, arrived in India on March 22, 1947. Plunging immediately into discussions with leaders of the Congress and the Muslim League, Mountbatten discovered that they were not any nearer to agreement than they had been at the London Conference with Attlee a few months earlier. The Viceroy then presented his own scheme—the Mountbatten Plan—which envisioned the partitioning of India. It did not satisfy either party wholly. But neither party had any illusions that its demands would be conceded in their entirety. Mahatma Gandhi refused to be party to the vivisection of India and kept away from the negotiations. In fact, he was not even a member of the Congress party at the time and had withdrawn from active politics. Jawaharlal Nehru was not pleased with the prospect of a divided India. But he reconciled himself to it because it would at least hasten the country's independence. Mohammed Ali Jinnah, the leader of the Muslim League, complained bitterly that the Pakistan conceded by Mountbatten was not the same as he envisaged but "a truncated, moth-eaten Pakistan," and yet preferred it to the prospect of not having Pakistan at all.

On the evening of August 14, 1947, mammoth crowds of cheering men and women and jubilant children lined New Delhi's streets as the leaders of the Congress proceeded to usher in an independent India at a solemn ceremony in the Constituent Assembly. At the appointed time, Jawaharlal Nehru rose to address the Assembly as millions outside the hall listened to him over the radio:

"Long years ago we made a tryst with destiny, and now the time comes when we shall redeem our pledge, not wholly or in full measure, but very substantially. At the stroke of the midnight hour, when the world sleeps, India will awake to life and freedom. A moment comes, which comes but rarely in history, when we step out from the old to the new, when an age ends, and when the soul of a nation, long suppressed, finds utterance. It is fitting that at this solemn moment we take the pledge of dedication to the service of India and her people and to the still larger cause of humanity.... Peace has been said to be indivisible. So is freedom, so is prosperity now, and so also is disaster in this One World that can no longer be split into isolated fragments."

Seventeen years earlier, a slip of a girl, no more than thirteen years old, had recited the words of the independence pledge which her father had drafted when he became president of the Indian National Congress for the first time. Today she was a young woman of thirty, happily married, the mother of two adorable children, and in command of the summit of domestic felicity. But it was also the crowning moment of her life for other reasons. Recalling the years of her childhood, Indira says:

"The absolutely overshadowing idea, of course, at that time was freedom for India and to do whatever was necessary for it, and since at that time one somehow didn't believe it would come in one's lifetime, it meant it would be a lifetime of hardship. And you may have heard that my own, sort of, heroine at that time was Joan of Arc. She died at the stake. This was the significant thing that I envisaged—an end like that for myself."

The national drama had a happier ending than she feared, although it was marred by the insensate communal passions which let loose a river of blood. Even personally, Indira did not end up at the stake; and her father, who had staked his all for India, was now the country's first citizen and Prime Minister. "I was so excited and proud," she reminisced, "I really thought I would burst!" Her elation was a mixture of private consolation and public satisfaction, although the latter was the dominant strand. She was proud, not so much for being the Prime Minister's daughter "but more as an Indian, I think, because of having taken part in the struggle and to feel it was worth it."

After Mr. Nehru became Prime Minister of independent India it was decided that he should move into the spacious sixteen-room mansion of the then British Commander-in-Chief on Teen Murti Marg. "I came over to look at it and was at once plunged in gloom," recalls Indira. She was entrusted with the task of redecorating the house, and she wondered if it could ever be made livable and would bear any semblance at all to a home. Staring down from the walls of the public rooms were life-size portraits of stern generals, resplendent in their bemedaled uniforms. She was ill at ease in their presence. "I felt they were watching my every movement, criticizing every unspoken thought. I couldn't be at ease until they were all taken down and hurriedly dispatched to the Defence Ministry." She was quite pleased with the result, although it posed another problem. "Their removal made the rooms seem larger and the walls seemed to stretch in their stark bareness." How was she going to fill those enormous rooms and long corridors? "I needn't have worried," she says in retrospect. "What house can resist fast-growing boys full of healthy mischief, aided by a host of animals?"

"We had always had dogs," she reports, "the good kind with long pedigrees, but others too, rescued off the streets, which were just as devoted." The boys, Rajiv and Sanjay, collected so many more pets as they grew older—parrots, pigeons, squirrels, practically every tiny creature common to the Indian scene—that she says, "We thought life was pretty full, looking after them on top of all the other chores." And then there was a strange new addition to the animal family, the acquisition and care of which Indira has written about:

> In Assam we were presented with a bear-cat [Red Himalayan Panda], although we did not know what it was until we reached Agartala and were able to study the book, *Indian Animals*, in the Commissioner's library. The tribals had told us it was a kind of bear, and my children, expecting it to grow large and strong, decided to call it Bhimsa [meaning, "like Bhim," the second of the Pandava brothers in the epic, *Mahabharata*, reputed for his physical prowess] even before they had seen the tiny ball of fur.
>
> We arranged a corner for Bhimsa in the children's bathroom, but somehow I could not house-train him and he always climbed on the towel-rack to do his business, besides racing all over the house. Finally we banished him to the garden, where a large wire-netting enclosure was made with a wooden house in a tree. And that is where he has lived ever since—except when he goes off to Naini Tal every summer. Much later we got him a wife, Pema (which means Lotus in Sikkimese), and now they have the most adorable little cubs—the first, I believe, to be born in captivity.

Mr. Nehru had grown extremely fond of the panda family, and he called on them morning and evening. They too missed him whenever he was out of town. "Once when my father was unwell," recalls Indira, "we even took Bhimsa to call on him in his bedroom. The only things that make them unhappy are loud noises and the scent of the dogs and the tigers."

There were already far too many dogs in the house and, to the discomfiture of the poor pandas, three tiger cubs also arrived in 1955. They were named Bhim, Bhairav, and Hidamba. Apparently, more trouble arrived for Indira along with the tiger cubs. She narrates the story herself:

A man came from the Lucknow Zoo to teach us how to look after them and advised us to have a cement floor in their enclosure. Unfortunately, he put the cubs into it before the cement had properly set, so that their paws were lacerated and infected. Two of them were cured with sulphur powder but little Bhim got worse and worse. Without our knowledge, the veterinarian on attendance decided to cauterize Bhim's paws, and forgetting that despite his ferocious roar he was still a wee baby, gave him such a walloping dose of sedative that he practically collapsed. My father and I were terribly upset. After much telephoning we were lucky to contact another veterinarian, who prescribed saline injections and a constant vigil night and day. One of our reception officers opted to stay half the night, while I would go to bed at 10 P.M. and be up at 2 A.M. to assume my duty. Mercifully, on the morning of the fifth day Bhim raised his head.

My own children had got used to playing with the cubs and did not care how boisterous they got, but for other children and visitors it was a boon to have Bhim still dazed and docile from his illness, and many who ordinarily would not come within ten yards of him felt courageous enough to stroke him! He recovered fast and only too soon was too big to be kept in the open in a house which had so much *va et vien*. Reluctantly we sent them off to the Lucknow Zoo, where you can still meet Bhim and Hidamba—magnificent beasts, their muscles rippling with power and grace. While they were with us they were petted by many distinguished people, including Marshal Tito and U Nu. The Marshal asked for one of them, and Bhairav now resides in Belgrade.

Before she could become her father's political understudy, Indira had to learn to be his official hostess at home. Her job was like "walking on a tightrope to adhere close enough to the formal side of protocol so as not to offend even the most particular of dignitaries and yet manage not to stifle the human element." By all accounts Indira succeeded remarkably well in this delicate task. Vimla Sindhi, who was one of the social secretaries in the Prime Minister's residence those

days, recalls the testimony of many guests to the perfect care Indira
bestowed on them. She would personally check every light bulb in
the lamps for functional failure and every faucet in the guest rooms
for leaks. She made sure that tall people were provided with high-
backed chairs and short people with footrests. She decided the menus
and selected the gifts for heads of government visiting the country.
The convention was for visiting heads of government to stay informally for two or three days with the Prime Minister, who was himself the head of government, and then formally in Rashtrapati Bhavan, the residence of the President, who was the head of state. Miss
Sindhi says that most guests who visited India more than once re-
gretted exchanging the warm attention of Teen Murti House to the
cold formality of Rashtrapati Bhavan, and some wondered if they
could not stay at the former all through.

Indira records that entertaining her Indian guests was "made more
complicated by the peculiar fads of our people." She is certain to
elicit the sympathy of many an American hostess who has had to
entertain an Indian when she laments:

"Apart from the main taboos of Hindus not eating beef and Muslims not eating pork, there are endless combinations and permuta-
tions. There are meat eaters who are vegetarians on certain days of
the week; there are vegetarians who eat eggs; others who eat fish; and
there was one distinguished guest who declared himself a vegetarian
and ended up by eating everything except chicken!"

Learning about the eating habits of people and the quantities of
food required was not easy. During her first year in Teen Murti
House, several receptions were held, mainly for diplomats, at the
in-between hour of 6:30 P.M. In India, around five o'clock in the
evening is teatime, and dinnertime does not arrive until eight or nine.
Indira discovered that only a small quantity of food was consumed.
At a subsequent party "for a slightly different crowd," her estimates
went all awry. Instead of helping themselves to a snack or two, they
relieved the bearers of whole trays of snacks.

"To our mounting dismay," she recalls the nightmarish experience,
"we saw the food being exhausted even before all the invitees had
arrived."

Her own error of judgment was compounded by the weatherman's faulty prediction. On advice from the meteorological department, the party was arranged outdoors. A thunderstorm announced itself out of the blue, the guests were herded indoors, two of them fainted in the suffocating humid air, and the food disappeared. Luckily, neither her father nor the guests noticed anything amiss. What "saved the day," she says, was "that sturdy standby, the *pakora* [a fritter usually of onion rings or slices of potato, eggplant, cucumber, banana, or spinach leaves dipped in a batter of spiced chick-pea flour and deep fried in oil] along with dried fruit and nuts!" She learned her lesson the hard way and admits that "since that dreadful day I take good care to have extra stuff available, and to make duplicate arrangements, outside and in, even if I see a speck of a cloud."

Various complications could arise when a lunch or dinner had to be served to a huge international gathering. One such distinguished assemblage of conferees gathered in New Delhi in 1956 for the celebration of the twenty-five-hundredth anniversary of the *mahaparinirvana* (the shedding of the mortal coils) of the Buddha. The delegates included the Dalai Lama and several other venerable Buddhist monks. Until almost the last moment it did not occur to Indira that the monks must eat their last meal before noon, whereas the other guests would not be free from their deliberations until 1:30 P.M. So she solved the problem by having seventy-five monks to lunch at 11:30 A.M. and the one hundred other guests at 1:30 P.M.

When Mr. Nehru moved into Teen Murti House and Indira had to keep house for him, she felt the need for a governess to bring up her children. She thought of Anna Ornsholt, the governess who had attended on Mrs. Pandit's three daughters and left for Europe when the girls went to study in the United States. Indira herself was well acquainted with the governess. After Kamala's death, whenever Indira came home to Anand Bhavan on her vacation from school in England, Anna proved a pleasant companion. Indira summoned Miss Ornsholt in 1947 from her native Denmark to help take care of Rajiv and Sanjay.

Nayantara leaves us a vivid description of the governess:

She was a tall, slim, erect Dane, with iron-gray hair, blue eyes, a smooth, unlined rose-and-tan complexion, and a swinging stride. ... She was an ardent believer in cold showers, exercise, and sunbathing. ... Tante Anna was contemptuous of people who did not do things for themselves. Under her tutelage we made our own beds, polished our own shoes, learned to sew and mend our clothes. ... "Sit up!" "Walk straight!" she was always commanding us. "How will India ever be free if you young people always sit hunched up?" She had more vitality than anyone we had ever known before. She was an enthusiastic vegetarian and frequently went on diets consisting only of raw vegetables, including raw potatoes and yoghurt. In her zeal she even tried to convert our cairn terrier, Tangle, to vegetarian food, but had to give up when the little fellow became listless on spinach soup.

She always wore a sari when she went out. It was unusual for a European woman to adopt so many Indian ways. She became Tante Anna to our friends, relations, and the servants as well, and people never ceased to be amazed at her abundant store of energy. She swam, played tennis and badminton with zest, and on summer afternoons when the searing heat and brutal glare of the sun had driven everybody into cool, darkened rooms for a nap, Tante Anna would get on her bicycle, bare-headed, and pedal to the bazaar a mile away to do some shopping for Mummie. The European community in town was convinced that she was quite mad.

In the autumn of 1951 the two Gandhi boys were admitted to an exclusive private school, *Shiv Niketan* (literally, Abode of Serenity), run by Mrs. Elizabeth Gauba, a German woman married to an Indian. The school admitted children between the ages of four and ten, and had on its rolls some forty-five pupils. Here Rajiv and Sanjay were subjected to the excellent tutoring of Miss Usha Bhagat, until she became Mrs. Gandhi's secretary in September 1953. Miss Bhagat taught the children Hindi, creative arts and crafts, and general knowledge.

Although her children were looked after at home by Miss Ornsholt and at school by Miss Bhagat, Indira made it a point to spend as much free time as she had with her children. She would bathe them and feed them and play with them in the evenings. She never left her children's bedside when they were ill. She recalls how pained she was to know of the callous attitude of a visitor toward children. "Years ago a lady came to see me once when my sons had some childhood ailment. She remarked: 'Children always have something or the other; that's why I am glad I don't have any.' How could I explain to her that the joy of having children far outweighs the worry and the trouble?"

Indira remembers Tagore's aphorism: "Every child comes with the message that God is not yet discouraged of man." She thinks it unnatural for women not to want children. "A child's need of a mother's love and care is as urgent and fundamental as that of a plant for sunshine and water," she theorizes. Her own abnormal childhood, full of loneliness and insecurity, tugged at her conscience to devote her full time to her children. But she admits honestly: "The main problem in my life was how to reconcile my public obligations with my responsibility toward my home and my children."

When the children were in Delhi, she says, "I took care to have my engagements during school hours so as to be free when the boys returned home." Later, when the children were sent away in 1954 to the Welham Preparatory School in Dehra Dun—one of the most exclusive private boarding institutions in the country—Indira never undertook her political travels when they returned home for the vacations. Feroze also made it a point to minimize his political activity when the children were home, would horse around with them in the spacious grounds of Teen Murti House, and, being an excellent carpenter, would make all sorts of interesting and amusing gadgets for them. The children loved ice cream and cheese—the latter a very scarce commodity in India—and Feroze combed the stores to find them for his sons.

Usha Bhagat testifies to the scrupulous regularity with which Indira wrote to her children. She never missed writing to them at least once a week and sometimes wrote oftener. She wrote from trains and planes and from whatever mode of transport she might be using at the moment. They were not the kind of impersonal, literary, or historical communications she had received from her father during her youth. They were personal, intimate, and down-to-earth letters, says Miss Bhagat, intended to take the children into the mother's confidence, to treat them as adults, and establish a firm emotional bond between them.

Indira also makes the same point. You may always be with your children and yet never really communicate with them, she says, and proudly relates an anecdote to prove her point that it is not the amount of time spent with the children that matters as much as the manner of spending it. "Once when Sanjay was quite small, a nursery school friend of his came to our house with his mother. The mother, a society lady of some means, commenting on my public work, remarked that I could not be spending much time with my sons. This hurt Sanjay, and before I could think of a reply he rushed to my rescue with the words: 'My mother does lots of important work, and yet she plays with me more than you do with your little boy.' It seems his little friend had complained about his mother's constant bridge-playing!"

More than the care of her children, however, Indira was absorbed by the attention she was forced to bestow on her father—a circumstance which was to trigger off her differences with her husband. Feroze had lost his father when he was still a child. He did not look upon his aunt as a guardian angel; and by the time his mother had come to live in Allahabad he was "lost" to the nationalist cause, for which he thought he was tormented by his elder brother and sister. Filial piety was therefore not a virtue Feroze understood. But it came naturally to most Indians, because of the institution of the joint family.

In the case of the Nehrus it was intense. Only months before his death, Motilal was still in prison. He was fortunate to have his son share his cell, for Jawaharlal took charge of his ailing father and nursed him with unfailing devotion. So deeply moved was Motilal that he wrote home:

Hari [his personal servant] could very well take a leaf out
of Jawahar's book in the matter of serving me. From early
morning tea to the time I retire for the night, I find everything
I need in its proper place. The minutest detail is carefully attended to and it has never become necessary to ask for anything, which had so frequently to be done at Anand Bhavan.
... Jawahar anticipates everything and leaves nothing for me
to do. I wish there were many fathers to boast of such sons.

Not many fathers can boast of such a devoted daughter either, as
Indira. During the seventeen years that Jawaharlal Nehru was Prime
Minister of India, he kept up a grueling pace of working eighteen
hours a day. Jawaharlal's needs as the nation's leader were far more
diversified than were Motilal's as a prisoner. A widower that he
was, he needed someone to supervise his daily needs of food, clothing, rest, and relaxation. Jawaharlal was an introspective person even
when he was in company. As the years rolled on, he was even denied
company, since his friends and political confidants were snatched
away by death one after another. Indira gradually filled the void in
her father's emotional needs.

Jawaharlal received his first great blow when Mahatma Gandhi
was assassinated in January 1948. Indira had been calling on the
Mahatma quite frequently those days. He was pained by the fear and
insecurity which still haunted the Muslims of Delhi four months after
freedom had come. The state of the minority of Hindus and Sikhs
in Pakistan was becoming increasingly intolerable, and thousands of
them were fleeing to Delhi daily. Their exodus from Pakistan had
a disturbing effect on the Hindus and Sikhs in the capital, who in
turn retaliated against the hapless Muslims. Gandhi argued that however much hate there might be in the feelings of the Pakistanis, the
Indians must not emulate them. On January 13, 1948, Gandhi commenced a fast of indefinite duration—the fifteenth in his life—to compel his own countrymen to follow the path of common sense. It had
an electric effect on the behavior of the Hindus and Sikhs, who
agreed to all the preconditions he had demanded for the safety of
Muslims. Scores of Muslim leaders, including ladies in their *burqas*
(full-length overall veils) called on him to dissuade him from persist-

ing with the fast. On January 18 the Mahatma finally broke his fast, satisfied with the public response.

At ten thirty on the morning of January 29, accompanied by her son Rajiv, her cousin Nayantara, and her aunt, Krishna Hutheesing, Indira had gone to Birla Bhavan, the spacious mansion of a business magnate, Ghanshyam Das Birla, where the Mahatma customarily stayed whenever he visited Delhi. "Well, well," he taunted them, "have all these princesses come to see me?" They had a pleasant time with him, seated in cane chairs on the lawn and enjoying the warm sun on that chilly afternoon. Content with the orange he gave him, Rajiv played in Gandhi's arms for a while and then chased butterflies on the lawn. As they left, the Mahatma remarked casually: "It's good you came to see me today, because the next time you see me, it will be in a crowd." The girls were a little puzzled to hear this, since he was amid crowds all the time anyway. But they hardly had any premonition of things to come.

The following day Indira and Nayantara were enjoying their evening tea when they were summoned urgently to Birla Bhavan. Gandhi was in the habit of holding a public prayer meeting every evening at five, when hymns of all religions were sung, and he gave a discourse or answered questions received in the mail.

On that evening of January 30, Gandhi had been closeted with Vallabhbhai Patel, the Deputy Prime Minister, and was late for his prayer meeting by ten minutes. Chiding his attendants gently for the delay and ascending the four steps which led to the grounds of the prayer meeting, the Mahatma folded his hands in the traditional gesture of greeting the assemblage. From his right emerged without warning a stoutish young man in khaki dress, who reciprocated the gesture and in a flash pulled out a seven-bore automatic revolver and shot thrice from point-blank range. With the words *"Hey Ram"* ("O Lord"), on his lips and his hands still folded, the frail, barechested figure stepped forward eerily and fell to the ground, a stream of blood making the green turf incarnadine.

Within minutes of Indira's reaching Birla Bhavan, Deputy Prime Minister Patel, who had been with Gandhi only a while ago, arrived. Jawaharlal was at a meeting when he received word of the incident, and he also hastened to Birla Bhavan. Hardly suspecting that the Mahatma would be dead, he strode into the room where the body was placed. Confronted with the incredible, the Mahatma's favorite disciple broke down, hid his face in Patel's lap, and cried his eyes out like an orphaned child. He collected himself soon and went to broadcast the news to the rest of the nation that still knew nothing about the tragedy. In words which matched their eloquence with the spontaneity of his grief, Jawaharlal intoned:

"Friends and comrades, the light has gone out of our lives and there is darkness everywhere. I do not know what to tell you and how to say it. Our beloved leader, *Bapu* [father], as we called him, the Father of the Nation, is no more. Perhaps I am wrong to say that. Nevertheless, we will not see him again as we have been seeing him for these many years. . . .

"The light has gone out, I said, and yet I was wrong. For the light that shone in this country was no ordinary light. The light that has illumined this country for these many years will illumine this country for many more years. . . . For that light represented something more than the immediate present, it represented the living, the eternal truths. . . ."

Gandhi's death made Nehru not only lonely but also helpless. He was habituated to run to him for advice or guidance whenever in doubt or distress. Two years later, Deputy Prime Minister Patel also died. Temperamentally and ideologically, Nehru and Patel were poles apart. Where Nehru was prone to reflect upon his Leftist inclinations, Patel was quick to act upon his Rightist sympathies. But although the two often collided with each other in the Cabinet's inner councils, Nehru derived from Patel, after Gandhi's death, a strange feeling of strength.

After Patel's death in 1950 Nehru came to rely on Rafi Ahmad Kidwai as on a walking staff. Large-hearted and impulsive, Kidwai was an old-style politician who went to work by feeling the pulse of the people. After Kidwai's death in the autumn of 1954, Nehru grew dependent on Maulana Abul Kalam Azad, the scholarly, urbane, nationalist Muslim with liberal leanings. After Azad's death in 1958 Nehru found an effective teammate in Govind Ballabh Pant, a stalwart in the politics of Nehru's own state and a loyal and dependable ally.

After Pant's departure from the scene early in 1961, Indira became her father's unfailing companion, filling the void in his political life. She gained confidence in herself, overcame her natural reserve, and emerged as a public personality. The younger elements in the party knew that Indira had her father's ear and used her as a channel of communication. She too realized suddenly her own political potential and commenced forming the nucleus of a following. She watched her father manipulate men and situations with the skill of a magician, and got herself schooled in his methods of dealing with Cabinet colleagues and the party's rank and file. From 1958 onward Indira was privy to most of her father's significant decisions affecting domestic affairs.

However, Indira derived the best practical education in elementary foreign affairs by accompanying her father on his numerous state visits to many countries of the world. From October 1948, when Mr. Nehru attended the first of the postwar Commonwealth Prime Ministers' Conferences in London, Indira was exposed to the labyrinthine ways of the chancelleries of the world. She also developed an acquaintance, fleeting and wholly social though it might have been, with the world's leading statesmen that was to stand her in good stead in the years to come. After the London conference she accompanied her father to Paris, where he addressed a special session of the General Assembly of the United Nations on November 3. It was a historic speech in which he enunciated for the first time the bases of India's foreign policy. He pleaded with the Assembly to take note of resurgent Asia's aspiration for political freedom, social well-being, human dignity, and the climate of peace.

Indira returned to London in 1949 with her father for what, perhaps, will go down in history as the most significant Commonwealth Prime Ministers' Conference of the postwar years. India, on which Britain conferred Dominion Status in August 1947, was now preparing to become a sovereign republic. Nehru, however, was keen on maintaining a close connection with Great Britain. He and British Prime Minister Attlee finally hammered out a solution under which the British Commonwealth was transformed simply into the Commonwealth of Nations, and India, which as a dominion owed allegiance to the Crown, now accepted the monarch merely as a symbolic head of the free association of Commonwealth members.

In April of the same year Indira accompanied her father on his first visit to the United States. Nehru's mission ended in failure, and the visit itself proved an unpleasant experience for him. To begin with, Nehru had acquired, as a student in England, much of the conventional British bias against the United States. He was by temperament an aristocrat, and shared with the British aristocracy a certain contempt for the Americans as the *nouveaux riches*. He was by intellectual inclination a Marxist, and shared with the British Left a deep-rooted suspicion of the Mecca of capitalism. He was by birth a Brahmin, and had inherited an innate antipathy for the crassness of the world's leading acquisitive society.

These factors were further compounded by the awkwardness of the situation. India was in the throes of famine, and he hoped to obtain from the United States wheat and capital for economic development—a situation very similar to the one his daughter was to face seventeen years later. Those were the days when the cold war was at its peak and the ruling American cliché was: "If you are not with us, you are against us." To the ardent advocate of nonalignment that Nehru chose to be, the supreme virtue lay in being with everyone and against no one. Despite the reprobation of disapproving American senators and congressmen, Nehru stood firm against receiving "aid with strings attached," and it was not until eighteen months after it had been requested that American surplus wheat began to reach India.

The half blunder and half braggadocio of American businessmen also distressed Nehru. At a dinner given in his honor, one of them boasted to him: "Mr. Prime Minister, just around this table are presidents of corporations worth twenty billion dollars!" Nehru's socialist sensibilities were deeply offended, and he exploded later in private that India was not for sale.

Indira, in contrast, had a pleasanter experience. Being so much younger than her father, and her mind still receptive to new ways of economic and social organization, she was curious to see and learn. She made many friends even on that first visit and was to make many more during a total of nine visits she undertook to the United States before she came as India's Prime Minister to meet President Johnson.

In 1953 Indira accompanied her father to London to witness an event which, for all its splendor and regalia, appeared a little outlandish in the second half of the twentieth century: the coronation of Queen Elizabeth II. On her way back to India she went on her first visit—a private one—to the Soviet Union. She saw the country, as she earlier did the United States, without any ideological blinkers and was honestly impressed by indubitable Russian achievements. She was interested in the Russian Government's policies toward its various nationalities, and particularly in its efforts to modernize the Soviet central Asian republics. Indira was eager to know if the Russian experiments held any lessons for India's similar problems. Like her father, however, she would not endorse the employment of coercive political measures for the achievement of ends, however desirable.

A wide gulf separated monarchical England from proletarian Russia. Indira discovered that as wide a gulf could separate a satiated Communist country from another that was insatiable. In October 1954 she went with her father to the People's Republic of China. A British correspondent covering the trip described thus her appearance at a Peking reception organized by a Chinese Communist women's group: "When Indira Gandhi entered the clinically furnished room there among the massed blue boiler suits of ideological orthodoxy and the square bobs of liberation, she resembled in some way a lotus flower that had been planted in a bed of broccoli." An official of the Chinese Foreign Ministry who had observed her in action is said to have exclaimed: "It's remarkable, she has a lot of the West in her but, dear me, how intelligent!" Yes, Indira Gandhi was intelligent enough to entertain apprehensions about Chinese intentions, but also intelligent enough not to decry their accomplishments simply because they happened to be Chinese or Communist. Two months later she went on an extensive tour of all but the Indochinese states of Southeast Asia.

The year 1955 signaled another landmark in the history of the postwar world. The widely billed Afro-Asian Conference was held in the Indonesian city of Bandung in April of that year. Although the Korean War had ended in 1953, Communist China was still eyed by most countries of the world as a sort of pariah in the international community. Nehru took upon himself the task of rehabilitating China in the esteem of Afro-Asian countries, and projected Premier Chou En-lai at the Bandung Conference as the very exemplar of statesmanship. Chou played to the hilt his assigned role of salesman of sweet reasonableness. Nehru was eager that the conferees should also subscribe to the *Panch Sheel* or Five Principles of peaceful co-existence, which were first enunciated in the Sino-Indian treaty signed in 1954 to legitimize the Chinese occupation of Tibet.

However, Pakistan and Ceylon, which are now neutralist with a vengeance, were then vehemently pro-West. They wanted to offer for adoption by the Conference five more principles of their own, one of which was a denunciation of the neo-imperialism of the Communist Powers. When Ceylon's Prime Minister, Sir John Kotela-wala, took Nehru unawares by introducing a resolution to that effect, the Indian Prime Minister was purple with rage. When he stalked out of a stormy session, Indira demonstrated how well she had learned her lessons. Long years ago, when she had refused to accompany her father to dinner at Lord Lothian's Elizabethan mansion on the pretext that she might lose her temper in the presence of Tories, he had admonished her: "You must learn to control your temper and mix with all kinds of people. You must know how these people think." That day in Bandung, when no one in the Indian delegation had the courage to curb Nehru's undiplomatic outbursts, Indira had the temerity to turn to him and say: "Papu, control your-self."

Indira's later tours abroad were more in the nature of jaunts. In June 1959 she went with her father on an official visit to the Soviet Union and the eastern European countries. In June of the following year she went along to London for the Commonwealth Conference and then visited half a dozen western European countries and three in the Middle East. In December 1956 she came with her father to

Canada and the United States during General Eisenhower's presidency. In June 1957 she toured the Scandinavian countries with her father, and in October of the same year they went on an official visit to Japan. In November 1961 they came to Washington again during John F. Kennedy's occupancy of the White House.

Indira's preoccupation with affairs of state, party, and her Prime-Minister father left her less and less time to be with her husband. It was obviously not a simple case of choosing to serve the father in preference to ministering to the husband. Usha Bhagat, one of Mrs. Gandhi's present secretaries, explains that if Jawaharlal had been just another father, Indira would have seen little justification to give him such great devotion. It sprang from her consciousness that he was primarily the leader of a great nation and only accidentally her father. But one of Indira's intimates contends that it is not so simple either. She says Indira had the subconscious desire of basking in the aura surrounding her father. She wanted to give her children an intimation of the immortality of their grandfather, such as the one she herself had experienced as a child.

Feroze appears to have been convinced that his wife could not give up the chores and allurements of life in Teen Murti House for the anonymous existence of a nondescript housewife. He could not quite appreciate the pride which his wife took in the Nehru family name. Although he genuinely admired his father-in-law, he thought there was something counterfeit in the cult developing around Nehru. He intensely disliked being introduced as "the Prime Minister's son-in-law," but that is how precisely he was introduced by the less understanding among his friends. This only encouraged him all the more to establish his own identity. As Indira found a substitute satisfaction in attending to her father's needs, Feroze sublimated his energies in attending to the needs of his constituents and to parliamentary affairs.

From the obscurity of a quiet back-bencher during his early years as a Parliamentarian, Feroze suddenly shot into prominence with his maiden speech in 1955. Using his brief but valuable experience in the insurance business, he exposed the shady deals of the Bharat Insurance Company and certain other firms controlled by a businessman, Ram Krishna Dalmia. The exposure led to the appointment of a Commission of Inquiry and ultimately to the nationalization of the life insurance business in the country. When Ram Krishna Dalmia was arrested, he was bailed out by his son-in-law, Shanti Prasad Jain, also suspected of having been implicated in some of the shady deals. In his anxiety to prevent the two from conspiring to get away scot-free, Feroze asked Mr. Nehru in the course of subsequent interpellations in Parliament: "Will the Prime Minister be pleased to state the relationship of the surety to the accused?" Nehru got the better of the exchange with the prompt reply, "The same as that of the questioner to the answerer," and the House roared.

Up until that time the press in India did not enjoy protection from being cited for contempt of Parliament, even if it committed no other crime than reporting Parliament's proceedings faithfully. As a service to his many friends in the newspaper world, Feroze undertook the responsibility for the sponsoring and enactment of the Parliamentary Proceedings Act of 1956, which gave the Indian press complete protection against proceedings in courts of law for the publication of *bona fide* and accurate reports of parliamentary proceedings.

In the second General Election of 1957 Feroze was returned to Parliament from his Rae Bareli constituency. He smelled the rat in some of the dealings of the nationalized Life Insurance Company of India with a young businessman named Haridas Mundhra. On December 16, 1957, Feroze took Parliament by storm, declaring:

"Mr. Speaker, sir, a mutiny in my mind has compelled me to raise this debate. When things of such magnitude, as I shall describe to you later, occur, silence becomes a crime. That public expenditure shall be subject to the severest public debate is a healthy tradition, especially so in an era of growing public enterprise."

Marshaling an array of facts and citing some startling statistics, Feroze argued a closely-knit case and concluded:

"I hope I have established collusion between the Life Insurance Corporation of India and Mr. Mundhra. I have, I hope, established a conspiracy in which public funds were wrongfully employed for financing the interests of an individual at the cost of the insured."

It was not Feroze's intention to embarrass either his father-in-law or his party. But the unintended did happen, and the Minister of Finance, T. T. Krishnamachari, had to resign. Minoo Masani, the leader of the opposition Swatantra (Freedom) Party, recalls Feroze's lament at the time: "*Array, kahan mara, kahan laga?*" ("Oh my, where did I aim and where did I hit?"). Another unintended by-product of the exposure was Feroze's own meteoric rise to national stature.

Although Feroze enjoyed the reputation of being a Leftist, he had a theory of human nature in politics which differed fundamentally from the half-baked notions of the surviving Leftists in the Congress Party who still lionize him. According to the latter, the administrators of public or state-owned enterprises are, by definition, virtuous and efficient, whereas the managers of private enterprises are, by definition, corrupt and inefficient.

Feroze believed in no such nonsense. He was honest enough to say: "An unfortunate thing has happened. But I don't think there is any reason to be ashamed of it. I am a champion of the public sector. I was one of the persons who championed nationalization of life insurance. I am not ashamed to face an inquiry. I would like the public to know, and I would like Members of Parliament to know that in the public sector, if such a thing happens, we are prepared to face an inquiry and get at the bottom of it."

Because of his conviction that his own party members could be as corrupt as any other, Feroze had suggested the formation of a high-powered committee of persons with judicial experience and reputation for integrity to examine complaints against his party's men in high positions and suggest the type of action to be taken. Unfortunately, on such matters Feroze's father-in-law adopted a narrow party stand, and the suggestion did not commend itself to him. Feroze knew that his party members were cowed down by the party whip. He therefore took it upon himself to become a one-man parliamentary opposition. In a country in which the opposition was not strong enough to replace the government, Feroze had rendered sterling service. With the exposure of the Mundhra affair, he had earned the sobriquet of "giant killer." Each time he walked down the central aisle there was a flutter in the treasury benches, in the ranks of the Opposition, and in the press gallery. "Feroze had a style of his own," recalls one of his parliamentary colleagues. "An expressionless countenance and a soft voice but words that easily bored holes in the enemy's armor."

Rafi Ahmad Kidwai measured up every inch to Feroze's conception of an ideal politician. Like the Democratic politicians of a former era in large American cities who collared the newly-arrived immigrants, found them jobs and places to live, and then pocketed their votes, Kidwai conceived of politics as social service. Feroze emulated Kidwai and acquired several of his personal attributes which he thought helped him to win friends, influence people, and chastise enemies. Among these assets were a persistent, pleasant but enigmatic smile, easy accessibility, and a willingness to help. Cab drivers, postmen, and hawkers hung around him as much as press reporters, politicians, and Parliamentarians.

A friend of Feroze's, Jagdish Kodesia, relates an anecdote typical of Feroze's handling of people in distress. Late one evening a group of *Bhaiyas* (milkmen—a breed unto themselves) had come to Feroze with a grievance. Their cattle usually grazed in a sort of no-man's-land. That day they had strayed a little, and officials of the New Delhi Municipal Corporation had impounded the cattle. Feroze listened to the milkmen, telephoned the Deputy Commissioner, and asked him to spell out precisely the limits of his jurisdiction. When the official professed ignorance of the finer details, Feroze needled him gently in Hindi: "I see. I guess you expect the cows to know what you yourself don't." The official felt like a buffalo and had the cattle released.

In the Central Hall of Parliament there was a nook which came to be called Feroze's corner, where his cronies gathered after the day's business. He would order innumerable cups of coffee for his hangers-on and preside over the hubbub of conversation and the ring of laughter. Red, rotund, and Pickwickian in appearance, he was always jovial, witty, and puckish. He was pointed and devastating in his criticism of politicians and their policies, but his criticism was free of animus. Mr. Jagdish Kodesia remembers the day when Feroze was amid an assortment of socialists from the Congress as well as other parties, including the Communist. "There are three main varieties of socialists," expatiated Feroze. "The first are like the guavas of Allahabad—white on the outside but red inside. The second are like the red radish—red only to look at but white inside. The third are like the beet-root—red both inside and out. The Congress Party abounds in the second variety!"

Politics was not the only interest of Feroze nor even the most absorbing. A man of elegant and refined taste, he kept excellent house in the quarters allotted to him as Member of Parliament on Queen Victoria Road. An acquaintance of Feroze, Miss Prema Mandi, describes the decor of his small one-bedroom house as follows: "A thick carpet of gray woolen pile lay in the center of the living room. Matching curtains adorned the doors and windows. Ferozebhai [an endearing term, literally meaning brother Feroze] was a do-it-yourself man—his hobbies were carpentry, lacquerwork, and printing—and so he made most of his own furniture. There weren't any sofas; just lacquered chairs of white wood with latticed seats of multicolored *nivar* [webbing]. Two book shelves stood in a corner, and on one of them was a framed color photograph of Panditji (Nehru), Indira, Rajiv, and Sanjay. On the mantelpiece was a big, white vase of cut glass. The bedroom was done up simply—a single bed and a massive writing table piled high with files and letters, all meticulously arranged, occupied almost the entire space. A black-lacquered armchair was by the table. On the mantelpiece was another vase of cut glass along with three photographs of Rajiv, Sanjay, and Indira. Ferozebhai just adored this picture of Indira. She was wearing a black coat and looked soft, fragile, and girlish in it. He loved to look at it most of the time.

"Ferozebhai wasn't very fond of modern furniture. He felt it was not as comfortable as the old-style furniture. As his visitors increased in number, he had latterly converted the veranda into an additional room. He had purchased from Mrs. Pandit a Victorian drawing room set, one of her wedding gifts. This he renovated and painted black. It was indeed very impressive-looking, and one couldn't help feeling regal sitting in it."

The most attractive part of the house was the garden, which

Feroze tended industriously. Everyone in New Delhi who visited his home remembers how hesitantly one stepped on the luxuriant lawn into which one sank ankle deep. The garden glowed under Delhi's winter sun like some fairyland, with row upon row of two to three thousand gladioli, roses, and other flowers in full bloom. Not even his friends dared pluck a single flower unless he clipped one for them with a pair of scissors. He often carried a bouquet for Indira even though the flowers were mostly for sale.

Feroze maintained a well-equipped workshop good enough to turn out a number of cottage-industry items. So exquisite were the products that his friends were happy to buy them from him, insisting on full payment. But Feroze worked as much for diversion as for money. Several of his friends in Delhi still display with pride the things he made for them. Mr. K. D. Malaviya's daughter-in-law speaks glowingly of the crib which Feroze made for her firstborn. Generous to a fault though Feroze was, he never lent his personal belongings to anyone for use, because he was certain nobody would care for them as well as he did. One of his proud possessions was his car—a 1952 gray model of the Morris Minor. Mr. Malaviya's son recalls one occasion when he needed a car most urgently and with what great reluctance Feroze parted with it—but not before warning him to handle it with care. Feroze spent long evening sessions with the Malaviyas. He was a sumptuous eater, with a partiality for rich foods. He relished the dishes which Mrs. Malaviya affectionately prepared for him. A lover both of innocent prattle and heated political argument, he found congenial the company of his former scoutmaster, the Left-leaning Mr. Malaviya.

Gossip in New Delhi is as all-pervasive as in Washington, D.C. It thrived on the suspected rift between Feroze and Indira—all the more because of the peculiar circumstances in which it was aired. Neither Feroze nor Indira ever talked to anyone about themselves. "He talked eloquently in Parliament," reminisces Feroze's sister, Tehmina, "but in private he maintained a stern silence about his domestic problems." Indira too never discussed her affairs with her father, and he was averse to prying into them. In the absence of direct knowledge, rumor and innuendo had the field for themselves.

Those ubiquitous eyes and ears—the domestic servants—would pur-
vey to the outside world "authoritative" information about the violent arguments Feroze and Indira sometimes had. Illiterate as they
were, and ignorant of the English language, the servants hardly knew
the difference between a political argument and a domestic quarrel.
It was sufficient for them that voices were raised. This is not to suggest that there was no rift at all between husband and wife. Mrs.
Gandhi herself admits its existence quite frankly and honestly, and
close relatives and intimate friends of both Feroze and Indira confirm it.

It is equally certain, however, that there was no "separation" between husband and wife in the known senses of the term—judicial or
physical. It is unfortunate that Welles Hangen's treatment of the
subject has led to a grave misunderstanding. According to his version:

> At times Feroze lived with his wife at the Prime Minister's
> house, but when he became a member of Parliament he estab-
> lished separate quarters in New Delhi. Although they had been
> separated, Indira was deeply affected by her husband's first
> heart attack. Menon [V. K. Krishna Menon, India's Former
> Defense Minister] is said to have promoted a reconciliation.
> Indira and Feroze spent a vacation together with their chil-
> dren in Kashmir, but found that their paths had become too
> divergent. They agreed to separate again. Rajiv and Sanjay
> usually stayed with their mother at the Prime Minister's house
> on vacation from their fashionable Dehra Dun boarding school
> in the foothills of the Himalayas.

The fact that Feroze should have maintained separate quarters
at all was the subject of much speculation and groundless comment.
Jagdish Kodesia, who visited Feroze frequently, asked him more than
once why he had to have a separate house. According to Mr. Kodesia, Feroze's response was: "As I am a Member of Parliament, all
sorts of people come to me. Some are pro-government, some are
vehemently anti-government. Some are bright-eyed fellows, and
others are dim-witted. Some visit me to have their grievances re-
dressed, others call on me for no reason at all. It would have been

wrong in principle for me to receive them all in the Prime Minister's house."

Miss Vimla Sindhi, the long-time receptionist in Teen Murti House, testifies: "Ferozebhai had his breakfast every morning with Panditji, Indiraji, and his children in the Prime Minister's house. He wasn't used to having lunch, but he dined again every night at the Prime Minister's house. There's also one other thing we mustn't forget. Ferozebhai, Indiraji, and their children were themselves regarded somewhat as guests at the Prime Minister's house. At the end of each month Ferozebhai was billed for the expenses of his family—and these were pretty high. Now, for Ferozebhai to have entertained his own guests at the Prime Minister's house would have proved inordinately expensive."

When asked to comment specifically on Hangen's report that Feroze and Indira had separated, a long-time intimate of both asserted: "I know Feroze went home to sleep every night except on occasions when he burned the midnight oil at his other quarters, working on a speech he was to make in Parliament the next day. You know, Feroze wrote out his entire speech in long hand, and he would then sit through the better part of the night typing it out. Indira sometimes went and joined him there for the night. But on most other nights he did go home to Teen Murti House."

The lady then exploded irately: "Now, I know he and Indira shared the same bedroom in Teen Murti House. What's more, there was only one bed in it! Now, if the Americans want to know the details of their sex life, I'm afraid I don't know. I wonder if there's anybody who knows or has a right to know."

Separation, as it is commonly understood, there certainly was not. Equally certainly, their marriage was not one long honeymoon—the kind that is defined as peaceful "coo-existence." They often waged cold war with each other, and if there was no Vishinsky-like vituperation in their exchanges, there was at least an eclipse of the understanding. It was ironical that this should have happened in a house presided over by the apostle of peaceful coexistence. Nayantara Sahgal says that the whole situation put Nehru in the most awkward position. "The unhappiest person was actually *Mamu* [Uncle]. He couldn't cure the situation. He had strong feelings about privacy and wouldn't intrude into his daughter's affairs or even pry out information from her. If you were in trouble and wanted his help or guidance, *Mamu* was extremely patient and would be glad to spend hours with you. But if you didn't approach him yourself, he just minded his own business. It pained him to see Indira unhappy. But he was helpless; couldn't do a thing about it. And what he couldn't cure he just had to endure." It must have been painful, too, for Mr. Nehru to reflect that what he had feared might happen, when Indira first told him of her desire to marry Feroze, should have happened after all.

What happened, Vimla Sindhi says, is that "two personalities, equally headstrong and strong-willed, highly individualistic and prepossessing, clashed with each other." They were young and proud, proud enough not to make up with each other, and too proud to seek the help of others. The evidence would point to an incapacity on the part of Feroze to adapt himself to a wholly new set of circumstances. When he married Indira she was merely the daughter of a nationalist leader who was in and out of jail, although one that was reverenced by millions. In March 1942 it never appeared, even to the more optimistic of observers, that in a matter of five years his father-in-law would become the Prime Minister of an independent India. The common man which Feroze prided himself as being was never again to be reconciled to the trappings of office.

Life in the Prime Minister's house imposed a strain on the naturalness and easy manner of Feroze's life. The dignity and decorum of his father-in-law's high office appeared artificial to him. He loved to associate with the common folk because he had always been one of them. He would rather stand at the street corner, chew *pan* (spiced aromatic betel leaf), and engage in lively conversation with a gallimaufry of companions than go on the rounds of diplomatic missions and hobnob with envoys extraordinary and ministers plenipotentiary. In contrast, Indira did not have to cultivate a liking for her new role. It came naturally to her and she felt perfectly at home in it. If it was not exactly blue blood coursing through her veins, she was never unmindful of her high birth. She was after all the granddaughter of an arch aristocrat and, as Shanta Gandhi recalls, Indira never tired of reminding her friends in the Children's Own School in Poona: "My grandfather is a very great man." It was characteristic of the fifteen-year-old girl to be attracted to fame. It was almost second nature for the thirty-year-old young lady to bask in its glory.

Indira was Prime Minister Jawaharlal's daughter. Feroze was only her husband. "How does it feel to be so-and-so's husband?" he was asked often by political adversaries of the Nehrus. A full decade was to pass before Feroze was recognized as a budding national figure in his own right. Before then, however, he was either condemned to anonymity or to condescending recognition. There was always one incident or the other to remind him of his subsidiary status. He would receive no invitation to a function to which Indira would be invited as the Prime Minister's official hostess. Or, if invited, he might be seated in some obscure corner, according to the dictates of protocol. The humiliation may have been even more pronounced as when, for instance, Bulganin and Khrushchev addressed a mammoth rally in New Delhi's Ramlila grounds in 1955. Mr. Nehru and his daughter were whisked to the grounds under police escort, while Feroze and some other Parliamentarians were prevented from getting in by the security men. At a meeting of the Congress Parliamentary Party later, Feroze took strong exception to the servants of the law trifling with the dignity and prestige of Members of Parliament, and the Prime Minister promised to look into the matter, but the damage was done.

Feroze started building around himself a defense mechanism and making a virtue of his indignant reaction. One of Indira's closest relatives says he went out of his way to cultivate Feroze and had personally invited him to weddings and other family functions of the Kashmiri clan, only to be rebuffed every time. Almost as a reaction to his wife's frequent trips abroad, he would appear to have determined never to leave the country. He felt it was demeaning to pull strings to go on a junket abroad. Shanta Gandhi remembers vividly his shocked reaction when she went to say farewell before leaving for Paris on a UNESCO fellowship. He asked her disbelievingly: "You too?"

He would visit his Rae Bareli constituency and return, having shed most of his clothes, all the bedding, and the warm blankets. "Whatever happened to your belongings?" his puzzled sister, Tehmina, would ask, and he would retort: "What do *you* all know about how my people live." A feeling of private hurt combined with a sense of personal martyrdom to create in him an alienation from family and friend. "It was an impossible situation," says Nayantara Sahgal, "and no marriage in the world could have withstood its strain." Feroze turned more and more to work as an escape. Over-work was compounded by deliberate disregard of discipline and indifference to health. In 1958, while Indira was on a visit to Nepal, Feroze suffered a heart attack.

It is interesting to note in passing the political capital the Hindu extremists made of Indira's and Feroze's domestic unhappiness. In 1950 Nehru was contemplating a root-and-branch reformation of Hindu law and social institutions. He favored the abolition of the nefarious practice of untouchability; the elimination of the caste system; the granting of inheritance rights to women; the abolition of polygamy and the introduction of monogamy; and the recognition of the right of either spouse to obtain a divorce on certain specified grounds. Under Hindu law marriage was traditionally considered an indissoluble sacrament, not a contract terminable by the parties at will. Some members of the Hindu extremist party, the Jan Sangh, and the right-wing reactionaries in Nehru's own party, the Congress, joined hands to mount a frontal attack on his program to reform Hindu society. At the same time, an insidious whispering campaign was commenced, alleging that the marriage of Indira and Feroze was on the rocks, and it was in order legally to end their matrimonial link that the Prime Minister sought to introduce the bill permitting Hindus to obtain a divorce. Neither tactic succeeded, and the bill was ultimately passed in 1955. The only concession which the bill's opponents gained was an empty one. The word "divorce" was omitted from the title of the bill, "The Hindu Marriage and Divorce Bill," but divorce itself was legalized. If Indira and Feroze had ever contemplated divorce at all, they must have dropped the idea after the unseemly agitation of the extremists. Being realists they must have calculated the probable adverse effect at the polls on their political fortunes and abandoned such a course of action, if they entertained it at all.

In the absence of Indira and her father, Govind Ballabh Pant came to the rescue, and Feroze was taken to the Willingdon Nursing Home. Tehmina came rushing from Allahabad. If it is true that a calamity often evokes the true feelings of its victims, this one proved how much Feroze and Indira loved each other to the end. Recalling to memory the scene in the nursing home, Tehmina says: "Feroze thought he was going, and seemed to be holding on to dear life just that he might see Indira. Every other half hour he would ask me: 'Where's Indu? Hasn't she arrived yet? When is the plane due?' I couldn't bear it. It was a pathetic sight." Shanta Gandhi remembers Indira's having admitted to her at one stage: "I don't like him, but I love him." It was a mature and understanding way of looking at her situation objectively and accepting it. At any rate, Indira was in a much happier situation than those who say they like their husbands but do not love them.

Under his wife's care and the treatment of Dr. H. L. Khosla, the superintendent of the nursing home, Feroze made steady progress. His condition seems to have drawn Indira closer to him. He himself was on the way to becoming recognized as one of the budding leaders of his party, and he resented much less than in the past the limelight which his wife enjoyed. Husband and wife went vacationing to Kashmir and left behind them the cares, worries, and disturbing memories of Teen Murti House. They do not appear to have needed the guidance or direction of any external agency to draw closer together. Asked if Hangen's report is true that he was responsible for bringing about a reconciliation between husband and wife, Mr. Krishna Menon disavowed any such role. Whatever the reason for reconciliation, there seems little doubt about the fact of reconciliation. Mr. Nehru was now an old man, and the day might not be far off when Indira would be free to devote more of her time to her husband and children. Feroze too looked forward to the day when he would build a little house on the plot of land he had purchased on the city's outskirts, into which the family could move. He also had visions of building a science college for his constituents in Rae Bareli and was planning a trip to Bombay for fund-raising.

Such was the stuff their dreams were made of, and dreams they were condemned to remain. In the first week of September 1960 Feroze experienced acute pain in the chest. Dr. Khosla, now his personal friend, advised Feroze to have complete rest. After five days, the pain had not abated. On September 7 he telephoned Khosla for an urgent appointment. The doctor instructed him not to move and insisted on coming to pick him up presently. Both anxious and reckless, Feroze drove himself from Parliament House to the Willingdon Nursing Home. After some preliminary discussion, Khosla offered him a cup of tea. But as tea was being poured, Feroze collapsed in his chair and was moved immediately to a bed.

As during his first heart attack, Indira was again absent from Delhi—this time in Trivandrum, the capital of the distant southern state of Kerala. She took off for New Delhi moments after receiving the news. Driving straight from Palam Airport to the nursing home, she found Khosla and five other specialists attending on her husband. His condition, however, was fast deteriorating, and there was little response to the treatment. He regained consciousness at four thirty in the morning, and from then on he appeared to be improving steadily. Indira, who had kept an all-night vigil, asked the others to retire and catch a short nap. In the morning Feroze had a sudden coughing spell. Indira, who was sitting by his bedside, held his head in her hands, but in a matter of moments he was dead—at seven forty-five on September 8.

Nehru rushed to the nursing home, but it was all over. He returned to Teen Murti House, stunned by the suddenness of the event, walked up the stairway to his room on the first floor, and sat there speechless for some time. He came down again, his face swathed in sorrow, and spoke to Mrs. Vijaya Laksmi Pandit and others about the funeral arrangements. Rajiv and Sanjay were sent for from school. When the news of Feroze's death was conveyed to his family, they suggested that his body be sent to Allahabad. The family was advised to consider, however, the large number of Feroze's friends and admirers in New Delhi who wanted to pay him their last respects. Unfortunately, the commercial flight had already taken off from Allahabad to Delhi and the train journey would not get them to Delhi till next morning. The Prime Minister's secretariat then requested the government of Uttar Pradesh to fly Feroze's family to Delhi in a chartered plane. On the afternoon of the eighth Faredun and Tehmina reached Delhi.

Meanwhile Parliament adjourned after observing a two-minute silence as a mark of respect for one of its most conscientious members. Among the hundreds of tributes to Feroze, Mr. M. R. Masani, the leader of the opposition Swatantra Party, emphasized Feroze's not-so-well-known qualities as an able administrator of one of the few well-run state-owned enterprises. (Feroze was chairman of Oil Refineries Limited, a state-owned company formed for setting up two oil refineries in eastern India.) Mr. Asoka Mehta, then chairman of the opposition Praja Socialist Party, eulogized: "Death robs Parliament of an outstanding member, and the underprivileged of a tireless champion. His sympathies were as catholic as his interests were wide. Our public life is not rich in dedicated men; that a man of Mr. Gandhi's attainments should have been plucked away in the prime of life aggravates our impoverishment." Acharya J. B. Kripalani, another member of Mr. Mehta's party, spoke the simple truth: "Feroze Gandhi belonged to no party. He was an Indian first and an Indian last."

In Teen Murti House during the afternoon of the eighth differences had arisen over the nature of the last rites to be performed. When Faredun Gandhi asked Mr. Nehru if Feroze had expressed any preference about last rites, the Prime Minister replied he was in the dark about it. But Feroze had once told Vimla Sindhi, the receptionist, somewhat in a jocular and vague fashion, that when he died she could make a bonfire of his remains. It was presumably on the strength of that half-serious wish that Feroze's body was being prepared for the cremation. At first Faredun was not opposed to the cremation. He was more concerned about where it took place, since he had some strong feelings about the "unclean" Hindu burning ghats. He asked the Prime Minister why the body could not be cremated right on the grounds of Teen Murti House. Mr. Nehru explained it would be against the law.

Faredun then suddenly remembered that back in February 1923, a month after his father's death, Feroze had gone through the *Navjote* (literally, a new spiritual light) or an initiation ceremony, confirming him in the Parsi faith. He therefore felt that even if Feroze's body was to be cremated ultimately, Parsi last rites should be conducted first. Mr. Nehru had no objection; nor had Indira.

All non-Parsis, except of course Indira and her two sons, were cleared out of the room. The *Gahesaran* ceremony, or the reading of the *gathas* of Zoroaster over the dead body, was then performed. The body, draped in the Indian tricolor, was carried from the house into an open truck. Indira, her two sons, her sister-in-law Tehmina, and Feroze's dear friend, K. D. Malaviya, sat in the truck. Prime Minister Nehru and President Rajendra Prasad followed the truck in their respective cars. Looking at the two-mile-long procession and the thousands of ordinary people whom Feroze had befriended now lining both sides of the road, Nehru exclaimed: "Oh, I didn't know Feroze had built up such a great following for himself!" By late evening the cortege reached Nigambodh Ghat. Rajiv lit the funeral pyre amid the chanting of Vedic hymns, and Feroze's mortal remains were consigned to flames.

Two days later Indira took the urn of his ashes by train to Allahabad and mingled some in the Triveni, or the sacred confluence of the three rivers. A major portion of the ashes, however, were buried according to Parsi rites in Allahabad's Parsi cemetery, and the rest in the ancestral cemetery in Surat, on the west coast of India. All this gladdened Faredun's heart, for he later discovered that in the will, under which Indira became the sole heir to her husband's property, Feroze had described himself as a Parsi Zoroastrian.

Her friends and relatives say Indira never sobbed, either before or since, the way she did on her husband's death. She was hoping to serve her husband after her aging father had departed from the earth. But the fates decreed the reverse. The husband was gone when she was still only forty-three, and for the next four years the young widow gave all her energies to the care of her father, nursing him through the stroke he suffered at Bhubaneswar during the Congress session there in January 1964 until his demise on May 27 the same year.

With Nehru's death ended the first phase of India's existence as an independent country, and also the bulk of Indira's terrestrial obligations. Until now she had hardly lived a life of her own. Asked whether, during the seventeen long years that she served her Prime-Minister father, she felt she missed something or was being forced to sacrifice her own interests, Mrs. Gandhi replied instantly:

"No, because one of the things I learned from my mother and father is that you must enjoy whatever you are doing or you mustn't do it. Because you can't do a good job if you are doing it grudgingly."

The Charismatic Politician

Just as her father in other circumstances might have written many more great books, Indira, with her background and opportunities might have blossomed into one of a number of possibilities. She is a woman of taste, with a highly developed critical faculty. I am sure she would have found some satisfactory and rewarding outlet for these qualities."

This judgment of Indira's cousin, Nayantara, is a sound one. She is a politician, not essentially but circumstantially. It is true that politics came as naturally to her as the air she breathed. She has been permeated with it since the age of four. But that politics was the politics of national liberation, agitation, and revolution. If she had been born at another time and an equally revolutionary but non-political cause had existed, it might have absorbed her totally. For politics defined as the pursuit of power or position Indira never had any great taste. When asked why she had an aversion for this species of politics, she replied:

"No, I didn't have an aversion. I had gotten married, I had two small children, and, as I say, whatever I do I believe in doing it well. I did not believe in leaving my children to other people. But at the same time, since I couldn't just sit at home, I was doing social work and other things. When there were riots I worked in the riot-affected areas."

Even before partition, Govind Ballabh Pant, the stalwart of Congress politics in Uttar Pradesh, had asked Mrs. Gandhi to run for the state assembly. She declined, pointing out that she had already refused an offer to run for the constituent assembly. Pant tried persuading Mahatma Gandhi to pressure her into acceptance. But not even the Mahatma could succeed. Even after her children had grown up and Mrs. Gandhi had sent them off to boarding school, she refused persistently every offer of office. If it was not aversion, then, that kept her out of power politics, it must have been a complete lack of personal ambition. For, as systematically as she refused office, the office went in search of her.

Asked when she felt she was ready for politics, she attributes her entry into it to accident rather than intention. "Quite honestly, I didn't give it a thought whether I was ready or not, because I was fully occupied. During the first general election, I went to one place—Chamba—instead of my father. That was in 1951. And that visit was such a success that throughout the election I was, sort of, taken in. I mean I was made to travel, speak and so on, wherever my father couldn't go."

Strictly speaking, even this did not mark her entry into politics. It was simply a service she was performing for her father by substituting for him when he himself could not nurse his constituency. Along with Lal Bahadur Shastri and Miss Mridula Sarabhai, who were managing Mr. Nehru's campaign in his Phulpur constituency in the state of Uttar Pradesh, Indira took care of the mechanics of electioneering. Congress Party officials were eager to rope her into the town's politics, but as before she dodged them. When she went back to Allahabad in 1953, it was, typically, for social work. On the occasion of the *Kumbh Mela* (the day hundreds of thousands of people take a dip in the sacred Ganges to wash away their sins) Miss Sarabhai had organized a camp, the *Gram Seva Dal* (literally, village service association), for helping the estimated seven thousand women and children who get lost in the melee. There were about a hundred women in the *Dal* and Indira was made chairman of the camp. After the *Mela* was over, Indira wanted to utilize the services of these women in the newly-established community development projects of the government. Since there was a dearth of women workers, she planned to enlarge the *Dal* and expand the training facilities for its members. A residential training center for rural women, the Kamala Nehru Vidyalaya, resulted from her efforts, and Indira was president of the institution for ten years.

Indira was assigned her first role of politician when she was named a member of her party's Working Committee in 1955 by the Congress president, Uchhrangrai Navalshanker Dhebar. She was given charge of the party's incipient Women's Department. Indira toured every state of the Union to activate the *Mandal* Committees—the lowest units in the organizational structure of the party. For the next four years she worked indefatigably for the uplift of rural women. She directed that attention must be concentrated on four issues. The first was the "Grow More Food" campaign. "It is really amazing how much can be grown in the smallest space, as I have myself seen in the tiny plots of land that are usually attached to blocks of flats in the big cities of Europe," she said, and asked women in India to develop "kitchen gardens." Vegetables could easily be grown in the kitchen back yard, she pleaded, and "they are just as decorative as they are good to eat." The second problem, closely related to the first, was the change, long overdue, in people's eating habits. Far too much cereal is eaten in India and far too little of protein foods like fish, meat, poultry, and eggs. In addition to growing more vegetables, she stressed the urgent need to set up fish and poultry farms.

The third problem of interest to Indira was savings. The massive economic development of the country was possible largely by internal financing, and only marginally through external resources. She insisted that people must learn to save even from their meager earnings and invest the savings in National Savings Certificates. The last problem was literacy and education. No development whatsoever is possible, Indira argued, unless social education on a large scale is imparted to rural women—the reservoirs of ignorance and superstition. Indira worked at these tasks with such demonic energy that her father was afraid of its consequences to her health. He wrote to Mrs. Mukul Banerji, then the secretary of the Women's Department in the Congress Party secretariat in New Delhi, expressing concern at his daughter's pace and imploring her not make his daughter work too hard. He also warned Mrs. Banerji not to breathe a word to Indira of his concern about her frail health, because she would be furious with him.

Allahabad, Indira's birthplace, would never give up its claims on the services of its favorite daughter. Mrs. Kamala Bahuguna, now president of the district Congress Committee of Allahabad, remembers the trivial dissensions with which the town Congress Committee was rived back in 1956. Matters could be set right only by someone who was not involved in this local factionalism. Indira was the one candidate, says Mrs. Bahuguna, who was equally acceptable to all the factions. So the Congress president, U. N. Dhebar, went out of his way to persuade Indira to accept the thankless job.

"She didn't need much persuading," says Mr. Uma Shankar Dikshit, a Member of Parliament and managing director of *The National Herald*. "No political leader of her stature would have touched a petty job like that with a pair of tongs. But she didn't mind it at all. She was prepared to work with them and for them, provided they all did too in the same spirit. She warned them that if there was no teamwork or if she detected any feuding or backbiting, she would quit forthwith. Things didn't improve much, and in about three months' time she really quit. Thereafter they pestered her repeatedly to head them again but she remained unmoved."

During the second General Election of 1957 Indira and Uma Shankar Dikshit together were responsible for managing Mr. Nehru's election campaign. The Prime Minister was too busy with affairs of government to visit his constituency more than twice or thrice. Mr. Dikshit recalls how Indira undertook one of the intensest campaign tours on her father's behalf. During the peak period just preceding polling date she would set out at six in the morning and not retire before midnight. She never delivered any long-winded speeches and relied on personal contacts. "At first she hardly had any audiences," explains Mr. Dikshit. "There were just a handful of people from neighboring houses in each village. But by the end of the campaign she became a great crowd drawer. In Fatehpur, I remember, she attracted a gathering of twenty thousand. It was the largest meeting anyone had ever addressed there."

More than speech-making Indira devoted her attention to training voters. In an electorate that was 80 percent illiterate, it was necessary to prevent the casting of as many invalid ballots as possible. She therefore trained a corps of workers to educate the electorate about the various political parties and their respective symbols and to instruct the voter on how to mark a ballot. There were eleven hundred villages in Nehru's constituency, and at the rate of about ten to fifteen villages a day she toured all of them before polling date. Although she visited every village personally, her workers scoured the areas to return and inform her of the villagers' grievances: lack of housing, roads, and hospitals. The workers were also asked to keep an eye on intercaste rivalries, which assumed tremendous importance at election time because of the tendency of various castes to vote for their own representatives regardless of the party to which they belonged. On polling day she made sure her workers had eaten breakfast by seven and left the camp to travel by bus, truck, or car to the various polling stations to assist the voters.

In addition to tending her father's constituency, Indira was invited by the party to boost the electoral prospects in doubtful areas. One of these was Gujarat. In November 1956, just before the second General Election, the Indian Parliament had divided the country into fourteen states. The boundaries of a dozen of these states accorded with the linguistic homogeneity of their inhabitants. There were two exceptions, the states of Bombay and Punjab, both of which were forced to remain bilingual, despite popular sentiment which demanded unilingual states. Bombay State consisted of two linguistic groups which spoke Marathi and Gujarati, while Punjab State consisted of two groups which spoke Punjabi and Hindi. The electoral fortunes of the Congress Party seemed quite bleak in these two states. To boost the morale of the party workers in the Gujarati-speaking area, Indira visited Ahmadabad, the textile capital of India, which had recently been the scene of bloody riots. The old guard of the Congress Party in Ahmadabad was thoroughly frightened. They had reason to be. The Chief Minister of Bombay State at the time happened to be none other than the redoubtable Morarji Desai, himself a Gujarati. A politician who put principle and party loyalty above everything else, he backed to the hilt the retention of Bombay as a bilingual state. The result was demonstrations, arson, and loot. Morarji retaliated by going on a fast. The mob reaction was only to hurl rocks at him when he addressed meetings.

Despite the reservations of the old guard, the younger elements of the Congress in Ahmadabad decided to invite Indira Gandhi to come and campaign for the party. She picked up the gauntlet early in January 1957. Yashpal Kapur, a scrappy young man with bubbling energy who had fled from the northwest frontier province when it became part of Pakistan in 1947 and who had served Nehru for a few years before becoming Indira's "Man Friday," describes what ensued. Indira insisted on traveling through Ahmadabad in an open car. The organizers agreed. But as a precaution they had arranged for three other cars to precede and two to follow hers. The streets were filled with dense crowds, many of them women. Instead of the expected stones, Indira's car was filled with garlands of flowers. "There was just one puny little student demonstration at the tether end of the tour," says Kapur. "Two small stones were hurled, one of which hit Indiraji's car, and the other hit mine. The whole affair passed off so tamely that she was frantically invited to Saurashtra [the hinterland of the Gujarati-speaking region]." The explanation for this incredible phenomenon was simple. The target of popular ire and mob passion was the government, with which the visitor had no truck. To thousands of Gujarati women, she was plain Indirabehn (sister Indira), the lucky possessor of charisma.

In January 1959, just before the Congress Party was readying itself for one of its periodic conventions, some of the disgruntled younger members of the Congress banded themselves together to form what they called the "Ginger Group." They issued a manifesto attacking the party leadership for complacency and tardiness in implementing its socialist pledges to the electorate. It was, in effect, a veiled attack on Mr. Nehru himself. Quite understandably, the public was amazed to learn that the signatories of the Ginger Group's manifesto included Nehru's own daughter and son-in-law. When asked why she joined them, Mrs. Gandhi asserts categorically: "I am sorry but I had nothing to do with the Ginger Group at all." Pressed to state if reports current at the time which linked her with the group were inaccurate, she answered: "No, no. I mean I fully agreed that the Congress should be gingered up and so on. But I didn't think this particular group would achieve it." Her judgment about the group, which was known more for its sound and fury than for the soundness of its views, was eminently sensible. Most of them have since been elbowed out of prominence through party infighting or defeated at the polls in the third General Election of 1962.

However, it still does not explain her motivation in signing the Ginger Group's manifesto. When it was put to her that her differences with her father might have been similar to the partly generational and partly ideological conflict which her father had with her grandfather, Indira said: "Well, I think it was mostly being of different generations, because in a lot of things I felt that he wasn't going fast enough or that something could have been done. But there again, one doesn't know the difficulties of the situation when one is not in power." Since 1959 Indira has been stamped politically as a Leftist, but she agrees now that it would be more accurate to describe her differences with her father as being those of temper rather than of ideology, and that they reflected her youthful impatience with her father's belief in the inevitability of gradualness. And then she added with admirable honesty: "When you are younger you are more intolerant also."

By now Indira had established herself so well as a national figure that her election as president of the Indian National Congress in 1959 was but the logical culmination of her political career. The position of Congress president had, however, lost much of its glamour since independence. Before 1947 the Congress presidents were the uncrowned kings of the nation, pitting India's popular might against the crowned heads of England. Once India became independent, it was the office of Prime Minister that suddenly assumed utmost importance. Nehru, as Prime Minister, consulted his party's president less and less. One Congress president resigned, complaining he had been completely ignored. Later, another Congress president was *made* to resign because his views conflicted with Nehru's. This conflict between the organizational and parliamentary wings of the party was obviated between 1951 and 1954, when Nehru was asked to don both caps in his dual role as head of his party and head of the government. In 1954 Nehru picked the meek and malleable Dhebar as Congress president. In 1958 the party resolved that the term of the president and the secretary should not exceed two years, and Dhebar resigned the following year.

Several versions about Indira Gandhi's election to the Congress presidency are current in India. When Jawaharlal first became president of the Congress, it was partly because Motilal pushed his candidacy very hard. There is a section which believes that Jawaharlal also groomed his daughter for the highest office of the party. Dewan Chaman Lall, Jawaharlal's contemporary in England and now a member of the Rajya Sabha, says: "Yes, he pushed her into the Congress presidency. She was in the knowledge of all the policies and thinking of her father. Of course, she was always in the background, but she was kept *au courant*. Nehru couldn't have done otherwise—he had a historic sense." But Indira's contemporary, Nayantara Sahgal, dissents. "*Mamu* never did anything specially to groom her. He didn't refuse to give advice if it was sought. If the subject of party presidency was discussed at all he might have argued one way or the other. But I don't think he ever said anything either way. He never pressured."

Two other versions establish that Nehru did not really push Indira into the Congress presidency. An Indian politician who discussed the question with Nehru says, "I told him she must be made Congress president so that she might succeed him as Prime Minister, if necessary. He insisted promptly, 'Oh, no. She is hasty and quick-tempered.' I retorted: 'Do you think you are any less short-tempered?' He laughed, and went on, 'I am at least close to the masses; she isn't.' I told him she could get to know the masses just as he did, and he concluded, 'Well, you think so? Maybe.'" Another person who was on the inside track at the Nagpur session of the Congress in January 1959 describes what exactly transpired at the last minute. "We were all staying at Raj Bhavan [the Governor's Residence]. Nehru was waiting for Indira to join him at lunch. As she was coming through the corridor, Dhebar, Pant, and Katju pounced on her and pressured her to accept the Congress presidency. Taken unawares she wavered a little and asked for time to consult her father. They insisted on her consent *before* she went to the table, and she yielded. When she got to the table, however, she was too nervous to broach the subject with her father, I think. The following day she told him she had accepted the offer of Congress presidency, but expressed doubt about her ability to do the job or even the desire to have it. Panditji (Nehru) exploded: 'You come to consult me now after it's all over? You have no choice now but to bend yourself and work.' "

Dhebar resigned, and Indira Gandhi was unanimously elected president of the Indian National Congress on February 2, 1959. It was a proud moment for the Nehru family, since she was the third in three generations to occupy the party's highest office. Her grandfather had been president of the Congress twice, and her father six times. It was an additional achievement for Indian womanhood, since Indira was the fourth of her sex to have become Congress president, her predecessors being Dr. Annie Besant in 1917 at the Calcutta session, Mrs. Sarojini Naidu in 1925, at the Kanpur session, and Mrs. Nellie Sen Gupta in 1933 at Calcutta.

Although Indira remained in office for only eleven months and then resigned, her stewardship of the Congress was quite distinguished. Her singular achievement lay in unseating the Communist government in the state of Kerala. After the second General Election of 1957 the Congress was returned to power in all the states except Kerala, where a Communist ministry headed by E. M. S. Namboodiripad, an astute Brahmin of considerable intellectual stature and ideological fervor, was installed. It was the first time in the history of the world that any Communist Party won power through the normal democratic process of a free and fair ballot rather than through the more familiar flying bullet. The Communists seemed to convince themselves that such a miraculous event might never again occur and went about infiltrating systematically the administrative machinery and the police force. This was followed by interference with the independent functioning of the judiciary, assassination of political workers of other parties, and diversion of state funds into the party's treasury. The feeling of insecurity of person and property was widespread, but when the people began to picket the Communist government peacefully, they were only fired on. The last straw to break the back of the people was the dismissal of openly anti-Communist teachers and their substitution by fellow travelers, the indoctrination of schoolchildren, and the methodical rewriting of school textbooks in which Lenin and Mao Tse-tung were glorified but Mahatma Gandhi was not even mentioned.

Indira visited Kerala in the spring of 1959 and convinced herself that "everything the Communists are doing is wrong." When she returned to Delhi she found that her father was averse to interfering in Kerala. For one thing, Nehru desired to avoid the impression that he was opposed to the Kerala ministry purely on partisan grounds— it being Communist and he being a Congress member. For another, he was touchy about stepping on the toes of the Soviet Union. Dismissal of the only Communist ministry in India might give umbrage to the Soviet leadership. Not being a member of the government but being the head of the party, Indira felt free to take a different stand. To the doubters who questioned the constitutional propriety of dismissing a duly elected government, she said: "The Constitution exists for the people, not the people for the Constitution. And if the Constitution stands in the way of meeting the people's grievances in Kerala, it should be changed." Addressing a mass rally in New Delhi, she declared: "When Kerala is virtually on fire it becomes the federal government's duty to go to the aid of the people. The misrule of the Communists has driven the people to desperation. The mass upsurge in Kerala and its ruthless suppression by the Communist rulers of the state have created a situation unparalleled in the history of our country; such a situation does not brook legal quibbling."

Aware of her father's touchiness on the subject, Indira approached the President of the Republic, Dr. Rajendra Prasad, and persuaded him that it was time to act. By Article 356 of the Indian Constitution, the President is empowered to assume direct control of a state if he is satisfied that its government is not being run according to the provisions of the Constitution. Yielding to her pressure, President

Prasad ousted the Communist ministry of Kerala on July 31, 1959, declared President's rule for the time being, and ordered fresh elections.

The tougher job of defeating the Communists at the polls now lay ahead. The chronic political instability of Kerala was partly due to multiparty contests rather than straight two-party contests, which resulted in no one getting a clear and workable majority. Indira therefore devised the strategy of forging a solid, united anti-Communist front of all democratic opposition parties. She sought the help and guidance of S. K. Patil, boss of the Congress Party in Bombay State and a tactician of consummate skill who loves the sport of Communist-baiting. Indira canvassed in Kerala from the southern tip of the state to Palghat in the north. Yashpal Kapur, who traveled with her, remembers a human wall, ten feet deep, lining her route wherever she went. "Gaily caparisoned elephants with their trunks uplifted and a cacophony of sounds emanating from bands of indigenous musical instruments greeted her enthusiastically. Every meeting was delayed four or five hours by the press of the crowds. She was scheduled to address a meeting at Trichur at eight P.M. We couldn't get there till midnight. But the vast maidan was still full when she got there and she held the audience spellbound until one A.M." Indira's strategy and persistence paid off when the special election was held in February 1960. The Communists, who had held sixty seats in the state assembly, were now trounced and managed to obtain only twenty-nine, while the anti-Communist electoral front augmented its strength, winning ninety-three seats.

Although the result was gratifying, Indira's strategy came under fire from certain quarters. One of the parties in her electoral front was the Muslim League. After the subcontinent's partition in 1947, the Muslim League dissolved itself in India. However, it was revived in Kerala subsequently. Since Nehru was a tireless advocate of the idea of a secular state, Indira was accused of subverting her own father's principles by entering into an arrangement of convenience with a "communal" or extremist religious party. Indira defended her action vigorously, asserting: "I don't believe the Muslim League is any more communal than anyone else in Kerala. Everything there is communal. Everything is run by the Nairs, the Nestorians, the Namboodiris, or some other sect. You have to deal with communal parties unless you want to forget about Kerala entirely."

Mrs. Gandhi might well have extended her observation to the whole of India. There are in India, if one wants to be honest about it, only Hindus, Muslims, Sikhs, Christians, Buddhists, Parsis, and Jews. There are no secular Indians as such. There are, of course, some Communists who claim to be completely secular. But in truth they simply subscribe to a secular religion, now spilt into two sects, the orthodox and the heterodox. The belief that there are secularly inclined people in India is largely a myth. Secularism is a superficial veneer displayed by a handful of highly westernized individuals. An Indian without a religion is like a dehydrated vegetable. Without his religion he is without his element. Indira Gandhi was only being practical and realistic in coming to terms with this supreme fact of Indian life, rather than wishing it away, as her father was prone to do.

A situation no less precarious than that in Kerala existed in Bombay State also. In the General Election of 1957, two newly-established political parties demanded the bifurcation of the bilingual state of Bombay into unilingual states—Maharashtra and Gujarat. The Congress managed to ward off their combined assault largely because of the skillful generalship of Bombay's then youthful Chief Minister, Yeshwantrao Chavan. Two years later, by the time Indira became president of the Congress, the law-and-order situation began to look increasingly alarming. The Communists had joined the bandwagon of linguistic agitation and the even tenor of public life in the state had been gravely disturbed. Chavan conveyed to the powers that be his considered judgment that unless the popular demand was conceded immediately, the Congress stood little chance of winning the election in 1962.

Indira felt that a final decision must wait until her firsthand observation tour of Bombay was completed. Since she had already visited the Gujarati-speaking areas in 1957, she now took a look at the other side of the fence, the Marathi-speaking region. "It was one of the most hectic tours she had undertaken," avers her secretary, Yashpal Kapur, "very much like the ones her father used to go on when he was in his forties. We traveled by car and she used to cover, on an average, two hundred fifty to three hundred miles a day. She would make what you might call whistle-stops—about thirty-five of them—and speak for not more than two to three minutes at each stop. There would be about three or four major addresses a day. Every morning Mrs. Gandhi would set out at five and call it a day after midnight.

"Just before we left Delhi, Paul Grimes, *The New York Times'* correspondent in India, rang me up to ask if he might come along and watch Mrs. Gandhi in action. I told him we could possibly work it out, and so he was with us on that Maharashtra tour. But he couldn't take the grind for longer than two days. On the third day he told me: 'I'm going to beat it. How can this woman do it?' "

It was a tour strenuous enough to exhaust someone in normal health. But in 1959 Indira had acute kidney trouble and only a handful of her intimate friends knew about it. Gripped in pain most of the time, she would press her abdomen with one hand and keep addressing her audiences without a trace of suffering on her face. "But when we got back," says Kapur, "she could hardly lie still. Writhing in pain, she would jump from the bed and almost hit the ceiling. The doctor had told me to give her a glass of water every half hour, which I did. She also scrupulously avoided eating tomatoes. But these precautions hardly seemed of much help."

As in the Gujarati-speaking area, so in the Marathi-speaking region also, thousands of people poured out from farm and village to get her *darshan* (communion through sight). Here, too, women predominated, and Indirabai, as they affectionately called her, was literally mobbed. "In Miraj," Mr. Kapur remembers, "there were a hundred thousand people inside a vast gymnasium and another hundred thousand outside. Those outside, who should have been demonstrating to press their claim for a separate state, were actually demonstrating to press their claim to get in. 'We have spent twelve annas [15 cents] to get here and we have to spend another twelve annas to get home. We haven't come here for fun; we want *darshan*.' They yelled for some time but cooled off when she started to speak and the loudspeakers carried her voice outside the gymnasium."

This Maharashtra tour was significant for revealing Indira's instinctive reaction to coercive public demands, although few people noticed it at the time. Condemning noisy demonstrations and upbraiding the troublemakers, she would ask: "What do you think you can gain from this *tamasha* [circus]? Nothing, I am afraid. I have come to meet with you and ascertain your feelings and aspirations. We don't have a dictatorship in India. We have a democracy. And in a democracy I believe people should get what they want. But I can assure you that you will get nothing by bullying me. I am not impressed by purposeless *Satyagraha* [civil disobedience], rioting, arson, and loot. In fact, I tell even my father never to receive anybody who threatens political blackmail or coercion."

Returning to the capital, Indira met with a number of Members of Parliament from the state of Bombay and ascertained their wishes on the question. She also appointed a nine-man body to study the entire question and report its recommendations to the Congress Working Committee. Her father had hoped to continue the bilingual character of Bombay State with a view to its serving as an example to the other warring linguistic groups in the country. Indira shared her father's idealism but not his illusions. A division of Bombay into the two new states of Maharashtra and Gujarat was decided upon by the Working Committee on December 4, 1959, and a bill to that effect was soon passed by Parliament, thus ending years of hatred feeding itself upon daily rioting and bloodshed.

The most important development in foreign affairs during Indira's stewardship of the Congress was the end of Tibetan autonomy and the effective occupation of Tibet by China. This did not come as a surprise—not at least to a handful of farsighted Indians who had been carefully analyzing Chinese intentions and actions. China had already occupied fourteen thousand square miles of territory in the northernmost state, Kashmir, while India was napping. It was through this Indian territory that China had built a highway, between 1957 and 1959, linking her own Sinkiang Province with Tibet. The Buddhist kingdom of the Dalai Lama, and his brother, the Panchen Lama, perched on the Roof of the World, had not so far seen anything on wheels. But with the highway completed, Chinese transport trucks and armored vehicles roared into Tibet. The process of "modernization" began, followed soon by extermination of the enemies of "progress." The Panchen Lama was successfully brainwashed and carted off to Peking. When the palace of the unyielding Dalai Lama was shelled, the living God of Buddhism fled to India, accompanied by thousands of the faithful. Nehru's Leftist advisers had warned him that the grant of political asylum to the Dalai Lama would infuriate Peking and that the risk was not worth taking. But Nehru sensed that if he did not take this risk he would become the target of public indignation within the country. He could not have forgotten that only three years earlier when the Soviet Union literally invaded Hungary, and he vacillated and equivocated, his more sensitive countrymen had wondered whether India had sat on the fence for so long that the iron had entered her soul. The asylum was granted, and the Dalai Lama settled temporarily in the hill resort town of Mussoorie.

The Congress Working Committee, presided over by Indira, endorsed the government's action and expressed deep concern and sympathy for the people of Tibet who were being subjected to near genocide. The flow of Tibetan refugees to India continued at an alarming rate, and they had to be properly settled and rehabilitated. Indira established the Central Relief Committee for Tibetans to undertake the task. Rather than make it the exclusive affair of her own party, she made it the common concern of all the political parties of the country, and, characteristically, chose Acharya J. B. Kripalani, a persistent critic of her father's policies toward Communist countries, as the chairman of the Relief Committee. After a few months, the Dalai Lama sought from the Government of India the same freedom of political expression which it allowed the politicians of Nepal who had obtained asylum in India. Still solicitous of Chinese sensibilities on the question, Nehru turned down the request. Indira found herself in an awkward position. Privately she was one with the Dalai Lama in his desire for freedom of expression. But she refrained from taking a public stand lest it should embarrass her father in the conduct of diplomacy.

Indira is also credited by her countrymen with having taken the initiative to build bridges of understanding with African countries. Since the convening of the Afro-Asian conference in Bandung in 1955, a few more of the erstwhile colonies in Africa had achieved independence. Indira established the National Council for Africa (which is now functioning as the Indian Council for Africa) to express solidarity with the African people. Herself poor and powerless, there was nothing very much concrete that India could have done for Africa, save let off a little steam on the issue of racism and administer a few whiplashes to the dying horse of colonialism. But to express a vague "Afro-Asian solidarity" was the thing for all "progressives" to do back in the 1950's, and Indira joined the trend of the times. Few could prophesy at the time that the Chinese aggression against India in 1962 and the subsequent flirtation of a few African countries with China would lead to the rapid liquidation within India of the sentiment of solidarity with Africa.

One other thing Indira did as Congress president was to appoint a National Committee for Algeria with a view to mobilizing moral support for the Algerian struggle for freedom from French rule. It was in furtherance of these two objectives that Indira had planned to leave on a goodwill tour of African countries on September 18, 1960. But her husband's death in the preceding week led to the cancellation of the tour.

Another accomplishment accredited to Indira Gandhi was the completion of the spadework for drafting India's third five-year plan. The first plan had commenced in 1951, the second in 1956, and the third was to commence in 1961. The party's Sub-Committee on Planning finalized its report during Indira's presidency. It conducted a week-long seminar from May 30 to June 5, 1959, at Ootacamund, a fabulous summer resort in the Nilgiri Hills of southern India. Removed by a comfortable distance from the unpleasant realities of the sweltering plains below them and elated by the elevation of their site, the seminarians did not find it difficult to set their sights high. They envisaged a 6 percent rate of growth of the economy during the third five-year plan, and 8 percent during subsequent plans; a rapid growth of industry and a simultaneous increase in agricultural production; maximum possible employment and a national minimum of social services; the reduction of inequalities of income and wealth; and the achievement of "a self-generating and self-accelerating economy."

The rapporteurs recorded that "while there were differences of opinion and of emphasis on certain matters, there was general agreement in regard to the broad objectives of the plan." The thirty-five participants in the seminar were of such varied political hue and economic stripe that the objectives had, of necessity, to be broad enough to please everybody in the Congress. Atop the hills at Ootacamund, one is literally in the clouds. So the Congress politicians promised the people the traditional apple pie a la mode in the sky for the future. For the present they dished out an omelet of stale leftover slogans. Little did Indira, whose grounding in economics is rather shallow, realize at the time that only six years hence she would be called upon to unscramble the omelet and take out the ideological eggs which her friends had beaten up so feverishly at Ootacamund.

The third General Election in 1962 made heavy demands on Indira's time and energies. Her father was too old to campaign even in his own constituency, and she had to take full charge of the canvassing. Besides, she had been elected a member of the Central Election Committee in 1961, and in that capacity she had to scrutinize the claims of those who wanted her party's label to contest the election. Along with Lal Bahadur Shastri, who also was a member of this committee, Indira went over every application with the utmost care so that the best claimants represented her party. Such diligence was certainly necessitated by the emergence of a new political party, the Swatantra (Freedom) Party, in 1959. This party, frankly conservative, was founded by a wily octogenarian, Chakravarti Rajagopalachari, to fight the recently-declared intention of the Congress to socialize the country's agriculture. Until then, the Congress Party had construed socialism to mean the establishment of a number of state-owned industrial undertakings in strategic sectors of the economy at the expense of the private entrepreneur. But in January 1959, partly under the prodding of the Ginger Group, the Congress was eager at its Nagpur session to announce "a new and dynamic agrarian programme based on the principle of cooperation." The party's resolution on the subject said: "The future agrarian pattern should be that of cooperative joint farming in which the land will be pooled for joint cultivation, the farmers continuing to retain their property rights and getting a share from the net produce in proportion to their land."

Rajagopalachari had defected from the Congress after years of membership in it. He was the first Indian to have become Governor-General of the country after it attained dominion status. He then was the distinguished Chief Minister of Madras State. After retirement from political office, he was greatly disturbed by the economic policies of the Congress. While the Congress professed to fight the concentration of power in the hands of private enterprise, Rajaji (as Rajagopalachari was called for short) was afraid of the growing concentration of power in the state, which in effect meant the ruling party. He charged that what the Congress was introducing in India was not socialism but state capitalism. He went further and maintained that the Congress Party was actually in league with the private capitalist, who welcomed the Congress brand of socialism because it created monopoly conditions which suited the Indian capitalist admirably. Rajaji now charged that the cooperative farming proposed by the Congress was nothing but a euphemism for collective farming as practiced by the Communist countries, and that the elimination of the private peasant farmer, who was the very backbone of a free society, was but the prelude to a totalitarian society. Thus was born the Swatantra Party to challenge the Congress in the election of 1962.

Since the Swatantra Party is, in the terminology of Indian politics, "the party of right-wing reaction," its establishment infuriated Mr. Nehru. He always used to reserve his favorite epithets and strongest invective for right-wingers. When asked to state his views about the Leftist and Rightist parties in India, Nehru once pounded the table at a press conference in 1962 and fulminated: "Right-wing parties are always the greatest threat. I think nothing can be worse than the right wing, because the right wing means going back to an ancient world, feudalism and all that. I can't stand a feudalist conception of

India. It means ignorance, decay, stagnation, and all that goes to the death of a nation."

An outward show of confidence notwithstanding, Congress circles experienced inner tremors about the potential challenge which the Swatantra Party posed to the hegemony of the Congress. Since more women than men had been voting in Indian elections, Indira advised women workers of the Congress party to concentrate on the "better half" of the electorate. She told them frankly of the new challenge: "The festival aspect of the first General Election of 1952 has now given way to a more serious consideration of the issues at stake. The years of freedom and progress have brought their own problems. The political scene is further complicated by the emergence of new parties making all sorts of claims. The voter is subjected to a barrage of propaganda from all sides and there is such a tremendous pressure on her that she often becomes confused." Displaying a passionate party loyalty which would have met even the exacting standards of Harry Truman, Indira campaigned vigorously to ensure the victory of her party.

As a charismatic politician, Indira Gandhi has no peer in India today. Her popularity, especially among women, is immense. "Not since the days of Mahatma Gandhi," said a veteran Congressman, "have I seen such enormous numbers of women attend meetings addressed by our national leaders—not even Jawaharlal's." However, the politician that lasts in his business is not one who is merely charismatic; he is also adept in the power-play of politics. Indira Gandhi suffers from some deficiencies on this score.

The Congress Party, both on the national and state levels, is composed of numerous factions. Indira must retain the confidence of a majority of these factions if she is to survive in office. However, factional politics disgusts her, as it did her father, even if it takes on the superficial aspect of an ideological argument. Writing about this some quarter of a century ago, Jawaharlal deplored:

> What am I to do with the finest principles if I do not have confidence in the person concerned? The party rivalries in many provinces illustrate this and we find extreme bitterness

and often an utter lack of scruple among people who are ordinarily honourable and straight. I cannot stomach this kind
of politics and I have kept absolutely aloof from them for
these many years. I function individually without any group
or any second person to support me, although I am happy
enough to possess the confidence of many."

Indira also keeps aloof from factions, but she does not enjoy their
universal respect as her father did. Jawaharlal's natural disposition,
political artifice, and an aura of greatness put him above the fray.
In contrast, Indira is frequently being pulled into the fray by factions
which wish to take advantage of her youth and inexperience. Ironically, she is paying the price for her father's mistakes. No Congressman of even the highest stature had the courage to question the wisdom of Nehru's policies while he was alive. "It wasn't that Nehru
was an autocrat," says a high Cabinet member who has served all
three Prime Ministers of independent India. "It is just that we had
so much deference for Nehru that we equated dissent with disre-
spect." India has paid a high price for some of Nehru's blunders, and
no one in India today—Congress Party members included—wants a
personality cult to develop within the country, with its implied notion of infallibility. This is a healthy development in the country
and, viewed rightly, is beneficial to Indira herself, insofar as she must
obtain for her policies the active consent of the party, where her
father took for granted its passive acquiescence.

Another grave handicap which Indira suffers from, especially in
the Indian political context, is her disinclination as well as incapacity
to articulate policy. The Indian mind in general revels in abstraction
and displays a distaste for action. The Indian politician in particular
has developed the intellectualization of politics into such a fine art
that he is often engaged in academic hair-splitting or is discoursing
upon distinctions without a difference. Strange as it may sound, even
the Indian Communists—both orthodox and heterodox—are cold-
blooded theorists rather than hot-blooded revolutionaries.

In this sense, Nehru was a typical Indian politician. Especially in
his later years, his monotonous monologues embraced the whole uni-

verse of problems as he glided smoothly from the discussion of one
to the dissection of another. Oftentimes he unburdened himself of
platitudes, but he possessed a remarkable gift for creating the illusion
of profundity in uttering them. Subhas Chandra Bose, a former President of the Congress and a fiery activist, once leveled a well-merited
charge against Nehru: "In recent years the Congress resolutions are
often too verbose and long-worded. One should call them 'theses'
or 'essays' rather than 'resolutions.' Formerly our resolutions used to
be brief, pertinent, and practical. I am afraid that you have had a
hand in giving this new shape and form to our resolutions."

Poor Indira is like her grandfather who detested "commonplaces,"
which he said were "the besetting sin of all Indian speeches." She
refers to a particular breed of Indian politicians with an annoyance
bordering on contempt: "I am sorry to say that articulation of ideas
means nothing to me because people talk a lot, and there is great
deal of hypocrisy; and if those persons are not living their ideas, obviously these ideas have no value."

Motilal and Jawaharlal openly aired their differences on economic
policy. The elder Nehru had no hesitation in declaring: "Pure idealism completely divorced from realities has no place in politics and
is but a happy dream, which must sooner or later end in a rude awakening." And he added: "The masses want bread. They have no time
for theories and dogmas imported from abroad. . . . The occasion
calls for skillful generalship, not academic discussions which take us
nowhere." Indira believes her country's chief problem is economic
and that it admits of none but hardheaded, practical solutions. When,
as Congress president, she welcomed the participants to the seminar
at Ootacamund on the third five-year plan, she had specifically requested them to bear in mind "the practical aspects" of planning.
What they offered her was verbiage that covered reams of paper.
It is not surprising that critics in her own party who now attack her
"new economic policy" do not question its practicality; they impugn
its ideological purity.

One other respect in which Indira is very different from her father
is both in the matter and the manner of decision-making. If two
opposing viewpoints were being actively canvassed, Jawaharlal never

entered the argument and kept his counsel to himself. After both sides had bloodied their noses, he sagely gave his advice, and they would exclaim that Solomon had spoken the last word. Nehru adopted this technique for one of two reasons: He either had no definite views of his own in a given controversy, in which case he would wait for the air to be cleared and then express his view. Or he had very definite views on the subject, in which case he maintained a diplomatic silence so as to avoid the impression of dictatorial interference, and then supported the side of his choice at the opportune moment. By employing this stratagem, Nehru got what he wanted, leaving the impression that it was what the people wanted; on this his reputation as a great democrat rested.

In contrast, Indira is already being accused of authoritarianism. She never waits for the dust of controversy to settle but hastens to express her view at the very outset in the hope that the dust will settle sooner. She acts as a kind of political yeast in the fermentation of structured public opinion. Uma Shankar Dikshit, who has observed her closely over the past many years, puts it this way: "She likes to face a situation rather than be faced with it. She doesn't believe in putting off action. Expediency or the line of least resistance doesn't appeal to her. If there's a conundrum, and two equally inconvenient alternatives are all she has, she won't postpone a decision. If public reaction to her decision is adverse, she will face that too and train all her guns on it. In this respect she is bolder than her father." When it was suggested to her that she had appeared diffident until recently in expressing her views and this might have been to avoid embarrassment to her father, she retorted: "I have never been diffident about my views, let me tell you. In fact, I think that at an earlier stage, as I told you, I've expressed them much more vehemently than I do now."

If Indira lasts in office long enough, she will project to the younger generation in India the image of a new species of politician. George Bernard Shaw used to say that a subject nation is like a man suffering from cancer; he can think of nothing else. Although India today is independent, her people do not feel free to branch out into a thousand different endeavors. Indira's mentor, Tagore, said fullness of expression is fullness of life; but to most Indians today, politics is the one and only preoccupation. They are obsessed with it as if they were still a subject people. Every question—be it agricultural, industrial, educational, demographic, cultural, or social—ends up as a political controversy. Asked whether she would share the view that, if more people in India did more things in a nonpolitical way life would be richer, fuller, and more meaningful for them, she said, "Yes," and added significantly, "but the politicians themselves should have a wider outlook and a wider range of interests. Rather than that life should be subsumed by politics, it is politics that should subserve all of life, so to speak."

12

The Lady Behind the Mask

Don't quote me, but the Nehrus are inscrutable. Looking at their faces you wouldn't know what goes on in their minds." This view of a Cabinet minister in a pivotal position, that Indira Gandhi wears a mask, is confirmed by many others. A close relative of hers points out how she sits motionless with a visitor, lending him a patient ear and maintaining an impassive face, till he has left and closed the door behind him. Most visitors leave disappointed because they do not get even a clue whether their pleas or representations fell on a receptive or hostile mind. Indira is, in a sense, even more inscrutable than her father. Although it was difficult to divine Jawaharlal Nehru's deeper intentions, his plastic face often gave away his immediate reactions. But Indira is so fully in control of her emotions that many people consider her a cold fish.

"The truth, however," says Dr. Ishwar Nath Topa, an uncle of Indira's, "is that the Nehrus are a people of volcanic emotions. They do try to control their emotions, but the more they try to do it, the more tense they become. With Indira this wasn't even an acquired characteristic. I remember carrying her in my arms during the evenings to Chandni Chowk in Delhi to buy her candy or some Indian sweetmeats. She was about four years old at the time. I used to tickle her, but she never even smiled. She would push my finger away firmly and remain tense and fidgety." The incommunicability of her emotions is often accentuated by her reticence. Although Indira holds strong views and expresses them freely and vigorously, as did her father and grandfather, she conceals her emotions much more successfully than both of them.

But when Indira is relaxed, which is not often, her friends say she is gay and carefree, and even talkative. She has the reputation of being an arresting raconteur, with an evocative memory and a ready wit. Her cousin Nayantara tells of the day they were together in London sometime in 1963 on a private visit. "We had planned to go shopping," she recalls, "but didn't have much money with us to splurge—thanks to the Reserve Bank of India [the watchdog of India's foreign exchange earnings, which doles out foreign currency parsimoniously for private visits abroad]. So we avoided the more expensive taxicab and went by bus. Indi [as she calls Indira] has the proverbial elephant's memory. She remembered all the bus routes and their numbers—from her student days! Anyway, we got aboard a bus, and since we couldn't find two seats vacant alongside each other, she sat in a front seat and I behind her. She turned round to me and began telling me of old times and her life in London. We both were so absorbed, I in listening and she in relating the story, that neither of us looked out for our destination. Not until she finished her story did we realize we had gone well past the department store we were to get off at."

Although Indira has a photogenic face, she is far more attractive than her pictures. At forty-nine there is a streak of gray in her black, wavy hair. Each gray hair, she assured President Johnson, represents a fund of political wisdom painstakingly acquired. Her sad, soft brown eyes, beneath a fairly wide brow, reveal an inner loneliness. Her straight, well-chiseled aquiline nose proclaims that power and dignity rest well on her five-foot-two-inch frame. Her ingratiating smile and spontaneous, girlish laughter put the visitor at ease, although her countenance ordinarily wears an aspect of severity in repose. A legion of imps twitch at the corners of her mouth when she is amused. A glacial look or a stony silence is sufficient to drive out an unwelcome visitor. A passing frown or a piercing scowl depicts the degree of her disapproval. Light in step, she walks swiftly, as her father did. If Jawaharlal detested anything, it was corpulence hanging loose on the female frame, and Indira always remained slim. "At first glance there is something forbiddingly regal about this child of the Indian revolution," wrote Welles Hangen, adding that "her long, thin face and Roman features," and "her slender sari-draped figure sweeping through the carpeted halls of the Prime Minister's residence in New Delhi" somehow reminded him of a Hapsburg empress.

Indira is among the best-dressed women of India, though never extravagantly so. She has learned to groom herself the hard way. Her teen-age requirements were not met adequately. When the poor girl arrived in school in Poona, says Coonverbai Vakil, all she had with her were those thick, canvaslike saris woven in khadi, which only hindered her gait. "She just couldn't manage with her mother's saris and kept tripping all the time. On the third day I sent for the tailor and had some printed khadi frocks made for her." Her schoolmates remember that Indira was not allowed to trim her eyebrows; her mother was very opposed to it. Later, her husband, Feroze, bought her expensive and tasteful saris from all over the country, and she acquired some jewelry too.

Her father, however, was quite austere in his tastes and even mistook the slightest decoration for ostentation. When she attended Queen Elizabeth II's coronation, her companions insisted that she wear some jewelry, which she did. "What for are you all decked out?" frowned Nehru. He was, however, silenced, and she kept her jewelry on. When her lady staff members or friends pestered Indira to use some of her exotic saris or jewelry, Indira always had a ready excuse: "Oh, I'm too old for them now. I'll keep them for my daughters-in-law." Whoever the lucky ones might be, the daughters-in-law will inherit only her saris; Indira gave away all her gold jewelry for national defense after the Chinese attack of 1962.

Handwoven textiles in India are fancy and exquisite and that is what Indira likes to wear today. But what she wears when is determined as much by political dictates as by her excellent sense of propriety and a feeling for the occasion. During her countrywide tours she wears the traditional saris of the state she is in, whether it is Maharashtra, Orissa, Bengal, or a south Indian state. And appropriately enough she covers her head in deference to tradition. Bangles too appear on her wrists while in the Indian country side. But in London or Washington she might prefer a rich silk sari, sport a becoming hairdo, and even wear a mink coat—which, of course, lends ammunition to ungallant members of the Opposition to ask ungenerous questions in Parliament. For her office wear she chooses white or cool-colored cottons for summer, and warmer shades of chocolate, brown, and yellow for winter. She paints her toenails, prefers low heels, and uses a light lipstick, but not for work. "She always had excellent taste," says Shanta Gandhi. "I remember her withering comments, as a student in London, when her eye caught an atrocious dress, a loud hat, or an ill-matched handbag." Personal grooming, about which she is meticulous, is not an obsession with her. "She detests flashy dress and she can't stand the 'drawing-room types' who are eternally preoccupied with physical appearance," says a Foreign Service officer. He testifies that Indira had his colleague's posting abroad changed because "his wife talked endlessly of trifles like clothing, jewelry and other shopping items."

India's woman Prime Minister's modest residence on Safdarjung Road, is tastefully and delightfully furnished. In the small visitors' room where guests wait their turn to meet her are placed two wooden sculptures and a flower arrangement, often done by herself in the past. A still life in oils hangs on the wall, and two color photographs —her father's and her husband's—stand on a table. In the gallery leading from the entrance to the drawing room are autographed pictures of President Radhakrishnan, Mahatma Gandhi, and of her father in a myriad mercurial moods. At the entrance to the gallery is a bronze statue of Ganesh, the elephant-headed son of Siva and the remover of obstacles to all endeavors. At its foot lie fresh flowers and garlands brought every morning by a stream of admirers. If the quantity of flowers is excessively large, they are sent away to hospitals and orphanages.

Alongside the gallery is Indira's bedroom and ahead of it the drawing room. In one corner of the drawing room is an exquisite sculpture of the Goddess Tara, and on an elevated stand is a bronze head of the Buddha. The fireplace is covered with a raw-silk board. The gray and blue sofas seat more than a dozen people comfortably. Seasonal flowers fill two large vases. A single rose bends in homage before a large color photograph of her father which stands on the mantelpiece. A shelf of books near by displays a varied collection: Theodore White's *The Making of the President*, Arthur Schlesinger's *Politics of Upheaval*, Louis Fischer's *Life of Lenin*, George Kennan's *Russia and the West*, and the *Russian Panorama* by India's former Ambassador to the Soviet Union, K. P. S. Menon. Among recent acquisitions are Tom Mboya's *Freedom and After* and Jean-Paul Sartre's *Words*. A biography of Swami Vivekananda, J. Krishnamurti's *Commentaries on Living*, and Aldous Huxley's *The Doors of Perception* obviously lend her some inspiration. And to arouse or satisfy her imagination are Eugene Ionesco's *Four Plays* and Joseph Campbell's *The Hero with a Thousand Faces*. Light filters through the bright yellow of a lamp shade, dimly lighting some exquisite Mogul miniatures on the wall.

In the center of the dining room is a dark-brown teak table that seats twelve. Hand-loomed curtains of beige ground and printed single figurines harmonize with the light walls. A work by Hussain, the well-known Indian painter, and Rafael Navarro's "Mexican Boy with Flute" hang on the walls. Beneath the latter is a cut-glass vase. A bamboo partition divides the dining room from an adjoining sitting room, studded with more sculpture in stone, that overlooks the side lawn. In the pantry are loads of cutlery, china, crystal, and demitasse coffee cups. In a fruit arrangement on a silver tray there might be fresh leechis, apples, and *langra* mangoes, Indira's favorite fruit. A *Round the World Cookbook* and a *Complete Vegetarian Recipe Book* peep out from a small shelf. *Eat and Grow Beautiful* proclaims another title; and there is *The Omelette Book* which Feroze must have mastered before acquiring his reputation for dishing out an excellent variety of omelet. Mrs. Amy Crishna, Indira's able and harried housekeeper, flits about the house, trailed by three pedigreed golden retrievers: ten-year-old Madhu, winner of the First Prize for the best-behaved dog when Sanjay entered him in a New Delhi dog show, eleven-year-old Pepi, and eight-year-old Putli.

Indira's daily meals are cooked by fifty-eight-year-old A. James, who has been the Nehru family chef since January 1946. The Prime

Minister is up at six in the morning. By eight she has bathed and is ready for breakfast, which she always has in her bedroom. She is generally served toast, a soft-boiled or scrambled egg, and coffee. Sometimes she likes an apple or a ripe banana. In the summer months she substitutes a glass of cold buttermilk for hot coffee. Every week Indira approves the lunch and dinner menu suggestions made by Mrs. Crishna. While James specializes in Western preparations, forty-two-year-old Vinod Behari Barua turns out the Indian dishes. "I've learned my cooking from Tulsi, the great Motilalji's cook," declares Barua, who has been with the Prime Minister's family since 1947. "She is most fond of *khichri* [rice and lentils cooked together]. Ordinarily, she eats one or two *phulka* [puffed-wheat pancakes]. She enjoys *daal* [lentils] and one or two vegetables. She is very happy when I cook *kulfa sag* [a leafy green vegetable] or *kurkura karela* or *bhindi* [crunchy, fried bitter gourd or okra]. Twice or thrice a week I make curried chicken or mutton, but very lightly spiced." Ever since the drought commenced two years ago, Indira has given up eating rice. "She isn't much of a dessert eater," adds Barua, "preferring fruit to sweet dishes." It is well known, however, that she is extremely fond of *khir* [rice and cream pudding], which she cannot hope to eat until famine conditions ease in the country. "She likes fish in any form," says James, "and I grill, bake or smoke it. She relishes stuffing very much and I stuff *brinjal* [eggplant] or *capsicum* [peppers] with meat and *paneer* [homemade cheese] or I stuff shoulder of lamb. For a change I prepare cutlets or Irish stew."

When her sons are home the cooking veers predominantly toward the Indian style because of Sanjay's perferences, which are distinctly like his father's. "He loves a *botidar salan* [a rich curry with chunks of meat]," testify the cooks, adding: "Rajiv doesn't have preferences. He is a *sadhu* [hermit]; anything goes." A relative says: "The whole family goes through different eating phases. Sometimes the fad is vegetarianism, which doesn't last long because the kids lap up ham and eggs any day. Indira herself may suddenly take a fancy for south Indian food." In general, however, eating is no elaborate ritual in Indira Gandhi's house, and she is attending official functions or touring the country so often that she eats at home quite irregularly.

"When she is on tour," explains Yashpal Kapur, "we send out instructions not to cook anything special for her. She insists on eating the food of the state or region she is in—Gujarat, Maharashtra, or south India, as the case might be. But we ask the hosts to use a little less *ghee* [clarified butter used as a cooking medium], *mirch* [chilies], and *masala* [spices]. I must say she is quite adaptable to different foods and is even enterprising. I remember her tour of the North-East Frontier Agency in March 1958 to examine social welfare projects. The tribal people of the region ferment two indigenous brews, *apong* and *zu*, from rice. She tasted both drinks, since tribal people take offense if you spurn their hospitality. She knew from past experience of travel with her father what these brews were like. So she warned me: 'Kapur, you better go slow with that *zu*. It's a pretty strong potion!' At Kohima, capital of Nagaland, we were served a dish of deboned fowl with something that tasted like *dal mot* [an elaborate preparation of fried lentils] and *apong*. She liked the meal. But the tour was an ordeal for me. It's customary for the tribal people to offer their guests boiled eggs and tea. Mrs. Gandhi ate the boiled eggs at a place or two but then started passing them on to me at every subsequent stop. By the time I returned to Calcutta I was so full of them that I was afraid I would begin to hatch!"

The Prime Minister's day begins with glancing through the capital's half a dozen daily newspapers. She notes the adverse comments, and passes the items on to the secretaries for investigation and follow-up action. At seven thirty her personal assistant, Mr. N. K. Seshan, arrives with official papers and a list highlighting the day's important business. By eight thirty Mrs. Gandhi steps out of the house to meet the scores of people gathered under the colorful *shamiana* erected in front of the house. Awaiting her might be student groups led by black-robed nuns or white-robed padres who wish to be photographed with the Prime Minister; a deputation of state assembly men; a group of petition-waving teachers; spokesmen of a company wanting to donate sizable sums to the National Defence Fund or the Prime Minister's Relief Fund; people who want to give wheat or rice for famine-stricken areas, or blankets, cigarettes, or playing cards for the Indian *jawans* [soldiers]; tourists, and simple folk who want nothing more than the Prime Minister's *darshan*. In about an hour she returns indoors and gets ready for office.

By 10 A.M. Mrs. Gandhi is in her large office in the South Block which houses a conglomeration of ministries and departments. Her secretaries, who work around the clock in shifts, produce the correspondence and present the urgent files. Then follow official appointments with her ministers, government officials, and ambassadors of foreign lands. She might have to rush to New Delhi's Palam Airport to receive or see off a visiting head of state or government.

Around 1 P.M. Mrs. Gandhi arrives home for lunch unless she has to attend an official luncheon. After a brief rest of about an hour she is back at the office for more work or for presiding over Cabinet meetings. Mondays and Tuesdays are the busiest days for the Prime Minister because of question time both in the Lok Sabha and the Rajya Sabha. Questions may be asked of her or of her ministers. If a minister is being badly badgered by the Opposition she might have to rescue him. During an important debate in Parliament she is forced to spend most of the time there to sense the mood of the House and of the Opposition.

Mrs. Gandhi leaves party affairs for the evenings. The meetings may be held at the party headquarters on Jantar Mantar Road, where Mr. Kamaraj presides. Matters discussed may range from purely organizational questions, such as disciplining dissidents or settling a factional dispute in some far-off state, to questions of government policy. Or the meetings may be held at the Central Hall of Parliament, where the Congress Party members of Parliament may caucus to map out legislative strategy. Civic receptions to visiting dignitaries are invariably accorded in the evenings, and Mrs. Gandhi would hasten to Delhi's historic Red Fort if one were planned. If she is herself not giving an official dinner in Hyderabad House or attending the President's state banquet at Rashtrapati Bhavan, Mrs. Gandhi is back at her residence by 9 P.M. People are certain to be waiting for her, and after disposing of them she has a quick dinner and then settles down in her bedroom with her files, as Madhu, Putli, and Pepi walk in and out wagging their tails. By midnight Mrs. Gandhi retires to bed.

The Prime Minister does not find the time now for physical exercise. In days gone by she enjoyed it immensely, whether it was horse riding in Allahabad, skiing in Switzerland, swimming in Kashmir's Nagin Lake, or hiking in the Himalayas. Nor can she indulge her hobbies unhindered, one of which is bird-watching. While living at Teen Murti House, Mr. Malcolm MacDonald, the then British High Commissioner, an ardent bird-watcher, would join her at dawn. The two of them obviously spotted many a bird, since the High Commissioner later published a book on the subject. However, Mrs. Gandhi's catholic tastes find satisfaction whenever the occasion permits. She always listens to music during lunch at home. She likes both Indian and Western music but has no favorites. "You know, I don't have any favorite artists and composers because my likes depend upon my moods and so on. I really like classical music best. But I also like folk music very much." She might have added folk dances to her list, for she is known to have joined folk dancers whenever in their midst.

Indira Gandhi is also a connoisseur of painting and sculpture. Here again she has no particular preferences and does not play favorites with anyone. "But she stands up for the right of an artist to belong to any school," says her aunt, Mrs. Sheila Kaul. "She becomes furious when she hears someone ridicule contemporary art. Not that she isn't a traditionalist. It's just that she can't stand anyone denying freedom of expression to an artist. And this isn't true of her views about art alone. Whether it is in philosophy or religion or morality, she favors a plurality of schools of thought." She has not stopped at mere appreciation of art. Several artists acknowledge the many acts of kindness she has done them, getting them both recognition and assignments.

When Jawaharlal Nehru was forced to reduce drastically his household expenses after his father's death, there was one luxury which he permitted himself without being apologetic about it: to continue to buy books. His daughter is equally fond of books, and her friends say that whenever she travels abroad she darts into airport bookshops to browse through or buy the latest books. She still makes the rounds of museums and theaters which she first learned to do with her father and subsequently with her husband. Like her father, Mrs. Gandhi is an ardent devotee of poetry. Mr. Sharada Prasad, her Deputy Information Adviser, testifies to this passion of hers: "When Mrs. Gandhi was in London in June 1965 to be present at the inauguration of the Nehru Memorial Exhibition by Prime Minister Wilson, she heard of a poetry reading that was to take place in Albert Hall. She didn't want to miss it at any cost, and luckily there wasn't any clashing official engagement. She slipped into Albert Hall quietly and incognito. No one even noticed her presence—not even the press —and she thoroughly enjoyed the poetry."

The lady Prime Minister's health has so far stood up quite well under the strain of sixteen or eighteen hours' work a day. Since her kidney operation in February 1960 she has had no other major ailment. She does get tired by evening after a long day's session in Parliament. Otherwise, she takes things in her stride. Four months after becoming Prime Minister she wrote to Mrs. Sheila Kaul: "I'm a little rushed for work but am not really tired." It is not so much the physical exertion as the mental strain that seems to tire her. As a Parliamentarian put it: "When old man Nehru stood up in Parliament, there was an immediate hush and everyone, even members of the Opposition, listened to him with deference. If the Opposition meant to be nasty, Nehru was a past master in the art of silencing it. But today these very Parliamentarians mob this poor woman the moment they see her in the lobby. They bully her for favors or threaten her with disfavor. Inside the House they are unchivalrous and even disrespectful to her. Quite obviously, parliamentary proceedings must impose a strain on her, at least until she masters the art of being on top of them."

The dissensions within her party also seem to be causing her some strain. "But most of all it's due to her own party men being so inconsiderate," says one of her personal assistants. "They trunk-call her from some God-forsaken place and insist that she tour their area intensively. When they are told, for instance, that the places are inaccessible and that she doesn't have the time, they offer to arrange for a plane or a helicopter, little realizing that they don't necessarily reduce the physical strain although they may cut down on the time a little. In any case, for how many people can she campaign? There are literally hundreds who insist on her giving them time." Reports of her alleged frailty or infirmity do, however, make the nation concerned about her health. But they also make her the recipient of popular sympathy and affection. If Mrs. Gandhi does not possess a robust physique she does enjoy reasonably good health. Edward Thompson was shrewd enough to observe, when she was studying in England, that she had a strong and wiry constitution, and that once past the stage of adolescence she would have no major complaints.

Neither her slight build nor her frail health have stood in the way of her displaying remarkable physical courage. In this respect, she is every inch her father's daughter. After the fall of Bom Dila in November 1962 under the Chinese blitzkrieg, the strategic town of Tezpur in Assam was evacuated. Mrs. Gandhi asked her father if she could go to Assam. When he remained silent she persuaded him at least to talk to the people over the radio. The broadcast over, Nehru asked her after nightfall: "Aren't you going to Assam?" "What do you mean asking me that question? I waited a whole day for your answer," she retorted. He said meekly: "Go, if you want to, but why ask me in the first place?" Overnight she made arrangements to leave by five in the morning. Lal Bahadur Shastri then tried his delaying tactics on her. "Proceed to Gauhati first and I shall be there too," he assured her. He arrived late and Indira Gandhi was cooling her heels at the government circuit house. Lunch was served on Shastri's arrival, and after that she said to all firmly: "Now, each one to himself and off we go." Shastri pleaded with her not to remain overnight in Tezpur, since its fall to the enemy seemed imminent.

Not only did she stay overnight in Tezpur, but she was up at four in the morning and drove twenty miles toward the war front. Morale was still high and twenty thousand people gathered to meet her. The people were furious that the police, the officials, and local ministers had all fled like cowards. She tried to calm them with an ingenious argument: "How can ministers stay? The invading Chinese Army would capture them and force them to declare a rebel government. That's why ministers and officials had to leave." The listeners seemed satisfied. Mrs. Gandhi subsequently visited Tezpur several times. She would visit refugee camps, meet with women and children there, and when she went later to the oil fields in Dibrugarh or the battle lines in the North-East Frontier Agency, she would tell their menfolk individually that their families were safe in refugee camps.

Indira Gandhi seems to have a knack for landing herself in trouble. In August 1965 she decided to have a five-day holiday in Kashmir and flew to Srinagar on the eighth. When she reached her houseboat she found it was empty. And so were many others. Officials at first gave her the lame explanation that the mosquitoes had driven everyone away. They then let her in on the secret that Pakistani infiltrators were once again flooding the northernmost Indian state, as they had done once before in 1947.

A Cabinet meeting of the state ministers was scheduled for the day. Since she happened to be India's Minister for Information and Broadcasting at the time, Mrs. Gandhi spent the day visiting the local offices of the All-India Radio and the Press Information Bureau. As evidence of Pakistani infiltration mounted and it became clear that the ninth of August had been designated as D-day for Srinagar's take-over, the state's ministers were gravely concerned. When the Cabinet meeting was in progress, Kashmir's Chief Minister, Ghulam Mohammed Sadiq, talked with Prime Minister Lal Bahadur Shastri on the phone and apprised him of the situation. Indira Gandhi asked Sadiq in the evening if there was any response from New Delhi; he shook his head. When no word had come even until midnight, panic seized officialdom in Srinagar. One minister confessed to Mrs. Gandhi: "I had joined Kashmir's popular militia in 1947 to fight Pakistani invaders. Everyone in Pakistan knows it. If these infiltrators get their hands on me now, they will decapitate me. I am nobody's fool and I am quitting." She assured him he could leave but that she would stay put and fight. The man changed his mind too when he sized up the determined woman.

Observers who had seen Indira Gandhi at the time say she was deeply disturbed by New Delhi's indecision. Prime Minister Shastri was slow to decide because he was waiting for the Secretary-General of the United Nations to make public the findings of his Chief Military Observer in Kashmir confirming large-scale infiltration of the Indian State by Pakistan. Shastri felt he would be on firmer ground if his action followed rather than preceded the Secretary-General's statement. On August 10, two detachments of the Punjab police arrived in Srinagar, and it was not until the twelfth that Indian Army reinforcements finally landed. On the thirteenth Indira finally left the trouble spot, assured that everything was under control. The episode earned her a new compliment. People in New Delhi said Indira Gandhi was the only "man" in the Indian Cabinet.

Once large-scale hostilities broke out between India and Pakistan in September 1965, Indira Gandhi was all over the battle front, clad in khaki camouflage. It was no time for public speaking and yet five to seven thousand gathered at each place in Abohar and Fazilka, which were under enemy shelling, and in Ambala, which was bombed. When she was proceeding from Amritsar to Pathankot she broke the journey after dusk at Gurdaspur. A man in a Jeep, awaiting her arrival, dragged her off to Pathankot, insisting that she address the thousands of people gathered there despite the blackout. She spearheaded the relief and rehabilitation activities as she had done so often before.

What is it that moves Indira Gandhi to action? It is not physical courage alone, but a sharp political instinct, a perfect sense of timing, and an inclination to nip trouble in the bud. Early in 1961, when fanatical Hindus rioted brutally against Muslims in Jubbulpore in the state of Madhya Pradesh, she was among the first to reach there. Again, in January 1965 she was the only Minister of the Government of India to rush from Delhi to Madras to reassure the people of the south that the north Indian language, Hindi, would not be imposed on them as the official language against their will. At the same time she reasoned with them to abjure the emotions and accept Hindi as the official language on purely practical grounds.

Numerous have been the social welfare activities which Mrs. Gandhi has begun or expanded in the country. She was president of the Indian Council for Child Welfare, vice-president of the International Union for Child Welfare at Geneva, chairman of the National Integration Committee to bring about the "emotional integration" of various linguistic and religious groups in India, member of the Indian delegation to UNESCO in 1960, member of the executive board of UNESCO, member of India's Advisory Board of Education, chairman of Bal Bhavan—a national recreation club for children, founder-president of the Bal Sahyog Samiti—a residential training center for underprivileged boys in Delhi, member of the governing body of the Tibetan Homes Foundation, and a trustee of innumerable philanthropic and cultural organizations.

This feverish plunge into welfare activities, primed by her intensely human concern for others, started quite early in life. As a little girl she would go on Sundays to the home of Sam Higginbotham, an American Protestant missionary who ran an agricultural institute outside Allahabad, and help his wife sort out clothes, toys, and books donated by Americans for Indian children. Young Indira also used to bicycle six miles to a leper colony to do voluntary service. During the civil disobedience movement of the 1930's Kamala Nehru had converted a large room in Anand Bhavan into an emergency ward for the treatment of noncooperators injured by gunshots, and Indira helped her mother nurse them. "She remembers one boy," writes Welles Hangen, "who was brought in with such a serious stomach injury that the doctors advised simply making him as comfortable as possible and awaiting the end. 'But he was my first patient,' she told me, 'and I was determined to see him through. I almost staked my faith in God on his pulling through.' She should still be a believer, because she met her patient again during the 1951 election campaign." Later, when she was at school in Poona, Indira used her spare time for the uplift of Harijan children and on slum-clearance projects.

Human concern does not dawn upon Indira Gandhi as an abstract proposition; it hits her as a concrete experience. During the Hindu-Muslim riots which occurred in Delhi in 1948 following the partition of the country, Mrs. Gandhi happened upon a little girl by the name of Satya whose legs had been chopped off. She took her home and nursed the girl till the wounds were healed. There was only one institution in the country—the Army Hospital in Poona—which could fit a handicapped person with artificial limbs. She informed the hospital that she was sending Satya there. Promptly came the reply that the hospital's facilities were meant exclusively for army personnel. She talked her Prime-Minister father into intervening, and the girl was finally admitted. Today Satya is married, has mothered a baby, and drives her own car.

It is the same kind of direct involvement with individuals which has led her to take an interest in logopedics. Mr. M. Gopala Menon, the resident director of the Indian Investment Center in New York, tells of this more recent phase of Mrs. Gandhi's social work. Mr. Menon, whose only son is afflicted with cerebral palsy, has been a Foreign Service officer and was posted in several countries of the world, where he could obtain no remedy at all for his son's condition. "One day, when I was taking leave of Mr. Nehru before proceeding on a new assignment," recalls Menon, "Mrs. Gandhi was there too, and she overheard her father inquire about my son. When I was reassigned to New York I had my son admitted to the Institute of Logopedics at Wichita, Kansas, where he was under the care of the world-famous specialist, the late Dr. Martin F. Palmer. When Mrs. Gandhi came to the United States on a lecture tour in 1961 she stayed with the Palmers for two days and acquainted herself fully with the rehabilitation work at the Institute. As it transpired, it was more than a passing interest. Now, you know, the Ministry of Health in India doesn't have enough money to curb even the death-dealing diseases. You couldn't possibly expect the Ministry to get interested in logopedic centers. Happily, because of the munificence of the Maharaja of Mysore, we could hope to establish one such center in his state. Although Mrs. Gandhi modestly disavows all credit for it, she has actually been its moving spirit. She discussed the whole project with the Institute in Wichita, cleared the hurdles back home, and has gone over practically every minute detail."

This sympathy for others persists in Indira even when she herself is most in need of it. While she was lying in New Delhi's Willingdon Nursing Home in February 1960 after a pyllograph had been taken preceding her kidney operation, she received word of Lal Bahadur Shastri's heart attack in Allahabad. She asked her secretary to call up the Shastri family and find out if they needed help. When they asked for heart specialists, Indira arranged for some to be sent immediately from nearby Lucknow and Kanpur. Two more specialists were flown from New Delhi in an Indian Air Force plane hastily procured through the late Vice Marshal Mukherjee. When her father died and the staff had worked all night at Teen Murti House, she asked them first thing next morning to shave and wash up. "Father wouldn't have liked to see you all with unkempt hair and shaggy beards," she said, and had breakfast served to them as soon as they returned, neat and presentable.

If Indira Gandhi is a charming hostess, she is also a very considerate guest, and both for the same reason—concern for others. On her more recent visits to New York prior to becoming Prime Minister, she was often the house guest of Gopala Menon. "I don't have as large an apartment now as I used to when I was Consul General," Mr. Menon says. "But Mrs. Gandhi never made us feel she was being crowded in. She kept her room in perfect order, since she was conscious there weren't the hosts of servants here that one has in India. Her meals never posed a problem for us since she likes the South Indian food of the kind we cook. But she really put us at ease asking us not to fuss over her. When she felt like it she would walk to the refrigerator and help herself. I remember one particular incident which shows how considerate she is even in the smallest of things. We had both white and whole-wheat bread in the house. She saw us eat white bread and that's what she ate, not knowing we had the other kind too. We never knew of her fondness for whole-wheat bread. She asked for a slice of it only after she saw me eat one and told us how much her father had enjoyed whole-wheat bread."

There are some who insist that Indira Gandhi possesses not a natural or spontaneous sympathy but a cultivated and contrived concern. "She isn't genuinely kind," says someone who has been observing her for many years, although from a distance. "It's more accurate to say she is prim and proper. I remember once when Feroze's sister had come to Delhi he had not bothered to find out where she was staying or whether she was comfortable. Now, no one could charge Feroze with inconsiderateness. It was just his way of being himself, easygoing, careless if you want to put it that way. But not Indira. She reprimanded Feroze for his ways and took her sister-in-law home to Teen Murti House. Now, I doubt if this proves she is more kind. I suppose she is more disciplined and has a keener sense of propriety than her husband."

"I don't agree with that," says her cousin, Mrs. Shyam Kumari Khan, a lawyer and Member of Parliament. "The trouble with Indira is she is so tongue-tied, the result of being lonely and detached for years on end. She has never really given vent to her emotions freely. She is usually keyed up and her intensest feelings are repressed. I know lots of people who take her silence for arrogance. And they don't think she is warmhearted either. They misconstrue her detachment for coldness. But I tell you there isn't another person who is more self-effacing. Indu doesn't even exist when she serves others."

Indira Gandhi has a large circle of acquaintances, but her intimate and trusted friends are few. These few insist that their distinguished Prime Minister friend is even sentimental. "She still sends us birthday cards," said one. "She still has with her two lounging chairs from her first home in Lucknow," says another. "I hadn't seen another girl in my school days who accumulated more junk than Indira did. She just wouldn't discard anything at all—the shortest pencil stumps or the weirdest knickknacks. But I wonder if it didn't have something to do with her insecurity as a child. Her father didn't even earn a penny those days and l am sure it must have affected the child's psychology. I think from then on Indira developed the habit of storing things away. At Teen Murti House, all the wrappings and ribbons from official gifts she carefully rolled away for reuse."

In no sense is Indira Gandhi a miserly or ungenerous person. But she does husband her resources most carefully, and no one seemed to know this better than her father. James, the family cook, narrates an amusing anecdote. "Panditji was once leaving for Simla for a few days' vacation. My family happened to be there at the time and I asked Panditji if I could have a few days off from work so I could join them too. He granted me leave but warned me to get back to Delhi before he did. And suddenly he asked me: 'Do you have enough money on you?' I kept mum for a while and then hinted I needed about sixty rupees very badly. He promptly took the money out of his wallet and gave me. When I returned from Simla, Panditji took me aside one day and said, 'Don't mention to Indu anything about the money I gave you,' and warned me with a smile: 'She might deduct the amount from your salary!'"

Mrs. Gandhi's sentimental attachment is not confined to persons or things alone. It extends to causes and institutions. Uma Shankar Dikshit tells of her intense attachment to *The National Herald*, the paper her father had founded, her husband had worked for, and of which she herself had been a member of the board of directors up until she became India's Minister of Information and Broadcasting. The *Herald* was once again in financial straits in 1954. The chairman of the board, Ajit Prasad Jain, who was later to become Minister of Food, arrived at an understanding with Mr. C. B. Gupta, "the machine politician" of Uttar Pradesh, to run the paper. Mr. Nehru was opposed to a change of editorial policy which Mr. Gupta was certain to make, and therefore preferred an outright sale of the establishment. "But Indira kicked up a row," says Mr. Dikshit, the paper's present managing director. "She was herself one of the directors at the time and insisted vehemently: 'The *Herald* must continue as an independent paper with an independent editorial policy, and I shall find the means for its survival.' She then organized a music concert in Delhi, presenting Mrs. Subbulakshmi, the incomparable South Indian singer, and it netted a hundred thousand rupees. Indira also had published on the occasion a concert program, *Jyoti*, containing several informative articles and expensive advertisements, which netted another three hundred thousand rupees. If it wasn't for her, the *Herald* should have gone the way of *The Independent*, her grandfather's paper!"

Unlike the rabid Leftists in her party who demand independence of thought for themselves and deny it to others, Indira Gandhi encourages it in everyone. These Leftists are denouncing her for her alleged departure from her father's strict and narrow path of ideological rectitude. The truth, if anything, is that she errs on the side of excessive approbation of her father's policies in her eagerness to ensure his place in history. But she recognizes the right of others to be critical of him. Mr. Hem Barua, the tall, stocky, balding Praja

Socialist Party Member of Parliament from the state of Assam tells of an incident which throws light on her devotion to freedom of thought. An outspoken critic of the Nehru policies, Barua was convalescing at the Willingdon Nursing Home. Paying him a surprise visit, Mrs. Gandhi noticed he was reading a book entitled, *The Art of Plain Talk*. "You don't need to read that book, Baruaji," she said, "since you do some pretty good plain talking all the time anyway." He told her he was reading the book to improve his English, whereupon she asked him to pass it on to her after he was through with it and promised to send him some herself. "That very afternoon," recalls Mr. Barua, "she sent me three books. One was *Design for Tomorrow* [written by a senior journalist, B. G .Verghese, who is now her Information Adviser], the second was the Dalai Lama's autobiography, and the third was Ronald Segal's *Crisis in India*. Now, the last one, as you know, is anything but complimentary to her father, and I must confess I was pleasantly impressed by her liberality of outlook."

A laudable quality of all the Nehrus—from Motilal to Indira—is their reluctance to impose their views on the young. Motilal and Jawaharlal had far more acute differences with each other over economic and political matters than did Indira and her father. Mrs. Gandhi has encouraged in her sons a similar sturdy independence of spirit. P. A. Narielwala, of the House of Tata, recounts the fearlessness with which young Sanjay expressed himself on a question which generally evoked strong convictions from his grandfather. "At the last dinner I was privileged to give Mr. Nehru before his death, Mrs. Gandhi and Sanjay were also present. On being told that Sanjay would soon be going to England for technical training, I asked him what he intended to specialize in. 'Automobile engineering,' he answered emphatically. 'Isn't aeronautical engineering the thing of the future? Aren't the prospects better in it?' I asked him: 'Perhaps they are,' Sanjay admitted, adding ruefully: 'But in India unfortunately the aircraft industry is in the public sector. And I'll never work for the public sector.' It came as a shock to me since I wasn't prepared for it in the least. After all, his mother, father, and grandfather were all champions of the public sector. Yet his mother didn't pull him up, and even his grandfather smiled indulgently!"

Indira Gandhi's coworkers praise her high-minded refusal to make capital of her position or of her relationship to her Prime Minister father. "I always had a constitutional antipathy for people in high positions," acknowledges Miss Usha Bhagat, Mrs. Gandhi's secretary. "When she first came to my kindergarten class with her two sons, my reaction was typical. I thought that as the Prime Minister's daughter she would try to lord it over us. I ignored her. Later, at a parents-teachers meeting, she smiled at me, since I happened to be her children's teacher. I turned my face the other way. I now know how mistaken I was. By the time I left the school, almost every parent had taken undue advantage of his or her position but not Mrs. Gandhi." In fact, Indira Gandhi goes to the other extreme and deliberately discourages others from deferring to her. Mrs. Mukul Banerji recalls the vehemence with which Mrs. Gandhi once opposed the intention of the Women's Department of the Indian National Congress to honor her. For some years now, November 14, Jawaharlal's birthday, has been celebrated in India as Children's Day. The women of the Congress wanted henceforth to observe November 19, Indira's birthday, as Women's Day. "But Mrs. Gandhi opposed our suggestion tooth and nail," says Mrs. Banerji, "and we lost. She won because of her genuine humility. She wasn't striking a pose."

The Indian Prime Minister has a lively sense of justice and fair play in matters big and small. When she was the chairman of a school, one of the teachers approached her directly, over the head of the school's secretary, for redress of a grievance. The secretary was annoyed with the teacher and Mrs. Gandhi was agitated by the secretary's attitude. "I appreciate all that you are doing for the school," she told him, "but anyone working with us has a right to cry on my shoulder." She allowed more of the same thing on a much larger scale when she became Minister of Information and Broadcasting in 1964. She was appalled by the service conditions of the artists employed by All-India Radio, a state-owned monopoly, in a country that styled itself socialist. She encouraged the artists to unionize themselves and met several hundred of them individually over the heads of directors of broadcasting stations throughout the country. Most of their demands were met: a five-year contract, fringe benefits, provident fund, and recognition of the employees' union. None of her predecessors had done anything like this in seventeen long years. She hastened doing it in the firm belief that justice delayed was justice denied.

Much of Indira's sense of justice is derived from her being a good sport. She makes sport of her awesome responsibilities, engages sportingly in self-disparagement, and roots for the underdog. R. Ramanujam, *Newsweek* magazine's correspondent in New Delhi, relates how she defended him while her own Deputy Minister was doing him in. "We had invited her in March 1965, when she was Minister of Information and Broadcasting, to give away the prizes at the annual cricket match between the capital's journalists and Members of Parliament. We won the match and since I was the captain of my team she presented the trophy to me. We then lined up to pose for a photograph. As I stood beside her, the massive wooden base of the trophy slipped from my hand and landed on her toes. I apologized to her profusely and she kept saying it was nothing, although I could see her toe trembling, something like a lizard that had its tail snapped. 'Ramanujam doesn't deserve the trophy,' her Deputy Minister gravely volunteered, 'if he doesn't know how to hold it.' But she knew I was feeling like a miserable wretch and sprang to my defense: 'Don't forget he knows how to win it!'"

Critics point to Indira Gandhi's administrative inexperience and charge her with having surrounded herself by inept advisers when she was Minister of Information and Broadcasting. It must be remembered, however, that her father had no more administrative experience than she when he was released from prison and invited to form the government. Her open mind on the question of changing the status of All-India Radio from a department of the Government to an independent statutory authority demonstrates that she had sufficient administrative insight to realize the evils of excessive administration. She was contending, in effect, that the forte of her ministry ought to lie in imagination rather than in administration. She had imagination enough to visualize the vast potential of television to popularize birth-control education and spread scientific methods of agriculture in India. In the face of Opposition charges that she was squandering money on "a white elephant," she went about determined to lay the foundation for a modest program of social education and the manufacture of TV sets in India. This accomplishment was not forgotten when Indira Gandhi became Prime Minister. The pun which made the rounds of the capital at the time was that India was blessed with three Prime Ministers—Nehru the visionary, Shastri the revisionary, and Indira the televisionary.

India's Prime Minister is very businesslike. When she was president of the Congress in 1959 she conducted party meetings efficiently. She put an end to long-winded speeches and her gavel came down sharply even when her father overstepped the time limit. She now conducts Cabinet meetings in the same efficient manner. But unlike the rubber stamp which to some extent it had become under Nehru, the Cabinet today has been reinvigorated by Mrs. Gandhi as a genuine team. Even in meetings with individuals she wants them to come to the point directly. Occasionally she tolerates a dawdler, and she herself may become a doodler—drawing mostly flowers or birds or a human figure for a change. She is a patient listener, largely because she has much to learn, knows it too, and is not ashamed of it. Her political youth and inexperience have shown through some of her minor lapses in diplomacy and statecraft, but she has so far avoided major blunders. "She is as shrewd as her father was," says one of her Cabinet colleagues, "and a much better judge of men than he, although he had a much better grasp of events than she has. Over the short term her decisiveness could hurt her; but in the long run it would help the country."

Another Cabinet member says her young age is her greatest asset. "It should help accelerate the process of public acceptance of a new leader. India herself is a young nation, and so are her people, their average life span being only fifty years. Mrs. Gandhi prefers to talk of determination rather than difficulties, and that appeals to the young." She is fair and frank with her colleagues. "But that doesn't mean you can take her confidence for granted," adds still another

Cabinet minister. "She never gives her whole confidence to anyone, only part confidence. You're always on trial."

Indira Gandhi's is still a developing personality. When Nehru was alive, he was likened to a banyan tree under the shade of which nothing else could grow. If there was any truth in that figure of speech, his daughter must have suffered the most, being constantly under the shade of that gigantic tree for seventeen years. She is now once again exposed to the sunlight and her personality may sprout anew and bloom afresh.

When Indira Gandhi was first asked at her press conference how it felt to be a woman Prime Minister, she replied: "I don't regard myself as a woman. I regard myself as a person with a job. . . . I feel neither excited nor nervous. This is just another job I have to do." Both an inner truth and an oversimplification lurk in the statement. Her father had brought her up just as he might have brought up his son had he lived. The stigma of being a woman was never attached to her as it was to thousands of middle-class women in India, and she grew up free from that painful consciousness.

Uma Shankar Dikshit bears out her contention: "I have met hundreds of thousands of women in India—not all kinds of women but only the kind that was politically involved in the freedom movement. They claimed they were advanced and liberated and progressive. But I always detected in them some little complex or inhibition or squeamishness. Not so with Mrs. Gandhi. She talked freely and frankly on any subject. In fact it is the men who would be embarrassed in her presence. I remember one evening we got back to Anand Bhavan after a long, hard day of electioneering. Mrs. Gandhi just dropped onto the carpet and reclined against the sofa. A maidservant came in to press her tired feet and Mrs. Gandhi agreed reluctantly. There were three of us men with her, and the conversation drifted from one subject to another till we came to childbirth. As we men listened dumbfounded, she explained to us all there is about childbirth, just as if it were one other natural function—like breathing or blowing your nose, for instance, which of course it might well be. As a man I wouldn't know. But that isn't how Indian women or even men regard it. 'It's really nothing,' she concluded. 'I just felt hungry and I asked for a piece of toast. As I was eating Rajiv came out. I was so sorry I couldn't finish my toast!' "

If Indira Gandhi does not regard herself as a woman, others do think of her as one, which she no doubt is. She says there is nothing special about being a woman Prime Minister because under the Indian Constitution a woman can aspire to be anything. And for two decades India has had women as Ministers, Members of Parliament, state legislators, judges, civil servants, Foreign Service officers, doctors, lawyers, journalists, nurses, secretaries, models, and now a Miss World. They did not have to fight for their rights. They had participated in the nationalist movement and fully earned their rights. But all this progress is not altogether new either. Throughout Indian history, the vast majority of women have worked in field and farm along with their menfolk, and enjoyed in fact, if not in law, a considerable degree of freedom and equality. Segregation of the sexes was more a reflection, under the brief influence of Islam, of feudal and middle-class morality than anything else. Poverty, illiteracy, and an ossified Hindu tradition have conspired to make the bulk of Indian women the repositories of ignorance and superstition, false modesty, and sanctimonious virtue. It is in comparison with this overwhelming fact that the oft-cited progress of a handful of Indian women appears more like window dressing.

In the Indian context, therefore, Indira Gandhi is, by any standard, an extraordinary woman, however much she might like to wear the mask of modesty. It is doubtful if she is even modest. When she insisted that her birthday should not be celebrated as Women's Day, one suspects that what she objected to was the cheap popularity that might go with it. Mrs. Gandhi is in fact a very proud woman; and varying Sir Winston Churchill, who thought Lord Attlee had plenty to be modest about, she might well claim she has much to be proud of. In addition to her pride, she has other qualities which make humans human—a streak of obstinacy, a perverse contrariety, occasional petulance, a trace of intellectual arrogance, a disposition to use those who want to be used. And all her perfect outward composure notwithstanding, she gives way to stress, runs into a room, and weeps, as all good women do.

Jawaharlal Nehru once complained that nations make gods of their great men and, having deified them, refrain from following them. This is never more true of another country than India. Since it is certain that her compatriots will deify her, she was asked which of her qualities or accomplishments she would like to be known for. The poor lady sighed: "Oh, my God! I really don't know." Her cousin, Nayantara Sahgal, is right in uttering a note of caution: "I think the one care one must take when writing about Indira is to avoid the pitfalls of exaggeration and sentimentality. No modern Indian woman can be truthfully cast in the age-old image of Sita or Savitri. It would be false and she would not wish it herself. Indira is not a saint or a martyr. She is a woman of character and unusual determination, a woman who has in her private and public life proved she can stand alone and face what comes her way. I find this more stirring than any cloying comparison with a mythical heroine."

But the Indians are a people burdened with a past—a long past—and they would certainly scour centuries gone by to locate the lodestar that Indira Gandhi resembles. They might find a parallel in a queen who ascended the throne of Delhi on April 29, 1236. As her father, the king, was nearing death, his courtiers asked him which of his sons he would want to succeed him. The king languidly replied that they would find his daughter a better man than his sons, turned his face to the wall, and died. And so the daughter it was. She soon laid aside her female attire, appeared both in court and in camp as a man, unveiled, and led the men to the battlefield riding her charger. A contemporary chronicler noted her qualities:

"Sultana [Queen] Raziya—may she rest in peace!—was a great sovereign, sagacious, just and beneficent, a patron of the learned, a dispenser of justice, the cherisher of her subjects, and of warlike talent, and was endowed with all the admirable attributes and qualifications necessary for kings.

"But," lamented the chronicler, "as she did not attain the destiny in her creation of being computed among men, of what advantage were all these excellent qualifications to her?" A band of intriguing Turkish nobles, known as "the Forty," assassinated Raziya.

It is difficult to give the exact count of Young Turks and old in the Congress Party who would like to assassinate Indira Gandhi. Like good Congressmen, however, they would ensure that the assassination was purely political and thoroughly nonviolent.

13

Between Scylla and Charybdis

WHEN Indira Gandhi was chosen president of the Congress Party, an Indian editor commented she had donned "a crown more of thorns than of roses," adding that she "has been sentenced to hard labour." When she was made Prime Minister, however, few cared to know what sort of punishment was being meted out to her. They were all too excited to give it a thought. The magnitude and complexity of the problems Mrs. Gandhi faces do not make hers an enviable job. There are some questions, like population control, which dictate but one clear course of action. But there are others, such as the economic development of the country and questions of war and peace, that admit a variety of solutions, all of which could be equally unpleasant and equally fraught with uncertainty.

The most frightening problem India is confronted with is the annual growth of her population. In 1966, the year in which the country's fourth five-year plan commenced, there were nearly 500 million people. Every year increases India's numbers by an additional 12 million people, or as many as in the whole of Australia. By the time India completes her fourth five-year-plan in 1971 there will have been an increase in her population of more than 60 million, or as many as in all of Britain. Of the total population, women between the years of fifteen and forty-four—the peak childbearing age—constitute 22 percent. Of these, 85 percent are married. Fortunately, the birthrate has remained more or less stationary, at 40 births per thousand of population both in 1951 and 1961. But the death rate has been falling rapidly and will continue to fall for some time to come. It was 27 deaths per thousand in 1951 and only 17 per thousand in 1961. Life expectancy in India, which stood at about thirty-two years in 1950, is now reckoned at fifty. The problem, therefore, is essentially the result not of a galloping birthrate but of a decreasing death rate. And the death rate has dropped mainly because of effective public health measures adopted and higher standards of living promoted by the government. It is ironical to think that if only the government of India were less of a good government than it is it would have less of a problem on its hands. But then democratic governments can hardly afford to be bad governments, save at the risk of self-extinction.

That the problem has been sadly neglected is clear from the financial allocations made for birth-control programs under the various five-year plans. During the first plan (1951–56) only one and a half million rupees were allocated; during the second (1956–61) 22 million rupees; during the third (1961–66) 270 million rupees; while the fourth (1966–71) proposes to spend 950 million rupees. Fortunately for India, the intrauterine contraceptive device (IUCD) or "the loop," as it is popularly called, promises to be a timely boon. A small S-shaped device which costs only about one cent apiece to manufacture, the IUCD can be inserted in the uterus as long as children are not desired, without any harmful effects, and removed temporarily for the purpose of conception. In addition, the manufacture of condoms is also being stepped up, as is the program for performing vasectomy or the sterilization of the male. The following targets indicate how ambitious India's birth-control program will be under her fourth five-year plan.

TARGETS (*in million*)

Year	IUCD	Vasectomy	Condom
66–67	2.33	1.38	1.83
67–68	5.09	1.90	3.56
68–69	8.46	2.57	4.66
69–70	13.70	3.39	4.66
70–71	19.69	4.51	4.66

However, it is one thing to lay down targets and spend the allocated money (the latter is never difficult to do) and quite another to achieve the desired results. As Mr. B. L. Raina, director of the Central Family Planning Institute in New Delhi, puts it: "Contraceptive technology is only a part of the total program. It is now even more imperative to build up basic organization, better supervision, and intensified educational activities in order to be able to apply the improved technology. Further coordination and mobilization of different resources that reach the public are required, and mobility, flexibility, and a sense of urgency are highly necessary." Unhappily, a sense of urgency about birth control is still hardly evident in India. Things are pretty much in the "talking" stage and hardly in the "doing" phase. Huge billboards urge the practice of birth control by citizens in New Delhi (where a modest number would anyway be practicing it), but there is not even the trace of a pilot program, for example, in the twin districts of Basti and Gorakhpur in the state of Uttar Pradesh, which this writer combed for ten days. They are among the most densely populated in the country! Nor are things encouraging even in New Delhi, as the mere proliferation of billboards would indicate. As soon as the boards went up, a delegation of squeamish ladies waited on Mrs. Indira Gandhi to protest against their alleged obscenity! The slogan in Hindi reads: *Loop Lagvaiyé: Parivar Niyojan Keejiyé* ("Have the Loop Inserted: Practice Family Planning"). Thoroughly innocuous, one would have thought, but it has apparently ruffled the sensitivities of some of New Delhi's virtuous ladies. One can well imagine the uproar which a birth-control program may create among psychologically unprepared women in the far recesses of the countryside.

The difficulty with birth-control programs is that the approach has to be, of necessity, to people individually and not en masse, since birth control touches upon the most intimate aspects of one's private life. The village woman in India does not know the rudiments of human reproduction; and even if she is persuaded to become receptive to the idea of birth control, her husband would more likely be hostile to it for various reasons grounded in ignorance. To deal with millions of illiterate couples on a scale vast enough to be significant

in terms of concrete results will involve considerable effort in mobilizing professional personnel and solving organizational problems.
Furthermore, male doctors would be useless for inserting the IUCD's
in the wombs of village women. There are frequent reports in Indian newspapers of villagers chasing away suspected family-planning
workers with long, menacing bamboo sticks. Only women doctors
can be of help. It is estimated that there are 12,500 of them in India
today, of whom 1,200 would be required for inserting of IUCD's
in the year 1966–67. By 1970–71 it is expected that there will be
17,500 women doctors, of whom 9,000 would be required for the
purpose. It is doubtful that the required personnel can be found and
organized effectively.

The major hurdle to the effective implementation of birth-control
programs will be the apathy of state governments. Under the scheme
for the distribution of powers in the Constitution of India, birth-
control programs fall within the sphere of state power. India's Health
Minister, Miss Sushila Nayar, herself a physician and a product of
Baltimore's famous Johns Hopkins University, is an ardent advocate
of birth control. But her enthusiasm comes to naught if the state
health ministers refuse to cooperate. In some states like Maharashtra
and Madras the program is catching on admirably. But in some there
is calculated indifference. And in some others it is actually being
sabotaged. The health minister of a populous North Indian state, for
example, argues that since the Muslims are prohibited by their religion to practice birth control, he will not force the Hindus (for
whom there is no religious bar) to practice it and thereby reduce
their own numbers! The argument is very similar to the one this
writer has heard some Protestants advance, opposing birth control
on the ground that it would diminish their numbers in relation to
the Catholics.

If India does not control her numbers, she will have to run at a
hectic pace just to be able to stand still. All her economic gains will
be swallowed up and neutralized by a runaway increase in population. There is a widespread popular tendency in the world to think
only of the equation between population and food. But humans require other things besides food—clothing, shelter, education, employ-

ment, health, transportation, and recreation, to mention but a few essentials. These cost money; and if money is not forthcoming for investment in the welfare of existing hordes of human beings, it cannot be found for the yet unborn. Pope Paul's observation that we must not limit the number of guests at life's banquet table is therefore singularly unimaginative.

If the population problem has not been tackled at all, the problem of food production has been attacked only intermittently and half-heartedly. In 1951 food grains production in India stood at about 50 million metric tons; it went up to 80 million in 1961. Since then it has actually declined, except in 1964–65, when it soared to the welcome figure of 89 million metric tons. Production in 1965–66 plummeted to 72 million metric tons because of an unprecedented drought. The monsoon refused to behave itself once again, and production is certain to be unsatisfactory in 1966–67 also. The planners in India would appear to have planned literally for the rainy day. It is the thought of the rainless days that should have troubled them. In 1951 irrigated land accounted for 56 million acres, to which 14 million have been added by major and medium-sized irrigation projects of the last three plans. But minor irrigation works have been badly neglected and little attention has been paid to digging tube wells on the required scale. Since nothing can be done about the vagaries of the monsoon, functioning wells should answer greatly the crying need for water on rainless days.

An easy way out of the recurrent scarcity situation has been dependence upon the import of food grains from the United States. In 1948 the total import of food grains amounted to 2.9 million metric tons. The situation improved gradually during the first five-year plan, and in 1955 only 0.6 million metric tons were imported. However, by 1960 imports ascended to 5 million metric tons and have been a persistent feature of the Indian economy since then, shooting up to 7.5 million metric tons in 1965. Last year, because of the drought, an estimated 10 million metric tons of grains had to be imported. India pays for these imports from the United States not in dollars but in rupees. Since the United States cannot use the bulk of the Indian currency she lends it back to India for various development projects.

The net result of Indian dependence on American agricultural surpluses has been psychologically harmful. The knowledge that she can depend on the United States has slackened India's own efforts. Not enough money has been put into boosting agricultural production. Secondly, the United States has accumulated so many rupees in India that she now holds more than a third of the entire Indian currency in circulation. If the present state of affairs continues, very soon the Americans will end up holding more than half the Indian currency. More and more Indians are agitated by this development. They feel it is dangerous for an already powerless country to put itself at the mercy of a great power for food—the very means of survival. Prime Minister Nehru was accustomed to argue that a military alliance with a foreign power would severely curtail India's independence and sovereignty. His prescription therefore was nonalignment. Today there are many Indians who feel that dependence for food on a foreign power is even worse than military dependence. As Napoleon said, even an army marches on its belly. Is it inconceivable, these Indians ask, that their country might be held to ransom when the very means of her survival is controlled by an alien power?

One reason for the depressed state of agriculture in India is the emphasis placed on rapid industrialization by the second and third five-year plans. The planners argued that because of an unfavorable land-to-man ratio, an essentially agrarian economy would limit overall prosperity and that, beyond a point, capital enrichment necessarily meant industrialization. The planners also found political justification for their proposal in a resolution which the Congress passed in January 1955 during its session held in Avadi. Among other things that resolution said, "Planning should take place with a view to the establishment of a socialistic pattern of society where the principal means of production are under social ownership or control." India's Planning Commission interpreted this as calling for "structural changes in the economy." Elaborating on it, Nehru himself said it meant "the expansion of the public sector both relatively and absolutely." In April 1956 the Government of India adopted anew an

Industrial Policy Resolution which established three categories of industries. The first category is the monopoly of the state. The second would be progressively state-owned and private enterprise would be gradually edged out of it. The last belongs exclusively to private enterprise.

An eminent Indian economist, B. R. Shenoy, attributes the present food crisis in the country to the "unduly large proportion of investment resources" funneled into the public or state-owned sector of the economy. He points out that the public sector industries contribute only 5 percent of the national income, whereas the private sector (which includes all the farmers) accounts for 88 percent of it. Yet, the sector which contributes only 5 percent to the national income is allowed by India's planners to draw 70 percent of the investment resources, while the sector that contributes 88 percent to the national income is condemned to make do with 30 percent of investment resources. "Disaster must strike sooner or later," says Shenoy. "The sector that was thus starved of investment resources would be unable to make its due contribution to the national product, as it would then suffer from the neglect of the necessary repairs and replacements, or from a slowing down of the rate of capital accumulation." During the decade 1951–61 total investment in the economy rose nearly three times, but gross capital formation in farm business declined by one half. The outcome of capital starvation in agriculture has been the general starvation of the people. The loss of productive efficiency in agriculture is reflected eloquently in the stagnation of agricultural production throughout the period of the third five-year plan, except in 1964–65, which was an exceptional year.

Unfortunately, no lessons were learned from all this, and Nehru himself preached pragmatism but practiced dogmatism. The public sector became the sacred cow of Indian economic thought. A plethora of new industries was established in the public sector without regard to productivity or profitability. In fact, profits were decried as the outcome of capitalist exploitation in the private sector, while losses of enterprises in the public sector were extolled as proof of their operating in the public interest. The distinguished Harvard economist, Professor John Kenneth Galbraith, when he was American Ambassador to India decried this as "post-office socialism," since only a post office, which is subsidized by the taxpayer, can afford to run at a loss, but no business, whether in the public or the private sector, can stay long in business by operating at a continuing loss. However, what inspired much of Indian planning was not economic considerations but political biases. When an eminent English economist was once asked to say wherein it would be economically sound to locate India's next steel plant, the public or the private sector, he replied tartly: "That, in India, isn't a question of economics but of comparative religion."

Whatever it was, it led to a good deal of misdirection, extravagance, and wastage of resources in industry, while all that agriculture could obtain was the ideological detours of the Congress Party. Precious time was wasted in arguing about the pros and cons of land reform, cooperative farming, and the pattern of agrarian ownership, a good deal of this slogan-mongering having increased the production not of food but of steam. India's Food Minister, Chidambaram Subramaniam, is now looking at the problem, for a change, through plain and not colored glasses. He sees it mainly as a scientific, not a political, issue. In fact he feels that the agricultural problem must be immunized from politics. What is needed, he says, is material inputs like adequate and timely supply of water, fertilizer, better seed, pesticides, improved implements, and modern agricultural machinery. Also required are supporting services like rural electricity to energize tube wells and irrigation pumps, agricultural research and extension work, land reclamation, soil conservation, and rural credit.

The yield of rice per acre in India is one of the lowest in the world —being a fourth of Spain's and Italy's, a third of Japan's, and half of China's and America's. More than 5 percent of India's wheat crop is exposed to a variety of rusts. Furthermore, owing to lack of storage facilities, rodents and pests destroy a great deal of grain. Thus, if nothing more is done than doubling the rice yield per acre, preventing the rust of wheat, and storing the grain carefully, India's food problem should solve itself. Even as things stand today, the Ministry of Food and Agriculture estimates that 50 percent of the food produced, worth 46 billion rupees, never reaches the consumer.

About 25 percent of the food produce is ransacked by rodents, 15 percent spoiled owing to inadequate storage facilities, and 10 percent lost in transport and processing.

Food Minister Subramaniam's decision to open the door a little wider for foreign private capital to enter the field of fertilizer production has proved fertile ground for fresh controversy. His Leftist critics charge that he has offered far too liberal terms to foreign private capital, but contend in the same breath that its response so far has been indifferent. The implication is that foreign capital is out to extract even better terms by exploiting India's helpless situation. This controversy has now reopened for consideration some of the old unresolved questions: the relative sizes and significance of the public and private sectors, the character of planning itself, the political implications of centralized economic planning, and the role of foreign private capital and government-to-government loans.

It must be said at the outset that no reasonable individual or party in India—not even the much maligned opposition Swatantra Party—is against planning as such. In fact, it is conceded that all governments must plan, as indeed private business houses and even housewives must. Again, nobody contends that planning in India has been an unmitigated evil. Some of its achievements are quite impressive, as the following figures for 15 years of planning (1951–1966) indicate. Although there has been a short fall in the production of food grains, the index of agricultural production as a whole rose from 100 to 158, and that for industry from 100 to 250; national income rose from 98,500 million rupees to 159,300 million, and per capita income from 275 to 325 rupees; steel production went up from 1.47 million tons to 6.2 million; cloth from 4,318 million meters to 7,580 million, petroleum products from 0.2 million tons to 9.8 million, and installed capacity of electricity from 2.3 million kilowatts to 10.2 million; railway passenger service went up from 6,650 million kilometers to 9,600 million, railway freight from 93 million tons to 205 million, surfaced roads from 156,000 kilometers to 284,000, commercial vehicles from 116,000 to 320,000, and cargo handled at major ports from 19.3 million tons to 50.2 million; the number of hospitals has risen from 8,600 to 14,600, birth-control clinics from nil to 11,474, and post offices from 36,000 to 98,000; 28 million new jobs have been created, 700,000 wells have been sunk, and 17,000 villages have been provided with a supply of potable water; per capita consumption of foodstuffs has gone up from 1,759 calories a day to 2,415 calories, per capita supply of food from 12.8 ounces a day to 15.4 ounces, and per capita consumption of cloth from 8.4 meters annually to 15 meters.

Economists who have been critical of Indian planning say that its chief defect lies in investing beyond what the aggregate real resources of the country warrant. Endemic in such planning, they assert, is deficit financing, which most necessarily causes inflation, malinvestment of resources, retarded savings, and therefore a deceleration of progress. In a scathing indictment of Indian planning, Professor Shenoy charges: "Most of our major economic ills of the past fifteen years—rising prices, mass poverty and distress, the growing opulence of the thin upper crust of the privileged, semi-stagnant or declining per capita income, lagging exports relative to production, chronic balance of payments difficulties, mounting reliance on foreign aid, and so on—directly stem from this futile attempt to invest nonexistent resources through credit creation."

Criticism of this kind is not confined to academicians or even to those with axes to grind. The governor of the Reserve Bank of India, an apolitical individual with a high public standing, warned recently that the country was "actually entering the stages of galloping inflation" and hoped that adequate measures would be taken by the Government to eliminate the factors contributing to inflation. He urged a greater degree of correspondence and harmony between investment expenditure and available resources, without recourse to the expedient of credit creation. Another person whose motives would not be impugned, the Comptroller and Auditor-General of India, while conceding that the primary purpose of state undertakings was not profit-making but social welfare and economic development, cautioned that a time must come, sooner than later, when these enterprises must make profits or perish.

The proliferation of bureaucratic controls and the resultant delay in implementation of plans, combined with the enormous scope which they afford for greasing the palms of officials itching to be bribed, is the subject of frequent editorial comment in Indian newspapers. It forms part of the larger question of administrative reform, which is currently being investigated by the Administrative Reforms Commission, headed by Mrs. Gandhi's rival for power, Morarji Desai. A grave defect would seem to lurk in the very nature of the federal-state relationship in India. The states charge that the federal government does not give them adequate financial help; the federal government, in turn, accuses the states of having failed to implement the provisions of successive economic plans. A purely political relationship of this kind, in which it is impossible to pin legal accountability on either party, can prove disastrous economically. For instance, the Committee on Public (state) Undertakings of the Indian Parliament brought to light recently the case of a cable factory in the state of Kerala. The undertaking in question obtained the license to manufacture in 1958. The process of completing the preliminaries and finding a suitable technical collaborator took five years. The land was acquired in 1963, while building the factory took two more years, and by the time production could commence it was the end of 1965.

A second defect is implicit in the nature of the bureaucracy itself. In the old pre-independence days, the British operated "a law-and-order state." Brutal efficiency was the keynote of the administration, and it was ensured, if necessary, by efficient brutality. But today the government runs "a welfare state," which, mistranslated, could mean a charitable institution. There is a widespread feeling that efficiency has gone out of the window and has been replaced by a namby-pamby goodness and mawkish sentimentality. Today's civil servants are bad enough as administrative caretakers; but as managers of state enterprises they look more nearly like undertakers. A courageous member of India's Planning Commission recently declared with admirable honesty: "Over the first three Plan periods, something like a total outlay of 20,000 million rupees has been invested in the public sector undertakings. Perhaps another 15,000 million or more will be invested in the public sector during the Fourth Plan period. It is vital to the functioning of the Indian economy, both in financial terms and in terms of essential goods and services, that these massive investments should bring in an adequate return. Yet, it is notorious that there have been grave errors of judgment and miscalculation in the formulation of some projects, serious delays in the implementation of several of them, over-capitalization and over-staffing in a very large number. In their operation, apart from technological deficiencies, high cost continues to be a distressingly persistent feature." Similarly, Mr. S. K. Patil, the Minister of Railways, has admitted that the worker strength of nearly one million on the payroll of the state-owned railroads could be halved without impairing efficiency and at the same time the wages of those not retrenched could be doubled.

Next, there is the problem of the undisputed existence of widespread corruption at all levels of the administration, both federal and state, its incidence in state administrations being much higher. No Indian would today contend that Congress Party members are less corrupt than a Communist or Swatantra Party member might be if in power, any more than Americans today would argue that Democrats are less corrupt than Republicans. Corruption is essentially a social or human problem. Unfortunately, during the seventeen long years of his stewardship of the Government of India, Nehru always treated it as if it were a political issue. Himself thoroughly incorruptible, he was inclined to shield his colleagues and the civil servants from charges of feathering their own nests, in order not to damage the reputation or political fortunes of his own party. The Administrative Reforms Commission, headed by Morarji Desai, has now recommended the appointment of an ombudsman on the Scandinavian model, with suitable modifications, and everyone in India hopes that Parliament will accept the recommendation.

Then there are the purely political arguments about choosing the right order of priorities in planned economic development. Such arguments, of course, are certain to arise in an underdeveloped economy with scarce capital resources. When the cake is small and the claimants are many, the clamor is bound to be great. The main opposing view is that the state must do what private enterprise will not or cannot engage in—education, social welfare, birth control—and leave industrialization wholly to the private sector. As the Swatantra

Party would put it: The business of government is good governance, not bad business. That party's view on foreign aid harmonizes with its basic approach. As its spokesman, Mr. M. R. Masani, debating the Finance Bill in Parliament, put it picturesquely: "We on these benches are not against international cooperation and acceptance of foreign capital. But we are against excessive dependence on government-to-government loans. We look upon these loans as a drug, if not poison, that has to be taken in very small quantities for very specific purposes. We look upon equity capital as vitamins, something which can be taken in larger proportions with benefit to the body."

There is another broad segment of the intelligentsia which agrees with the objectives of planning but disputes the mechanics of the ruling party. It accepts the need for "a mixed economy" but argues that the right mixture has not yet been found, and that what the ruling party has built is just a mixed-up economy. This segment consists of both Rightists and Leftists, and their prescriptions for the right mixture vary with their political complexions. As for the Communists and their views, here is how a member of the Congress Party's Working Committee put it: "What do they know about planning for India? Do they even know India? They are a bunch of sheep who just follow the lead from Moscow or Peking. They haven't had an original thought of their own in all these years. Look at what's happening in Russia, Yugoslavia, and the eastern European countries. They are all moving away from the highly centralized planning of the old type which produced a number of white elephants. The emphasis now is on the productivity and profitability of enterprises and on the quality and exportability of their products. Communists in other countries have to produce results. So they use their brains. Our Communists don't have to produce results. So they have their brains washed out. In fact, all this trouble in my own party has arisen because it has been infiltrated in the middle and late fifties by a number of fellow travelers. Some of these loafers would go to Moscow on official delegations and come back and tell us that the only way to industrialize is the Russian way. The others would go to China and come back and rave about the Chinese agricultural methods. Since the Chinese aggression, the Peking loafers in my party have more or less quit. They would have been hanged otherwise. But the Russian loafers are still very much with us. And all the noise and trouble of the last few months is caused by them. If it hadn't been for that we should have had a far more united and effective party."

India's first two plans were moderately successful. With the start of the 1960's, however, a new direction was needed. But by then Nehru was in his seventies, too old and stale to rethink the political postulates or reformulate the economic presuppositions which had animated his policies. He alone was acceptable to all the factions and he alone had the stature to do what Lenin had done for Russia with his NEP or new economic policy: to change the policy drastically and still make it appear that no change was effected. But such changes as Nehru countenanced were more a case of *plus ça change plus cela même chose*. The whole edifice came crumbling down with the Chinese attack of 1962.

Nehru was not really wrong in his foreign policy. It would be more true to say he was so right that he was rendered obsolescent by it. His basic contention was that the two superpowers were committing a monumental blunder by dividing the entire world into two armed camps. With the kind of weapons they possessed, they could make this planet extinct and man obsolete. The arming of their allies (denounced as satellites by the other camp) by the two giants was fraught with grave consequences to the peace of the world, Nehru argued. He prophesied that the recipients of this sophisticated weaponry would misuse it for settling old scores against their neighbors. Finally, with the pronounced pride of a pagan, he decried the religious zealotry and the ideological acerbity with which the cold war was being waged, creating a psychosis of suspicion, fear, and hatred.

Like the good professor that President Woodrow Wilson was, a good preacher Prime Minister Nehru was. He hit upon the catchword *Panch Sheel*, or Five Principles. All the five principles were as old as the Congress of Vienna. Only the word was new. Nehru, like Wilson, was hypnotized by his own sermons and mesmerized by his own phrases. *Panch Sheel* was the Word, and the incantation of it as a *mantra* or magic spell was the order of the day. Like the cock which imagines that the sun rises because it crows, the vast majority of the Indian people, led by Nehru, imagined that the peace of the world was being maintained by the power of their lungs. Little was it realized that peace was being maintained by the two superpowers themselves. Never in the history of man did any two countries possess such enormous power; and never did any exercise it more responsibly than have the United States of America and the Union of Soviet Socialist Republics.

Ironically, it is Soviet Premier Nikita Khrushchev who has done the most to render Nehru's foreign policy obsolescent. It was he who took the Soviet Union away from Stalin's erroneous path of external aggression and internal repression. Khrushchev was also the first world statesman to have actively pursued a policy of genuine peaceful coexistence and retreated hastily when by miscalculation he went to the brink of the precipice. But once Khrushchev removed the vestiges of the cold war, he also obliterated the very context in which alone Nehru's policy of nonalignment had relevance.

Mao Tse-tung is the second person who has done a good deal, though not as much as Khrushchev, to reduce Nehru's policy to shambles. By attacking India, exposing her military and diplomatic ineffectiveness, and forcing her to seek arms aid from the two very powers—America and Russia—with whom Nehru said others should not align themselves, Mao Tse-tung struck the last nail on the coffin of nonalignment. The third person to have done something to render Nehru obsolescent is President Mohammed Ayub Khan of Pakistan. Nehru had warned that small nations have neither the power nor the inclination to fight "the Communist world" or "the free world" and that when they acquire weapons on that pretext it is only to have territorial disputes settled in their favor. By attacking India in 1965 President Ayub proved Nehru right. In the process, however, he shattered India's faith in nonalignment.

What happened in September 1965 shocked India much more than what happened in October 1962. In 1962 both America and Russia came to India's aid in the face of the Chinese invasion. But in 1965 neither America nor Russia came to India's aid when Pakistan attacked her. Worse still, both countries bullied India in her worst predicament. When the United States first gave arms aid to Pakistan in 1954, India had protested vigorously that the arms would be used against her. President Dwight D. Eisenhower had explained that the arms were intended for the containment of Communism and gave India the solemn assurance that should Pakistan misuse the weapons in any aggressive venture against India, the United States would rush to India's aid. But no such miracle occurred in 1965. India had to face the music all alone, as President Ayub orchestrated belligerently with deadly instruments worth 1.5 billion dollars which the United States had generously given him. Rather than implement the pledge which President Eisenhower had given India, President Johnson added insult to injury. In his eagerness to appear scrupulously neutral and pay India back in the Nehru coin, he suspended all military and economic aid to both warring countries. This was hardly fair, since the great bulk of the aid which India received from the United States was economic. However, when the six-week war ended, India had done a little better than Pakistan on the battlefield and gained some strategic mountain passes in Pakistan-occupied Kashmir.

Then came the *coup de grace* from the Soviet Union. Premier Aleksei Kosygin invited both President Ayub Khan and the late Prime Minister Shastri to talk peace in Tashkent. Everybody in India was certain that Russia, which had befriended India consistently since 1955 and supported the Indian case on Kashmir as legally valid and unexceptionable, would sympathize with Shastri. Just before leaving for Tashkent, Shastri had assured the Indian Parliament that he would not give up at the conference table the costly gains which had been won on the battlefield. But the Russians put such high pressure on Shastri to give up his stand and return to the *status quo ante bellum* that he had to comply meekly.

The disillusionment in India with both the superpowers is now complete. There is some vague talk about rethinking the premises of Indian foreign policy. It is being argued that dual alignment is as dangerous as nonalignment, and the only valid position is sovereign independence buttressed by adequate military strength. A similar rethinking has obviously gone on in Pakistan. The country which once boasted that it was the staunchest Asian ally of the United

States has veered now toward nonalignment. If the Indians have redefined nonalignment as dual alignment with America and Russia vis-à-vis China, the Pakistanis seem to be saying that true nonalignment is treble alignment with America, Russia, and China vis-à-vis India.

If Pakistan and China were to stage a combined assault against India, as they threaten they will, and both America and Russia were to observe an indifferent neutrality, as they have demonstrated they can, then India would really be in the soup. She must therefore acquire her own independent nuclear deterrent. So goes the latest argument in a widening circle of Indian politicians. The development of a nuclear armory, however, is an extremely expensive proposition even for a country of massive resources. For a poor country like India, it is an unthinkable thought, asserts another section of Indian opinion. If scarce resources are diverted from sound economic development to unsound military preparedness, it would lead to domestic disaffection and chronic political instability, thus inviting the very foreign intervention we dread most, argues this school of thought, and recommends that a *modus vivendi* be sought with both of India's belligerent neighbors.

Of her two neighbors, Mrs. Gandhi should find it easier to establish a *modus vivendi* with China than with Pakistan, notwithstanding the present-day excessive Indian obsession with the Chinese menace. The euphony of the slogan, *Hindi-Chini Bhai Bhai* ("Indians and Chinese are brothers") which once rent the skies in India has now given way to the harshness of an unnatural hate. The politicians in India have popularized the contention that "China has stabbed us in the back." But there was no need for India to have bared her back in the first place. Sharing a long and undefined border with a country with which she had no direct relations for the past many centuries, India should have made it the first order of business to get a clear Sino-Indian agreement on where exactly the border lay. India may have all the legal rights on her side. If so, prudence demanded that they be recognized as such by the Chinese Government also. But instead of talking turkey with the Chinese, Mr. Nehru went about posturing on the world stage and neglecting vital Indian interests. In contrast, the Chinese leaders went about their business silently, in disciplined fashion, actualizing their industrial and military potential, and forging a first-rate army. The Indians, on the other hand, reveled in the organized confusion of their competing linguistic claims and conflicting religious loyalties at home, and proclaimed to the world that their army was "an army of peace"—a reference to the role of the Indian army in the peace-keeping operations of the United Nations in the Middle East and the Congo. When Mr. Nehru threatened to "throw the aggressors out," the Chinese hacked to pieces "the army of peace."

It should still not be difficult for Mrs. Gandhi to reestablish a dialogue with the Chinese. China is undoubtedly on the road to becoming a great power, conscious as she is that the only thing which is of any consequence in international relations is power. Indians must make peace with the fact that they cannot hope to compete with China or Japan for an equal status in Asia. For the foreseeable future India must be content with the position of a third-ranking power in the continent, draw Japan away from her posture of splendid isolation, and create with her cooperation a new balance of power in Asia. With Nehru India has already lost her honor with China. There is no reason why with Mrs. Gandhi India should lose the peace too.

If India must make peace with China's superior might, Pakistan must reconcile herself to a secondary position in South Asia. The tragedy is that it will not be easy for the Pakistanis to learn to do it. For almost two decades before the partitioning of India, the Muslim League, aided and encouraged by the British, had vied for a position of parity with the Indian National Congress. With India and Pakistan coming into existence as two independent countries, what was once an interparty conflict within the same country was transformed overnight into an interstate conflict. Unfortunately, the British did nothing between 1947 and 1954 to heal the wounds of the two countries they were partly responsible for inflicting. The temptation to continue as the arbiter of South Asian affairs was perhaps too strong to be abandoned by a country which had been the home of imperialism for two centuries.

With the establishment of the South-East Asia Treaty Organization in 1954, the United States displaced Britain as the power with the dominant interest in South Asia. American policies in the region, and especially the insistence that the principle of self-determination be applied in Kashmir, helped India and Pakistan draw farther apart. It must be borne in mind that India was partitioned in 1947—two years *after* the Charter of the United Nations was adopted. Yet, the Wilsonian principle of self-determination which was inscribed in the Charter, and in which Americans have an emotional vested interest, was not relied upon by any of the three parties—the British, the Congress, and the Muslim League—for settling the political issues of the subcontinent. The reason for discarding the principle of self-determination is that the Hindus and Muslims of the subcontinent are one people, even if they profess mainly two different religions. The Muslims of the subcontinent are not a nation apart from the Hindus any more than American Catholics are a nation separate from American Protestants, or Lebanese Christians are a nation different from Lebanese Muslims. Today the Indians and Pakistanis continue to be one people even if they inhabit two different countries. But this simple wisdom somehow eluded most Americans, and they cannot escape partial responsibility for the strained relationship between the people of the subcontinent.

An improvement in Indo-Pakistani relations must begin at the beginning and not at the end, which the knotty problem of Kashmir is. It must begin with the recognition that the partition of the subcontinent was a folly of monumental proportions. To say this is not to suggest that the two countries must be united forcibly, which is what the Pakistanis dread most—without justification. It is simply to advance the plea that we must look at the past dispassionately before we can build for the future. That task should be a little easier now that the three main actors in the drama which led to partition—Mahatma Gandhi, Jawaharlal Nehru, and Qaid-e-Azam Mohammed Ali Jinnah—have exited from the stage. All three of them blundered at one time or the other, and those blunders can now be safely interred with their bones. As long as one of the main actors in that past drama, Nehru, was alive and at the helm of affairs in India, a fresh approach toward Pakistan was not possible. Not having been emotionally involved in that wrangle, Indira Gandhi is fully capable of taking a new look at Indo-Pakistani relations. It would be a pity if the Pakistanis held against her the fact of her being Nehru's daughter.

Indira Gandhi's chief dilemma is that she must work through her party and for her people, and yet it is these very two who might defeat her purposes. The factions in her party have not yet accepted her as the undisputed leader, as they had her father. The Rightists have not yet forgiven her for thwarting Morarji's ambitions. The Leftists still accuse her of departing from her father's principles. The Syndicate still insists that she must play ball with it. As if this were not enough, the rain gods have been unkind to India again, and the situation may well be exploited by the disgruntled elements of the Congress to unseat their present leader.

Mrs. Gandhi's relations with the party president, Kamaraj, have not been smooth since her assumption of office in January 1966. Not equipped to understand the intricacies of policy and afflicted by the occupational disease of doing things purely for his party's gain, Kamaraj has been impatient with some of Mrs. Gandhi's decisions, especially in an election year. She, on the other hand, has not hesitated to say, "The Congress is great but this country is greater still."

A breach between the two, however, does not seem likely. A Cabinet Minister on whose advice she relies heavily and who has had a prominent part in getting her chosen as Prime Minister puts it this way: "Mrs. Gandhi and Kamaraj are complementary to each other. Neither is dispensable to the other. They are like two dissimilar peas in a pod. But the pod has to have the peas."

Mrs. Gandhi can always go directly to the people and use her popularity with them as a counterweight to the machinations of her party men. Nehru did this very effectively. But in one respect she is very different from her father. Whenever he was fed up with his party, Nehru made theatrical gestures about quitting. But he was far too enamored of office to carry out his threats. However, the threats did produce the desired effect of making the party scurry after him and do his bidding. Mrs. Gandhi is not enamored of office. She had given up the presidency of the Congress Party in the face of a concerted bid to keep her in it. There were good excuses to quit then. Her husband had heart trouble; her own kidney trouble was acute enough to warrant an early operation; and her father needed her more than ever. But all these were mere excuses. The real reason for quitting was her disgust with things as they were shaping up in her party. "It is more important to do well even if you stay for a short time than just want to be the Prime Minister or anything else," she said to this writer in all earnestness, and is quite capable of acting on it.

Would that her party consisted of a few more individuals like her who put country above party and a sense of duty above the glamour of office! Of the Kamaraj Plan under which Congress Party members were supposed to have resigned from office in order to rejuvenate the party, a wit has said that all that is now left of the Kamaraj Plan is Kamaraj himself. This is certainly true. For a long time now India has had a gerontocracy more than a democracy, where politicians prefer natural death to political demise. Quite naturally, this has affected the psychology of others, and no one in India seems to retire for good. Retired generals of the Army become Ambassadors; retired Ambassadors become vice-chancellors of universities; retired vice-chancellors become members of public service commissions; retired Chief Ministers become Governors; retired Governors become Members of Parliament; retired civil servants become directors of private companies or chairmen of public sector enterprises—and so goes the never-ending circus. Inevitably, there is a lack of vigor and vision in the "ins" who are mostly old, and frustration and fretfulness in the "outs" who are all young.

It is doubtful that Mrs. Gandhi will have any better luck with her people than she has had with her party. She wants to revitalize her nation and spur it to make new sacrifices for the common good. But Reinhold Niebuhr is probably right in saying that while an individual cast in the heroic mold is capable of sustained self-transcendence, the multitude is not. For a quarter of a century under the leadership of Mahatma Gandhi, there were many who were willing to die at the altar of freedom, and for a little less than two decades under Nehru's leadership they were prepared to give their all for

India's future. They are now tired of giving. Like the Irish politician of old, they ask what posterity has done for them that they should do anything for posterity.

For one other reason also Mrs. Gandhi will experience difficulty moving her people to act. If the Americans are amorous of devices and contemptuous of ideas, the Indians are amorous of ideas and contemptuous of devices. It is as if there were a dissociation between the Indian's sensory nerves and his motor nerves. Perception and interminable reflection become ends in themselves, not the primers of action.

But it is perhaps necessary not to be too harsh on the Indian. Many Western thinkers and their disciples in India attribute this failing of the Indian to his alleged otherworldliness. This is anything but true. If Plato and Aristotle have stressed the ideal of the golden mean largely because of the excesses of the ancient Greeks, successive sages in India have stressed the pursuit of spirituality only because of the crass materialistic instincts of the Indian. It is precisely because of the Indian's violent temper that so many teachers have emphasized the virtue of nonviolence, with the not too happy result that the Indian often argues the case for nonviolence a shade too violently. Again, it is the innate streak of intolerance in the Indian that has prompted the seers of all faiths in India—Hindu, Muslim and Sikh—to extol the virtue of tolerance. It must therefore be said to the credit of the Indian that he knows his nature only too well and tries to curb it consciously.

There is perhaps reason to give thanks that the Indian is what he is. For, if the 500 million people of India were simultaneously to become victims of rising expectations, heads would doubtless roll in a physical convulsion without sparking a real revolution. It is easy for Indian planners to talk glibly of "self-reliance," a "self-generating economy," and "the take-off stage" (this last, thanks to Professor W. W. Rostow). The truth is that it will take at least a century before living conditions in India can become tolerable. Until then they must at least be made bearable, and there is no better attitude than the Indian to make them so.

The late Mrs. Eleanor Roosevelt once told this writer: "Whenever

I go to India my heart bleeds in sympathy not so much for its people as for its Prime Minister. I wonder how he even has the courage to get up every morning and face those problems he knows he can do so little to help solve." She would have applauded Mrs. Gandhi's courage even more. Every morning the lady Prime Minister of India faces either an unpleasant situation which leaves her no choice or a situation which offers her equally unpleasant choices. But her people are happy with the pleasant thought that no matter what they have to face every morning, the newspapers will carry a picture of the pleasant face of their Prime Minister.

A Glossary of Indian Terms

Accents indicate pronunciation:
ā *as in English* far, é *as in English* hay.

achkan, a knee-length coat with Russian-type closed collar

alpana, a decoration made on the floor in intricate patterns with colored liquids or powders

Amar rahé, (May he) remain immortal

Anand Bhavan, Abode of Joy, the name of the Nehru family home in Allahabad

apong, a liquor brewed from rice by tribal people in northeastern India

āshram, a retreat, hermitage

Bāl Bhavan, a recreational club for children in Delhi

Bāl Sahyog Samiti, a residential training center for underprivileged boys in Delhi

Bandé Mataram, "Salutation to the Motherland," the name of the patriotic song composed by the Bengali poet, Bankim Chandra Chatterjee

béti, daughter

Bhagavad Gita, the "Song Celestial," the name of one of the holy books of the Hindus

bhavan, a mansion, house or abode

bhindi, okra (in the United States) or lady fingers (in other English-speaking countries)

botidar sālan, a rich curry with chunks of meat

burqa, the veil worn by Muslim ladies

chhātim, a beautiful tree of compound leaves with seven leaflets, also known in Sanskrit as the *saptaparna*
churidār, tight-fitting jodhpurs

daal, lentils
dal, an organization or association
darshan, visual communion
Dewān, the Prime Minister of one of the former princely states of India
dhania, coriander
Dhwaj Vandan, flag salutation
Divāli, the Hindu festival of lights

Gahesaran, Parsi last rites
ghee, clarified butter, used as a cooking medium
grām, village
grām séva dal, a village service association
Grihya Sutra, a Hindu philosophical work

Harijan, literally, "child of God," the name given by Mahatma Gandhi to a member of the former untouchable class
Holi, the festival in which colored powders are smeared on faces and colored water is squirted on clothes

jāgir, an estate
Jana Gana Mana, the title line of India's national anthem, written by Rabindranath Tagore
janata, the people or the masses
jawān, a soldier
Jaya Homa, a sacrifice to victory
jhoola, a swing

Kalā Bhavan, an art center
kanya dān, the giving away of the daughter in marriage
karéla, bitter gourd
katori, a small bowl
khādi (also *khaddar*), homespun or handwoven cloth
khichri, rice and lentils cooked together
Kotwāl, chief of police

Kumbh méla, the auspicious day on which hundreds of thousands of
    Hindus gather to immerse themselves in the river Ganges
kurkura, crisp, crunchy
kurta, a sheathlike upper garment

lāthi, a long, heavy stick, usually of bamboo
lezim, a rhythmic exercise

Mahābhārata, one of the two great Hindu epics
Mahāmantri, literally "Great Minister"
Mahāparinirvāna, the shedding of the mortal coils and the attainment
    of nirvana by the Buddha
Maharshi, a great sage
Maktāb, an indigenous or traditional school, especially one run by
    Muslims
māli, a gardener
māmu, uncle
mandal, of the locality (in the context used)
mandap, a canopied square specially erected for the performance of
    a wedding or religious ceremony
Māngalya māla, a floral offering to a bridal couple
masāla, spices
math, a monastery
meenakari, enameled decoration
méla, a fair or festival
mirch, green or red chilies
munshi, a clerical assistant
Mushāira, a lively session in which Urdu poets recite mostly their
    own poetry

nahar, a canal
Nām sanskār, christening ceremony
nannhi, the tiny one
Naoroj, the Kashmiri New Year's Day
Navjote, the Parsi "thread" or initiation ceremony
nivār, webbing

pakora, a fritter
pān, spiced, aromatic betel leaf

Panch Sheel (sometimes written as one word), the Five Principles expounded by Nehru as the basis of India's foreign policy: mutual respect for each other's territorial integrity; mutual non-aggression; mutual noninterference in each other's internal affairs; equality and mutual benefit; and peaceful coexistence

pandit, a learned man. Also used as an honorific prefix to a proper name or as a proper name itself

peepul, an Indian tree

Posh puja, a part of a wedding ceremony in which flower petals are showered on the couple

Pradhān mantri, Prime Minister

Priyadarshini, dear to the sight

Puja-ghar, the room in Hindu homes that is reserved for prayer and worship

Rām navami, the birthday of Rama, one of the ten incarnations of the Hindu god, Vishnu

Ramāyana, one of the two great Hindu epics

Rig Véda, the first of the four most ancient sacred books of the Hindus

Ritu Rāj, literally, "Lord of the Seasons." The title of one of Tagore's plays, translated as "The Cycle of Spring."

saag, a green, leafy vegetable

sabha, a society

Sādhu, one who has renounced worldly desires

Sāhitya Sabha, a literary society

Sāmānya Sabha, a mock parliament

samiti, an organization

Samskāra, a sacrament

Sangeet Sabha, a musical concert

Sāntiniketan, literally, "the Abode of Peace." The name of the school established by Tagore.

Sapta pādi, the part of the wedding ceremony in which the couple walks hand in hand around the fire seven times

Sāri, the garment worn by Indian women

Satyāgraha, literally, "truth-force," the technique of civil disobedience popularized by Mahatma Gandhi

shahanāi, a wind instrument
shamiāna, a colorful, tentlike canopy
shikār, a hunt
Shiv Nikétan, literally, the "Abode of Serenity"
sloka, a verse
swarāj, self-rule

tamāsha, a circus or show
thāli, a round metal tray
tilak, the round decorative mark worn by Hindu women on their
  foreheads
Trivéni, the confluence of the three rivers, the Ganges, the Jumna,
  and the legendary Saraswati

vakil, a pleader
Vasant Panchami, the Hindu festival which heralds the coming of
  spring
Védic paddhati, the path of the Vedas
Vijaya Dashami, the Hindu festival signifying the victory of light
  over darkness

zu, a brew made by tribal people in northeastern India

Index